Once in a lifetime, a book comes along that pulls all the strands of social history, migration, world politics and food into a comprehensive, entertaining book that is both enlightening and thoughtful. *Have You Eaten Yet?* arrives at a perfect time and is more relevant than ever. A must for anyone interested in how politics, culture, family and food merge together to create a most unique global phenomenon.

— KEN HOM, OBE, author, chef and BBC-TV presenter

A fantastic and important book. The social history and personal individual stories that Kwan shares brings to life what it means to be a Chinese immigrant navigating life in a foreign land. He highlights the strong sense of identity that so many Chinese immigrants possess, consciously or unconsciously, connecting them to their Chinese heritage, through food, so that no matter how disconnected or displaced, whether in Trinidad, Cuba, or Madagascar, one can draw from it, be nourished by it and share it. Kwan brings us closer to understanding our human experience, whether Chinese or non-Chinese, immigrant or non-immigrant, so that we may take away the human stories that ultimately bind, connect and inspire us all.

— CHING HE HUANG, Emmy-nominated television broadcaster,
host of *Ching's Amazing Asia* and bestselling cookbook author

This book is aptly titled. "Have you eaten yet?" is a colloquial Cantonese greeting akin to "You are well?" Just as food is quintessential to Chinese culture, these stories nourish the soul and warm the heart. With a masterful blending of rich textures, contours and flavours, Kwan takes us on a lively journey of the omnipresent Chinese restaurant capturing the enduring spirit of the Chinese diaspora. I hear their voices jumping off the pages. This is how history should be told!

— DORA NIPP, historian, lawyer and CEO of the Multicultural
History Society of Ontario

Seeing the world of the Chinese diaspora through the restaurants they created is brilliant. The stories shared are about adaptiveness and resilience, but also about innovation and invention and the creation of new flavours and culinary experiences that have shaped the history of the world. It's not an exaggeration to say that the kinds of restaurants that Kwan describes were the model for small family-run businesses as a portable technology of the Chinese migrant networks that transformed the globe. If who we are is a product of what we eat, then the invention of Chinese restaurants as a worldwide phenomenon that spanned every ocean and continent has shaped all of us.

— HENRY YU, history professor, University of British Columbia

In my many decades of traveling across continents and oceans, I've come across many enclaves of Chinese immigrants. "Have you eaten yet?" is a phrase I hear often in communities populated by those who came from Canton, the province of my family. More than a casual social greeting, the question conveys to me a sense of familiarity, of culture, history, tradition and of home. It took the keen eye of a great storyteller like Kwan to spin all that to a most enjoyable and meaningful book. Have you read the book yet? If not, what are you waiting for?

— MARTIN YAN, host of *Yan Can Cook* on public television,
   chef-owner of M.Y. China Restaurant, San Francisco

Kwan was ahead of his time in taking the form of the culinary travel documentary but merging it with a deep sense of community histories and the vast networks of diaspora. Chinese food may be everywhere, yet through Kwan's research and storytelling, we realize that in each niche it finds itself, it acquires something unique in its translation.

— OLIVER WANG, sociology professor, California State University,
   Long Beach

An amazing first-person New Yorker–style global ethnography of quiet emotional intensity that I could not put down. As a Chinese restaurant kid, Kwan's words made me tear up, as he really gets those interstitial moments between local patron and diasporic Chinese restaurant worker. Kwan nails the agony of what it's like to be a part of and apart from China/Chinese people.

— JENNY BANH, Asian American studies and anthropology professor, California State University, Fresno

An intimate yet sweeping lens on the Chinese diaspora through the institution of the family-run restaurant all around the world. From the jungles of the Amazon, to the heights of the Himalayas, to tropical islands of the Caribbean, to the fjords of Scandinavia, Kwan explores how, as immigrants, all our stories are all different yet all our stories are the same.

— JENNIFER 8. LEE, journalist, author of *The Fortune Cookie Chronicles* and producer of *The Search for General Tso*

Travel the globe in this fabulous memoir with the author, eating your way from Saskatchewan to Madagascar, and savour the stories, flavours, sounds and culinary adventures of Chinese restaurateurs as he brings you into their kitchens, replete with savoury welcome. Kwan has a unique gift for creating meaningful intimate connections with everyone he meets, for reading their history alongside his own, and honours the restaurant workers with his heartfelt storytelling. All readers will find something here that rings true for them.

— GLENN DEER, Asian North American studies and English professor, University of British Columbia

Have You Eaten Yet?

STORIES FROM CHINESE RESTAURANTS
AROUND THE WORLD

CHEUK KWAN

PEGASUS BOOKS
NEW YORK LONDON

HAVE YOU EATEN YET?

Pegasus Books, Ltd.
148 West 37th Street, 13th Floor
New York, NY 10018

First Pegasus Books paperback edition June 2023
First Pegasus Books cloth edition January 2023

ISBN: 978-1-63936-578-4

10 9 8 7 6 5 4 3 2 1

Printed in the United States of America
Distributed by Simon & Schuster
www.pegasusbooks.com

In Memory of Tony Chan and Jim Wong-Chu

Table of Contents

Foreword

EVERY ONCE IN A LIFETIME AN AUTHOR COMES ALONG THAT PULLS ALL THE strands of social history, migration diaspora, regional politics and, above all, food, into a most comprehensive and thoughtful tome. Cheuk Kwan has done just that.

I loved following Cheuk and his film crew on their odyssey of discovery from Canada to Israel, Kenya, Peru, Mauritius, Norway, Turkey, South Africa, Argentina, Madagascar, Cuba, India, Brazil and Trinidad.

What makes *Have You Eaten Yet?* such good reading is Cheuk's fascinating insight into each region—how the Chinese diaspora has impacted the cuisine and how the Chinese have been impacted by the region—weaving in history as well as delicious descriptions of how Chinese food has adapted itself to its environment.

As a Chinese chef who has achieved global fame through my bestselling BBC series, I have always been obsessed with learning more about how Chinese food has impacted the world. Cheuk, in his unique, insightful and interesting book, has filled that gap. I am most thankful to him for this.

The writing is gripping, addicting, amusing, funny and at times quite raucous; however, don't take my word for it. Find out yourself and I know you will agree. Fasten your seatbelt for a great reading experience.

KEN HOM, OBE

Chef, author and TV presenter

Introduction

THE RAIN IS COMING DOWN HARD.

I'm nursing a drink at a bar somewhere on the outskirts of Antananarivo, Madagascar, when a smallish Chinese man of dark complexion sits down next to me and starts making small talk in Mandarin. Where are you from? Where are you going? What's your name? By this time, I've figured out that he is Cantonese, so I switch to our common dialect.

"What's yours?"

"Just call me Ah Wong," he says. *Ah* is a colloquial Chinese prefix used with a shortened form of someone's name, usually one-syllable, to express familiarity—like my friends calling me Ah Kwan. Wong is a common Chinese family name, and there are tens of millions by that name in the world.

"What are you doing here?" My turn to ask.

"Just prospecting here and there in the mountains."

"For gold?" I am curious. The island's Central Highlands are rich with precious mineral deposits.

"Oh, it's a long story. It's been four months, leaving soon." Wong is evasive.

So, what is he *really* doing here? I've watched enough Hong Kong gangster movies to recognize this cagey dialogue. For all I know, he may not even be a Wong.

Earlier in the evening, on my arrival from Johannesburg, I was picked up by Paul Lee Sin Cheong. We drove for what seemed like an eternity on back roads, through blinding rain, in the dark, to get to this bar.

Paul, a Sino-Mauritian who has lived in Madagascar for twenty years, is part-owner—"Just for the fun of it"—of this restaurant-cum-boarding house where I'm staying for the night.

"Let's eat," Paul says.

Having travelled all day from Cape Town, on the other side of the continent, I'm famished. The dinner is mouth watering. We have Mauritian-style fried rice and the Creole classic rougail de boeuf—beef braised in a rich tomato stew with onions, garlic, chilies, ginger, thyme and coriander.

At the end of the meal, Paul asks the kitchen for soupe chinoise.

"Try this, this is a national dish in Madagascar," he says, pointing to the steaming bowl of wonton soup. "There are two major cultural imports from China in this country. This is one of them, the other is the rickshaw that you will see where you are going."

Madagascar is one of the last places on Earth I would expect to find Chinese settlement. And now I find out that wonton soup and rickshaws have contributed to the rich cultural tapestry here on the Big Island.

—·—

"Have you eaten yet?"

This colloquial Chinese greeting is akin to asking "How are you?" In a culture where food plays such an important role in life, asking if someone has eaten shows that you care. Because of war, famine and poverty, people in *old* China did not always have enough to eat. Perhaps that is how these words became an expression of concern for someone's well-being.

However it evolved, it's a greeting that you hear worldwide among those with Chinese heritage. And we *are* truly worldwide. There's a Cantonese saying: *yat wok jau tin ngaai*, literally, "journeying to the sky's edge with a wok."

You can find a Chinese restaurant everywhere you go.

And the cuisine has morphed, becoming American, Cuban, Jamaican, Peruvian. Or what have you. As Samson Yeh in Kolkata told me when we were talking about Indo-Chinese food, "We adapt to new environments, not the other way around."

He might as well have been talking about the Chinese diaspora.

I am a card-carrying member. I was born in Hong Kong—a British colony before it was handed back to China—and spent my formative years in

Singapore, Hong Kong and Japan. I attended universities in the US, immigrated to Canada and worked in Europe, the Middle East, Africa and Asia, speaking three languages *and* two Chinese dialects.

In 1976, I travelled westward on a round-the-world route from San Francisco to Toronto, where I would report as an immigrant. It was on that journey that I first ate at Istanbul's China Restaurant, whose owner—my *Let's Go Europe* guide informed me—had "walked from China." That culinary encounter inspired me to make the *Chinese Restaurants* documentary series, which brought me back to that very same restaurant twenty-five years later. For four years, I scoured the world for good eats and intriguing stories from the Chinese diaspora. It was an odyssey of more than 200,000 kilometres that took me from the Amazon to the Arctic Circle.

Family-run Chinese restaurants are global icons of immigration, community and good food. They are found in every corner of the world: cultural outposts of brave sojourners and purveyors of dim sum, Peking duck and surprising culinary hybrids. Running a Chinese restaurant is the easiest path for new Chinese immigrants to integrate into the host society. It's a unique trade where no other nationalities can compete, and it provides work for new arrivals, whether legal or illegal, helping them get on their feet.

But food is just an entry point.

Take a look behind every kitchen door and you will find a complicated history of cultural migration and world politics. The Jade Gardens and Golden Dragons that populate towns and cities from Africa to South America are intricately connected to the social schisms and political movements that propelled the world into modern times.

This global narrative is made from the myriad personal stories of entrepreneurs, labourers and dreamers who populate Chinese restaurants in six continents, and the social, cultural and political forces that shaped their stories.

There are more than 40 million of us in the Chinese diaspora, and it's serendipitous how we find each other in unexpected corners of the world. As I travelled the world meeting with far-flung members of the Chinese diaspora, one question always came to mind: Are we defined by our nationality or by our ethnicity? Nationality is a legal construct that can be easily given—or taken away—while ethnicity always stays with us. It's in our blood.

Even though I have held different passports and passed through different cultures, deep down I know that I'm ethnically Chinese. Somehow I have retained my Chinese cultural traits along the way. As second-generation Chinese Canadian journalist Nancy Ing-Ward once told me: "We may no longer speak the language, or embody the culture, but we all carry that invisible baggage of ancestral China on our backs."

Then she dropped a truism: "Like we always have to have our rice."

I once met an elderly Chinese man in the city then known as Leningrad, walking on the other side of a bridge that spans the Neva River. After we nodded to each other, I made a point of crossing over to chat with him. He invited me to his Soviet-era apartment. After dinner with his grown daughter and his Russian wife of forty years, he shared the story of how he had come to live in the Baltic city so far from home, and of the trials and tribulations they faced as an interracial couple in the Soviet Union.

Chance encounters like this one are precious moments in our life journeys. We all seem to be interconnected, in so many degrees, across blurred boundaries of geography, history and politics. But as disparate as we are, and as many different dialects and languages as we speak, we all share a set of common values: we believe in the importance of family ties, Chinese culture and education, and, most of all, we share an undying love of Chinese food.

Like, if it tastes good, we will eat it.

CHAPTER 1

Noisy Jim

OUTLOOK, SASKATCHEWAN, CANADA

"HIYA, CHUCK, THIS IS NOISY. SAY, WHEN I GET TO SEE YOUR *MOOVIE?* YA'KNOW, the one I *staar* in."

As I drive to the town of Outlook, Saskatchewan, I remember that voice coming over the phone. I remember particularly the gregarious and charming way Noisy Jim spoke, elongating vowels in his Taishanese-accented English.

"When you come see me again, eh? And how's my *Toisan doy?*" Jim always asked about his "Taishan boy," Kwok Gin, director of photography on my documentary series. Like Che and Cher, he goes by one name: Kwoi.

When I was looking around for someone to shoot the world with me, a friend of mine, Daisy Lee, told me about Kwoi. He'd shot a couple of her films. "He's the only one you ever want on your shoot. Just don't mind the way he looks."

Kwoi walked into our first meeting dressed all in black, keychains hanging from his belt, wearing a cowboy hat, white-rimmed spectacles and sandals. He is short and dark, with lots of facial hair, and likes to say that he's always been mistaken for an Indigenous person. At first I was afraid that he would attract too much attention to himself during a shoot—I like my crew to blend in with whatever we are shooting, like chameleons.

My directorial style is, as Bruce Lee once said, to "be water," to go with the flow. Kwoi got it, and he soon became my eyes and ears. He flourished with his Steadicam in the kitchen, thrived in navigating tight spaces, and came up with neo-Taoist aphorisms like: "If you groove with everyone's energy and flow, there is a harmonious madness that won't let you collide into any accidents."

I had found the right guy.

Noisy Jim and Kwoi both spoke Taishanese, one of the dialects from the Sze Yup (Four Counties) region, in southeastern China's Pearl River Delta, in Guangdong province—the homeland of most of the Chinese immigrants who left for Canada at the end of the nineteenth century.

Now it is November 2001. Noisy Jim died four days ago.

I received a call the previous afternoon about his funeral—just time enough to grab my Sony camera and catch the next flight out of Toronto. After overnighting near the Saskatoon airport, I'm now travelling south-southwest on the same road that Kwoi and I drove two years ago, at the launch of our five-continent, fifteen-country exploration around the Chinese diaspora.

Ever since I immigrated to Canada in 1976, I wanted to explore the history of those who came before me. And there's no better way to tell the story of the Chinese diaspora than through the stories of Chinese restaurant owners. There isn't a small town anywhere in Canada that doesn't have a Chinese restaurant.

I first heard about Noisy Jim from Tony Chan.

Tony and I have been comrades-in-arms advocating for a distinct Asian Canadian identity. We co-founded, in 1978, *The Asianadian*, a progressive magazine dedicated to the promotion of Asian Canadian arts, culture and politics. For years, we talked about how to share the stories of Chinese restaurants in Canada. Tony got there first, in 1985, with his TV documentary *Chinese Cafes in Rural Saskatchewan*.

Noisy Jim had "a starring role."

Twelve years later, I travelled through the Canadian Prairies with video artist Paul Wong, photographing small-town Chinese cafés and their owners in places like Cold Lake, Swift Current and Vulcan. We visited the New Outlook Cafe. Jim was every bit as entertaining and animated as he was in Tony's film—a storyteller with a wide-open heart. By then, he was seventy-five.

In a few years, the older generation of Chinese café owners like him would not be around to tell their stories.

I promised Noisy Jim I would return to make a star out of him again.

Three years later, I returned to Outlook with Kwoi to start filming our *Chinese Restaurants* series. After our trip, my editor told me I didn't have enough footage on the story. Rookie mistake—it was my first shoot.

Jim had called me over the intervening years, to see how I was doing or just to say hello. I had called Jim a month earlier, and his family told me he was in the hospital and very ill. It didn't look like I would be able to get back to see him.

It's déjà vu when I arrive in town about an hour before the funeral: the same old sleepy town that Kwoi and I visited almost two years earlier. It's almost noon. The main street is deserted. A notice posted in the front window of the café announces that it is closed for the funeral, perhaps the only day the restaurant has closed since it opened forty years ago.

—-—

On a frigid January day in 2000, with the mercury at –30°C, Kwoi and I drove the two hours from Saskatoon to the town of Outlook. We were deep in the Canadian Prairies: a vast, flat countryside with a big sky and endless wheat fields. The late-afternoon sun cast a golden hue on a landscape dotted with railroad crossings and grain elevators, criss-crossed by empty roads and emptier train tracks.

It was both bleak and strangely beautiful.

Five kilometres from town, at a T-junction, a road sign pointed left, just over the South Saskatchewan River, to "Outlook Pop. 1,200." The sun was setting. We rode into town like gunslingers in a John Ford Western.

The New Outlook Cafe was in a corner building, across from a car dealership, halfway down Saskatchewan Avenue—a main street with no traffic light. The restaurant's sign protruded diagonally at the corner, so you couldn't help but notice it.

Inside, three rows of booths, seating fifty, ran down the length of the room and led to the kitchen. There was also a lunch counter at the service area, facing a Coca-Cola fridge, stainless-steel display shelves for desserts and the omnipresent coffee maker.

A sign advertising "Noisy Jim's Homemade Apple Pie" was posted on the far wall.

Jim was convivial as he refilled coffee and chatted up his customers, very much the proud owner of the Chinese café.

Well, not quite.

When Jim retired seven years earlier, he sold his business to Ruby Lee and Ken Chan, an immigrant couple from Jim's village in Hoiping county. But he continued to show up every morning at six to serve coffee to his loyal customers, just as he had since 1959.

"I wake up at four every morning," said Jim in his hoarse voice. "Okay, they get too tired working long hours, so I get up and help them, open up for them. I'm not doing anything else, so why not get up and help other people, eh?"

"Is there anything in this for you?" I asked.

"They offer me but I never take it. Because the moment I take any pay, I'm not a free man." His voice boomed across the room. "This way, I come and go when I like. And I don't like to owe anybody a favour. I like it when I do you a favour and you go help others. I'm happier this way. That's my way."

According to Lloyd Smith, a customer of thirty years, Jim couldn't give up the habit. "He even takes the coffee home with him. He can't get used to his home coffee." Lloyd had the keys to New Outlook's mailbox in a nearby town. He picked up the mail for the restaurant, which Jim still opened and read before passing it on to the new owners.

"This is not a bar town, it's a café town," Lloyd pointedly told me. "The town's social life is at the café. We come here and visit with each other. It's more fun than watching television at home anyway."

The Chinese café is more than just a place to eat; it is an institution in towns across the Canadian Prairies: a community centre, a place where families grow up together. The bond that Jim created with his customers was so deep that, for many years, he gave them keys so that they could open up in the morning and make their own coffee if he wasn't there yet, or even go into the kitchen to make their own breakfast. On their way out, they would leave money in a wooden box on the counter.

Generations of locals were loyal to the restaurant: farm workers, having their first coffee at dawn; school bus drivers, stopping by every morning after their runs; mother-daughter pairs, having a lunchtime chat; and retirees, dropping in for a second visit of the day.

Lisa Cooper, a Royal Canadian Mounted Police officer, ate lunch there every day because "it's just too far to go home, and you get a nice home-cooked meal."

As Kwoi shot in the kitchen, I crossed the room to talk to three men in their mid-thirties. Jeremy, wearing a John Deere hat, said there was a time when they spent upwards of six hours a day in this place, "just sitting around, drinking coffee and eating whatever, playing cards."

Jon, his buddy in a Blue Jays baseball cap, told me he first came with his parents when he was seven. "And I've liked Chinese food ever since, so I just kept coming back."

Curtis, the third diner, noted that as soon as they sat down, "Jim would know exactly what we want—cheese, fries and gravy."

Prairie cafés are not really Chinese restaurants. They don't serve anything remotely resembling Chinese food. They are about a nice cup of coffee with bacon and eggs in the morning; a generous cut of pork chops with mashed potatoes and gravy at lunch; and maybe a coffee and dessert after dinner.

"And, as much coffee as you want for a dollar . . . Better food than McDonald's," Jon added.

I asked Jim what kind of food he served.

"Canadian . . . Chinese. Well, it's not really Chinese. It's what you call American Chinese food, eh. Egg roll, chow mein, chop suey and all that. It's not the same as what Chinese people eat, right?"

Chop suey is American Chinese, of course. Or, as Jennifer 8. Lee, in her book *The Fortune Cookie Chronicles*, calls it: the biggest culinary joke one culture plays on another. In Cantonese, *chop suey* means "odds and ends." In other words, whatever is left over. The dish is essentially meat and vegetables stir-fried together in a cornstarch-thickened soy-and-sesame sauce. Bean sprout is a popular ingredient because it is cheap.

There are many legends surrounding the dish's creation. But it is generally accepted that it was created sometime at the turn of the twentieth century by Chinese immigrants—most likely unemployed railroad workers—who settled in California. The ingenuity of the dish is that it can be made with any ingredients.

This creative use of leftover ingredients is not limited to early Chinese workers. High-end chefs do it, too. I once sat in on a morning menu meeting with Susur Lee, who has for years dazzled Toronto diners with his epicurean Sino-French fusion. The first thing he asked his staff was: What do we have in the fridge and the pantry?

—•—

Chinese immigrants first arrived in what is now Canada in 1858 to pan for gold and to provide domestic services for gold diggers in British Columbia's Fraser Valley. Many travelled north from California when its gold rush ended. Chinese migrant workers have always referred to San Francisco as "Old Gold Mountain" and to Vancouver as "New Gold Mountain."

From 1881 to 1884, more than 17,000 Chinese were recruited from Guangdong to build the transcontinental Canadian Pacific Railway. Valued for their agility and hard work, they often performed the dangerous task of dynamiting the mountains.

Many died. It's said that a Chinese worker sacrificed his life for every mile of rail.

The completion of the railway in 1885—when the western and central sections were linked in the mountains of British Columbia—was documented in a photograph of the ceremonial "last spike." All the people looking at the camera are white. Not one Chinese man is present. Their labour, sacrifice and struggles were erased from this historical record.

With the railway's completion, Chinese labourers, who received only a third of the pay of other workers, were no longer welcome. With no means to go home, they were forced to seek employment in the few jobs Chinese were permitted to hold: washing, cooking and cleaning. Women's work, as it was called at the time.

After 1885, the Canadian government made it even more difficult for Chinese to immigrate by imposing a head tax—starting at $50 and eventually rising to $500. In 1923, even this path was closed when the government passed the Chinese Exclusion Act.

For twenty-four years, until the act was repealed in 1947, Chinese workers were no longer allowed into the country. But people found their way to Canada regardless. They came as "paper sons," assuming the identity of a deceased Canadian resident. Jim arrived in 1939, using the papers of a Chinese boy named Chow Jim Kook.

"In those days, everyone was selling papers. All you do is find the paper of someone who's dead around the same age. And you take over that person's identity, name and all."

Jim's father had helped a friend in Canada who was in financial trouble. When this friend came back to their village, he gave Jim's father the identity papers of two boys who had died. Jim took the place of one of them. He can't remember how old he was at the time—perhaps twelve, perhaps fourteen—but he used the date on the boy's birth certificate. He also had to learn everything about that boy: his parents, his siblings, the town he lived in, the school he went to.

"They asked all those questions when you go to the immigration office in Hong Kong. And when you come to this side, they asked the same questions again. So, I've got to have all that information to give the right answers, eh?"

My father was also a paper son of sorts. For many years, I wondered why he was called a different name by our relatives and family friends. It turned out that his birth certificate was lost during the war; when it came time to apply for a passport to go overseas, he assumed the identity of his elder brother, who died at an early age.

Jim remembered sailing from Hong Kong to Vancouver on Canadian Pacific's *Empress of Russia*. It was September 1939, and Canada declared war on Germany as the ocean liner docked in Honolulu. According to Jim, the ship was chased by two German submarines in the Pacific Ocean.

In his retelling of the voyage, Jim said he was accompanied by a younger brother and an older sister. The sister, who had lived in Canada, taught him his ABCs en route. Jim was vague about how the three were related. Was the sister the daughter of his "paper father"? Was the brother another paper son from the village? Or was he Jim's real brother? Jim wouldn't say. Maybe he wasn't even sure himself.

After arriving in Vancouver, Jim took a train to Moose Jaw, then to Outlook, travelling on the very railroad that Chinese labourers had helped build six decades earlier. He didn't dare stop on the way because he was in Canada illegally, travelling under a false identity and assumed name.

"If we stop anywhere and somebody else know, eh, they could report me to the government. We don't want anyone else to know."

—•—

Jim's "paper father," Chow Yuen ("Fat Cook"), came to Canada in 1911. He paid the $500 head tax and—as he hailed from the Qing dynasty in China—he wore a pigtail. Chow first worked for a Vancouver doctor as a houseboy, making $4 a month.

"That's a lot of money then," Jim pointed out. "And after three years, people could make enough to buy a few acres of land in China."

In 1929, Chow opened the Outlook Cafe with several partners. Jim worked there when he first arrived and, after a couple of years, he went to Dawson Creek, British Columbia, to help build the Alaska Highway. He returned to Outlook after the war.

After the repeal of the Chinese Exclusion Act in 1947, Chow asked Jim to accompany him on a trip to their ancestral village in China.

"Did you know why you were going back to China?" I asked.

"My father didn't tell me, but I knew why. You know how Chinese are. When your father says go, you go," Jim explained. "We'd more respect for our parents in those days."

"So why did he want you to go?"

"To get married." He gave me a sheepish look.

"He wanted you to go back to China to find a wife?" I pretended to be incredulous.

"Yah, he took me with him, and I know what would happen. Although we're already in this country, all my uncles and cousins go back to China to find a wife, eh."

"Did you want to go?"

"Not too much, but I did go."

"Did you find a wife?"

"I don't know what you call find my wife, yah, but I lost my freedom then." He flashed a mischievous smile.

Jim was twenty-four, maybe twenty-six. It was an arranged marriage with a bride he had never met. But he returned to Canada a year later without his new wife, May Wong. "I can't bring the wife at the same time. I had to come back here to apply for her from the immigration office in Saskatoon."

May flew to Canada three years later, accompanied by Jim's cousin Chow Fong. Like Jim, Fong entered Canada as a "paper son" to work for his "father" in a Chinese café in nearby Rosetown.

Later in the evening, while Jim and May were playing mahjong in the restaurant with Fong and his wife, Mae Yee Quan (Fong went back to China in 1955 to get married), I asked May whether she had followed Jim to Gold Mountain willingly.

"She's got no choice," Jim answered for her. "When she said 'I do,' she's gotta do." He gave me another naughty look.

Jim often told people he had "lucky sevens," five daughters and two sons. His children were all born on the West Coast, where May and Jim moved in 1952, first to run a grocery store on Granville Street in Vancouver. When there was too much competition, they left for Prince Rupert, 1,500 kilometres north on the Pacific coast, to run the Commodore Cafe.

Seven years later, Jim and his young family returned to Outlook to work for Fong at the newly opened Modern Cafe. A year later, Jim opened the New Outlook Cafe, just two doors down from his cousin.

Jim had studied for a ham radio licence in nearby Rosetown. He wanted to be a radioman. He could also have been a tax inspector, an accountant or a forest ranger in British Columbia, where he could have telegraphed forest conditions using Morse code, which he had learned. But his father told him to stay put at the restaurant because those jobs were not for Chinese people. (Chinese Canadians of that era were barred from many professions.)

"I could've been something else," Jim said with a tinge of regret. "All those opportunities were opened to me."

He never wanted his children to end up a "washy washy cooky cooky" like him. "And they don't want it either. It's hard work, long hours and low pay. And if we calculate all the hours we work, we're lucky if we get 50 cents an hour."

"Your children must be very proud of you," I said.

"They should be. I brought them up right. I gave them all an education." He grinned with pride. "And they helped, cleaning, washing dishes at the restaurant, although they didn't get paid every time they helped."

While I was in Outlook, I made a side trip to meet with Grant Kook and Barbara Larson, Jim's second- and third-youngest children, in Saskatoon. Grant joked he and his siblings were the cheap labour force for their parents' restaurant. He remembered washing mountains of dishes, lugging heavy wooden crates filled with glass bottles of soft drinks and handling the cash register.

Barbara reflected on growing up as a restaurant kid. "I think we have a lot of resentment. We'd assimilated in our community, our friends were all people in town. But we had to help out in the restaurant, so we didn't have a lot of free time. But now, looking back as an adult, we realized what our parents went through and that there's a lot that they gave up for us."

"I didn't realize it when I was young, but my dad's always helping to raise funds for the community for various projects," Grant remembered. "He's silently helping families in the community who are facing hardships, be it financial or otherwise."

When the community put on a retirement party for Jim, it was overwhelming for his children to see how many people came out to show their support. Jim always told his children: it's family and community first. He always lived by that code.

—•—

Although Fong and Jim were cousins, they acted more like twins. I pointed out that they both assumed the identity of another Chow. Jim's actual name is Chow Hung Kong; his paper name Chow Jim Kook. Chinese put the surname first, followed by given names, but that often got turned around when they moved to other countries.

"There are lots of Chows in our village," said Fong.

"That's right, and the Chows from the same village are all related," Jim said. In China, it's not unusual for an ancestor to take root in a village and grow a whole family in place. Often, villagers who share the same surname can trace themselves back to the first settler.

I was born in Hong Kong, then a British colony. Grandfather Kwan had come from the village of Gau Gong (Jiujiang in Pinyin romanization, literally Nine Rivers) in Nanhai county, not far from Guangzhou (Canton). It has been said that the first Kwan to settle in Gau Gong had come from central China during the Southern Song dynasty, some 750 years ago. The genealogy book in the village ancestral hall traces back twenty generations from that single forefather. (Alas, only sons are listed, and only the eldest from each generation is carried over to the next.)

Dialects, even those from the same branch of the language like Cantonese, developed so differently—sometimes even between two villages across a river—that people from different areas don't understand each other. A lack of physical and social mobility can do that. People from my village speak a Gau Gong dialect that's almost incomprehensible to people elsewhere. And I look to Kwoi to interpret Jim's Taishanese.

In Canada, Jim's "last name," Kook, became his surname. I asked him whether, by losing his Chinese family name, Chow, he felt he lost his identity.

"All these years, everybody calls you Jim . . . Jim . . . what the heck, it's just a name anyway. All you pick is a name, it can represent anything. It doesn't matter to me. As long as they don't call me Stupid Nut or something."

And why was he called Noisy?

"Can't you tell? He makes so damn much noise," Lloyd, the old-timer with the mailbox key, turned around to explain. "He's been excessively loud as long as I can remember."

"It was his idea. He makes a phone call and says: 'This is Noisy.'" Clarence, a retired farmer sitting next to Lloyd, gestured as if he was answering the phone.

"Some mornings, he's so loud and so noisy that you can hardly hear yourself talk." Verna, an elderly woman of Finnish descent, rounded out the explanation. A lot of Finns and Norwegians came in the 1920s. Now they have Greek, Vietnamese and Iraqi neighbours.

"The Chinese immigrants want to be here, they want to create something they're proud of," said Clarence. "Their heart's in it. It's just a whole different attitude than a lot of other groups that come in."

I asked Jim whether he considered himself Chinese or Canadian.

"I call myself Chinese Canadian. Besides, my papers say I was born in Canada, eh?" He winked. "I'm myself. I'm me. Canadian, Chinese, Japanese, Italian. Don't matter. I'm me."

Chinese railway workers who settled along the Canadian Pacific Railway became model citizens, despite the prejudices and discrimination they faced. But Jim saw this also as his special mission in life: "We're here to serve the community. You have to open up for the people in that community. It's your duty to serve. That's your obligation."

He also found that people are friendlier in small communities. "In big cities, many times you don't know who your neighbour is." And his customers helped. They took care of each other, and the restaurant. Whenever the coffee pot was empty, they would go make another pot. And if they were refilling their own cups, they would go around refilling everyone else's.

Jim always cared about Outlook. He used the restaurant to raise money for the local high school hockey team. If the players couldn't afford hockey gear, he would buy them used equipment. He also helped raise funds to put in artificial ice for the rink and to keep the bus fully fuelled so the team could travel to other towns to compete.

A lot of people wanted him to run for mayor, but Jim thought it was too much hassle.

Lloyd laughed when I mentioned this to him. "It wouldn't be a good thing for him. It's not that he doesn't get into politics, but he'll get mixed up. Like he won't remember which party he's actually belongs to. Probably start another war by just casting an opinion."

Mayor or not, Jim *was* Outlook. And he agreed. "I've been here more than sixty years. I'm a pioneer. So, Outlook's mine. I own it."

We took a day trip to Moose Jaw, to visit the cemetery where Jim's paper father was buried. It was a two-hour drive on bare, windswept roads with nothing but snow and whiteness outside our car windows. Jim and Fong bantered non-stop in the back seat. I told them they looked funny with their furry hats and ear flaps.

Moose Jaw was known to be one of the wildest towns of the Canadian West. There's a network of tunnels under its main street where Chinese railway workers lived for many years. They were dug around 1908, when whites savagely beat Chinese railway workers, who they thought were taking their jobs. Western Canada was gripped by hysteria about the "yellow peril," and Chinese workers literally went underground, digging secret tunnels under Chinese businesses where they could hide until the situation improved.

During Prohibition in the 1920s, Chicago mobsters, hiding from the FBI, used these tunnels for gambling, prostitution and warehousing bootleg liquor. They even hired Chinese to help them with smuggling, or simply to cook and do laundry. Al Capone is rumoured to have hidden here. Moose Jaw resident Nancy Gray told a reporter for the local newspaper that her father was called to the tunnels to give Capone haircuts. The tunnels are now a tourist attraction. Capone's Hideaway Motel sits next to the train station.

The grounds of the Rosedale Cemetery were covered with thick snow. It took a little while for Fong to finally locate Chow Yuen's tombstone. Jim, walking ahead of us, was reluctant to come over.

"Yah, that's him all right," he said when he finally turned back.

"Where is your mother's grave?"

"Down that way." He pointed, but didn't go there.

"Do you want to be buried here?" I asked this question a lot. The older generation of Chinese immigrants has a deep-seated desire to be returned to China when they die, even if only as bones and ashes.

"Don't talk things like that. Chinese don't like." He walked away, thumping awkwardly through the snow. So did Kwoi, who was having trouble holding his camera steady.

"Boy, that's quite a head trip for me," Kwoi said after we got back to the car to thaw out his camera—in that temperature, the mic cable froze and a moisture spot inside the lens refused to go away.

Kwoi's father left Taishan as a paper son in 1948—the year before China became Communist—to join *his* grandfather, who had paid the head tax to enter Canada early in the twentieth century. Seven years later, Kwoi's father had saved enough money to visit his family, who by then had fled China for Hong Kong. He stayed for a year, just long enough to see the birth of his first son, Kwoi. When he was nine years old, Kwoi came to Canada to live with a father he didn't know.

Kwoi and Jim's life stories are eerily similar, which explains their we-are-all-from-the-same-village bond. And I could see how this trip to the cemetery has triggered many suppressed emotions for both of them.

On our way back, we stopped by the National Cafe on Main Street, next to the kiosk that sells entrance tickets to the tunnels. The fifty-five-year-old restaurant is owned by Tap Quan, a relative of Fong's wife, Mae. Much larger than the New Outlook or the Modern, it seats 180 on two floors.

While having coffee, Jim and Fong reminisced about the pioneer spirit and family values that Chinese immigrants share: as Fong put it, "Working together as a family, no matter which family one comes from."

"You know what? I run out of things, I could borrow from him anytime," Jim pointed to Fong. "When his coffee urn broke down one morning, he came over to my place to take some coffee back."

"There's no competition. We're in the same family," Fong assured me. "We work hard. We call it 'hard life, happy life.'"

"Hard work don't kill you, eh." Jim was warming up. "As long as you enjoy your work, don't matter what it pays. They pay you big money to work in a big company, all those hassles, and if you don't enjoy it . . . you get ulcers."

"Do you believe in God?" My question came out of nowhere.

Fong chuckled.

Jim turned dead serious, "I don't know. Sometimes I do, sometimes I don't. But I do believe in spirit. Who's doing the talking to you? Your soul. To me the body is like a car. Who makes the car go? The gasoline or the man driving? Who makes you walk? Who makes you think? Your soul. Your spirit."

<hr />

It seems like the entire town has shown up for Jim's funeral at the Outlook Civic Centre. Jim's relatives came from as far away as Toronto and Vancouver. There are six pallbearers and twelve honorary pallbearers. The entire hockey team shows up as colour guards.

John Vavra, a family friend, gives a heartfelt eulogy: "A lot of alumni came back after twenty-five years of being away, they walked into the restaurant and Jim greeted them by name and said, 'Would you like such and such?' They said, 'Why would you say that?' He said, 'Twenty-five years ago that's what you always ordered.' Anyone who has that kind of memory of people holds people in high regard. And I think that Jim, in his delightful, rough-hewn way, has shown us what service is all about."

In China, tradition dictates that the deceased be carried around the home three times before interment. There's no question where the hearse will go today. Noisy Jim circles the block three times for a final farewell to his New Outlook Cafe.

The Woodlawn Cemetery, on the outskirts of Saskatoon, is spacious and beautifully laid out. There's a large section with Chinese tombstones, each prominently carved with a surname common to the Prairies: Yee, Mak, Chow, Ma.

May sobs uncontrollably, held by her sons Grant and Steve, as the coffin is lowered.

After everyone has left for the reception at a Chinese restaurant in town, I stand alone at Jim's grave. Two years earlier, Outlook was the first stop of my global quest for stories from the Chinese diaspora. And how appropriate it was that I started here.

CHAPTER 2

Port of Refuge

HAIFA, ISRAEL

ON A MOONLESS NIGHT IN DECEMBER 1978, A FAMILY FRIEND DROVE KIEN Wong, his wife, Mei, and their four daughters, aged two to fifteen, to the banks of the Mekong River from their home in Cholon, the Chinese district of Ho Chi Minh City (Saigon).

They hid at a chicken farm until midnight before boarding a fishing boat packed with refugees and sailing toward the open sea. From there, they would climb aboard the Hong Kong–registered freighter *Tung An*. Wong had paid the equivalent of US$4,000 in gold taels to leave Vietnam.

Over the next sixteen days, the *Tung An* sailed around the South China Sea with 2,700 refugees on board. Thailand, Malaysia and Brunei turned them away. The ship finally anchored in Manila Bay, but the Philippines would not allow the passengers ashore either.

By then, twenty children had died.

Those on board survived a two-week stay in Manila Bay only due to an international humanitarian effort to provide food, water and medical supplies. Just as the Philippine government prepared to tow the ship back to international waters, thirteen nations announced they would accept the refugees for settlement.

Like many Vietnamese refugees, Wong would have liked to go to Australia, the US or Canada. Or even France, as he spoke a bit of the language. Instead, he was the first to volunteer to be interviewed by an Israeli official.

"I was guided by the hands of God," Wong told me when I first met him. As the part-time minister of an evangelical church in Vietnam, he welcomed the opportunity to spread the gospel in the Holy Land.

—•—

Kwoi, David Szu and I land at Ben Gurion Airport in February. It's mid-afternoon, but it might as well be the middle of the night. Menacing dark clouds hang low over the entire region, and an incessant rainstorm keeps blowing our car sideways as we inch along the ring roads of Tel Aviv in the middle of rush-hour traffic.

"We are in Noah's Ark territory," Kwoi deadpans.

I am travelling with two very disparate companions.

Kwoi can be very unassuming and dark humoured, despite the flamboyant way he dresses—his white cowboy hats and thick-white-rimmed glasses. He wants to go into an Israel Defense Forces (IDF) surplus store, if there's such a thing, to buy army fatigues.

Meanwhile, David is a clean-cut young man from Taiwan who just finished college in Toronto. He is attending a local film school where Kwoi teaches and was added to the crew to be second camera and on-location sound—we realized that Kwoi couldn't do everything by himself.

Three hours later, the rain clouds lift to reveal a setting sun over the Mediterranean as the coastal highway from Tel Aviv bends around Mount Carmel and deposits us in Haifa, the third-largest city in Israel.

Haifa is a model for the co-existence of Arabs and Jews, with about 70 per cent of the population being Christian Arabs living in Lower Haifa. Under the League of Nations' Mandate for Palestine, Britain invested in turning the city into a central port for Middle Eastern crude oil. It also became a focal point for immigration.

It's eight o'clock. We are in an Arab district of cloth merchants, spice sellers, car mechanics and shish-kebab purveyors. The pelting rain has stopped, and the streets are gleaming. Hardly anyone is out at this time of night. Just a few cars go by with dimmed headlights.

"Was your flight delayed?" Wong asks as I walk into Yan Yan Restaurant on Ha'meginim Street. I tell him about the rainstorm of Biblical proportions, and he laughs.

Kien Wong is a robust man of medium height with a tanned face. Tonight, he's dressed in a white pullover and beaming, having just celebrated his sixtieth birthday with a surprise visit from his sister Kuk from Vietnam. He hasn't seen her since he fled the country more than twenty years ago. Kuk's two sons also came from Canada for the celebration.

The restaurant seats no more than thirty. Its customers are mostly budget-minded tourists and seamen from ships docked just down the street. There's a table of Canadians from Montreal: mother, daughter and her Israeli boyfriend, with whom Wong chats easily in Hebrew. He tells them stories about his travels to Hong Kong and Canada, where immigration officials were curious as to how a Chinese could be travelling on an Israeli passport.

"Yum. This is really good," says a seaman from the next table, a John Travolta look-alike from Louisiana. "I never thought I would find Chinese food in Israel."

When the server arrives, I notice that she is Japanese. As she hands us our menus, she is surprised when I greet her in Japanese. She tells me she's from Yokohama and married to an Israeli. I tell her that I went to high school in her city.

"Don't bother with the menu," Wong says as he comes over to order for us. "Tonight's special is St. Peter's fish caught this morning from the Sea of Galilee."

I've never heard of tilapia being called St. Peter's fish, but then I realize that the French call the fish St. Pierre. The British have another name for it, John Dory, while people in Hong Kong sometimes call it *doh leh*, after Dory.

Wong sits with us while we wait for our dinner. "Opening a restaurant is not something I wanted to do. I knew it was tough. Besides, I didn't have the skills." Many of his fellow refugees went to work in Chinese restaurants, but he chose a job at the Ford plant in Nazareth.

"A lot of Israelis asked me to cook," he recalls. "They said, 'We don't look Chinese, you do. You should be the chef.'"

At this time, the St. Peter's appears on the table. The whole fish is lightly coated in flour, flash-fried to crispiness, and served—with a noticeable sizzle—in a pour-over sauce of ginger, scallions, rice wine and soy. A classic Cantonese rendition and a cousin to the steamed whole fish.

"I never thought I would find Chinese food *that good* here in Israel," I tell my team, echoing the Travolta look-alike.

The three of us are all discerning eaters under normal circumstances, having grown up in Hong Kong and Taiwan, where food culture is an essential part of everyday life and where fresh ingredients are always available.

And this St. Peter's is absolutely fabulous.

After ten years in Afula, where Vietnamese refugees first settled in government-provided housing, Wong felt the urge to try the restaurant trade. He needed more income because his four daughters were entering university.

"I hated to leave. There are great pastures in Afula. Sometimes you see shepherds and sheep in the country, very beautiful." He is describing the land of milk and honey that I've read about—I attended Catholic schools when I was young, and I know my Bible. He first worked in Chinese restaurants in Nahariya, Haifa and Tel Aviv—"I was a chef in a very famous restaurant in Tel Aviv," he tells us—and learned the skills to run a restaurant of his own.

"Actually, it is not hard to open a Chinese restaurant. If you can make almond chicken, green pepper and beef, sweet and sour pork, throw in spring rolls and salad, you're in business." Wong recites the hit parade of Chinese restaurant menus. "Israelis only want to eat these dishes. If you asked them to eat something else, they would refuse."

Though not strictly kosher, Yan Yan Restaurant nevertheless replaces pork with chicken in its sweet and sour dish. Wong later introduced his customers to ingredients such as tofu, dried scallops and Chinese mushrooms when he opened a grocery store called Chinatown on Jaffa Street, next to the Port Inn where we are staying.

When I was looking for a Chinese restaurant in Israel, it was a challenge to find one run by ethnic Chinese. Most owners were Israelis, with Chinese as cooks or managers. Many even employed Thai cooks, adding a distinctive Thai flavour to their Israeli-Chinese cooking. Tom yum kung was often on the menu.

Just as I was getting disheartened in my search, I spotted Yan Yan. "Merry Christmas" and "Happy Chinese New Year" signs on the front window were handwritten in proper Chinese calligraphy, a good indication that I'd found a Chinese owner.

Wong returns to clear the dishes. He retired a few weeks ago, handing over the restaurant to his eldest daughter, Cee Wong, and her husband, Vinh Hei Fung. But Wong still helps out, going into the kitchen when his son-in-law is overwhelmed with takeout orders. I spot Mei, Wong's wife, wrapping spring rolls in one corner amid the cacophony and organized chaos typical of a Chinese kitchen.

Being the eldest daughter—fifteen when the family arrived in Haifa—Cee dropped out of school to help, but she doesn't regret her decision. She wanted to help her father so her younger sisters could have a better life. Fung, who arrived with the same group of refugees from Manila in 1979, also started out working in Chinese restaurants. Both believe their children will eventually take up the same business. They are very much at home in Israel. Coming from a diasporic Chinese community in Vietnam, they feel they can belong anywhere: in Israel, in Australia, in America.

But there's one problem.

"Israelis don't treat you as one of them," Fung reminds me. "They don't trust you with sensitive matters."

Cee was turned down by the IDF when she tried to enlist.

—•—

In October 1977, the Israeli freighter *Yuvali* rescued sixty-six Vietnamese "boat people" in the South China Sea. Four other ships of different nationalities had passed them by. By international convention, those picked up at sea had to be accepted into the ship's country of origin.

Israeli Prime Minister Menachem Begin went a step further, granting them the immediate citizenship they accorded Jews under the Law of

Return. He equated the refugees' plight to that of Jews fleeing Nazi Europe: "We never have forgotten the boat with 900 Jews, the *St. Louis*, having left Germany in the last weeks before the Second World War . . . traveling from harbor to harbor, from country to country, crying out for refuge. They were refused . . . Therefore it was natural . . . to give those people a haven in the Land of Israel."

Concurrently, Canada also faced its own call of conscience. Despite the thousands of Vietnamese lingering in refugee camps in Southeast Asia, only 9,000 settled in Canada between 1975 and 1978.

As a new immigrant, I fully recognized the intrinsic value of a multi-cultural Canada and wanted my adopted country to open its doors to help alleviate the humanitarian crisis. I joined an action group organized by activists from Toronto's Chinese community. Petitions, rallies and marches were held almost every weekend. Alliances were formed among social agencies and labour organizations.

That public outcry led to Canada eventually accepting 60,000 refugees between 1979 and 1980. Being part of that public outcry launched my personal journey of community activism.

Southeast Asian refugee settlement became the norm among Western democracies. Eventually, Israel accepted three groups of 360 boat people from Vietnam over the next two years. Wong and his family arrived in January 1979 with the second group of 100 refugees, almost all of them ethnic Chinese.

"There was a welcoming reception at the airport, with people waving Vietnamese and Israeli flags," he reminisces. "We didn't feel like refugees; we felt like honoured guests."

"We're people from all around the world," Shimon Lipschitz adds, now joining us at our table. He runs a neighbourhood garage not far from Yan Yan and drops by in the evenings after his shop closes.

Born to German Jewish parents who immigrated to Israel after the Second World War, he empathizes with Wong's displacement, even calling Wong his blood brother. Lipschitz rhymes off the names of countries in Europe, the Middle East and the former Soviet Union from which Jewish immigrants arrived.

"Even some from Asia," he adds. "And they brought their Asian wives."

This is classic diaspora. Having travelled around the world several times over, I have always maintained that the Jews, the Indians and the Chinese are the three largest diasporic peoples—you can find them in the four corners of the globe.

I am intrigued by his reference to Jews from Asia and tell him that successive waves of Jews had settled in the open city of Shanghai during the first half of the twentieth century. There were Baghdadi Jews who came via the British Empire in the late 1800s, Russian Jews fleeing the 1917 revolution and European Jews who fled in the early days of Nazi rule.

"Twenty thousand European Jews sailed from the south of France through the Suez Canal to reach Asia, only to be turned away by British India," I add. "Japanese-occupied Shanghai was one of the few remaining places in the world that would accept them."

In fact, Jewish migration to China began centuries earlier. Sephardic Jews came via the Silk Road in the eighth century during the Tang dynasty; a tribe known as the Kaifeng Jews settled in the tenth century in the Song dynasty capital Kaifeng. They have long since assimilated and are indistinguishable from Han Chinese, but their existence in China was specifically recognized: a fourteenth-century Ming emperor conferred seven surnames to Jews in China, among them Jin (gold) and Shi (stone).

I am curious about Wong's own integration. "How's Mr. Wong's Hebrew?"

"His Hebrew is good," Lipschitz says. "You speak English, you can manage, but if you speak Hebrew, you are king. Doesn't matter from where you come."

——

The sun breaks out the next morning. Wong has chartered a bus to take a group of Chinese expatriates and their families to the Chinese ambassador's residence in Tel Aviv to celebrate Chinese New Year. The group includes post-doctoral physicists, oceanographers and molecular geneticists.

The ride is festive. Loudspeakers blast Mandarin songs as our bus rolls down the Mediterranean coast. Palm trees, blue sky and a bright sun give a false sense of a tropical paradise—we're actually in the midst of an unusually cold Israeli winter. It snowed in the Negev Desert for the first time in fifty years.

Our group is joined by more than 400 others at the reception, some from as far south as Eilat on the Gulf of Aqaba. They mingle, drink and eat throughout the afternoon. Children, speaking Hebrew among themselves, run around the garden and gobble steamed meat buns from the buffet. The pungent smell of mao tai fills the air. The ambassador gives a welcome speech, urging his guests to love their motherland. And a toast to China.

It's late afternoon when our bus drops us off at Jaffa, the ancient port city to the south that has since been absorbed into Greater Tel Aviv. While the other passengers sightsee and shop in the restored Old City, Wong brings me to a windswept lookout with a panoramic view of Tel Aviv's waterfront. Here, he tells me about his conversion to Christianity in high school and about his work, as an adult, as a part-time Christian minister while running a successful family business.

"But when the Communists came, everything went downhill," he says. "That's when God told me to leave." He was thirty-nine.

After arriving in Israel, Wong began to have doubts about his choice. He had wanted to preach, but he couldn't speak Hebrew. His only audience would have been other Chinese speakers—but Chinese seamen never stayed long enough. Even his compatriots began immigrating to Canada and the US in the 1980s.

Wong now tells the story of Jonah and the Whale. Jonah had sailed from Jaffa only to be swallowed up by a whale during a storm. Wong tells the story like a homily: "Jonah was impatient, and it was God's way of testing him. I took from this story that we should be willing to obey God's commands. He asked us to have patience, to follow His wishes."

The answer to Wong's prayers finally came thirteen years after he settled in Israel.

In 1992, expatriate Chinese began to arrive when the two countries established diplomatic relations, opening doors to cultural and scholastic exchanges. Then came migrant construction workers and apple pickers.

"That's when I understood why God wanted me to stay here. It was to build a new home for these newly arrived Chinese."

—•—

I want to get a better sense of how well the family has assimilated and decide to visit Wong's other three daughters elsewhere in Israel.

Dao Wong, the second youngest, became the first Chinese immigrant to be accepted by the Israeli army—"I wanted to give something back to my adopted country," she says—and the first homegrown flight attendant of Chinese heritage at El Al, the national airline.

Dao's story became even more impressive when she was fast-tracked into the foreign service. She smiles with pride when she tells me that while negotiating arms treaties in Washington, DC, her US State Department colleagues really warmed to a Vietnam-born Chinese holding an Israeli passport.

The stories of Dao and, to a lesser extent, her younger sister Mai—who followed Dao's footsteps to become the first ethnic Chinese to enlist in the navy and is currently flying with El Al—are famous in and around Israel. Newspapers and magazines have profiled them.

Dao now works for a bank in Jerusalem and lives with her Polish Israeli husband Amit Rochvarger in Modi'in, a new housing estate built on the bare rolling hills by the Tel Aviv–Jerusalem highway. Rochvarger was first attracted to Dao ten years earlier, when they were students at Jerusalem University.

"It took me some time to realize that she's not a Chinese foreign student but almost a *sabra* like me," he says, using the Hebrew term for Israel-born Jews. "After that it was finding an excuse to speak to her. We were taking a course together, so I asked to copy her homework."

On his first visit to the Wong family, he passed the "chopsticks test" and noted that "we have the same Polish mother jokes." I sit with him while his infant son Tzur ("rock" in Hebrew) sleeps on his lap. Dao is preparing lunch, her kitchen full of Chinese produce and condiments, with the ever-present rice cooker.

Rochvarger epitomizes sabras born after the Six-Day War. Young, hopeful and not overtly religious, he offers plenty of insights on and criticism of his country. His Israel has less to do with Zionism than with survival as a modern Middle Eastern state.

"In Israel, nationality doesn't exist, since nationality is equated to the Jewish religion. There is no such thing as an Israeli national—if you are an Arab or a Christian, you can only be a citizen." To someone who comes from a left-wing family that believes strongly in Israel's brand of socialism—kibbutz, army and equality—"this is sheer craziness."

Not being Jewish in Israel can create a lot of day-to-day bureaucratic problems in birth and marriage. Rochvarger and Dao were married in Cyprus because Israel does not recognize marital unions between Jews and non-Jews. "Still, nine out of ten people in Israel won't marry a foreigner unless they convert to Judaism. So, there's still a problem living here," he says.

I broach the subject of security and tell him I can't get over the fact that soldiers even carry Uzis into bars and clubs on their days off. "For people outside of Israel, it's a very disturbing thing to see," he says. "In Israel, it's a very normal thing. But Israel is not a normal country. You learn to live with it."

Rochvarger is Jewish more in nationality than in religion. His conversion to Christianity by his future father-in-law was purely to facilitate his marriage to Dao. Living with two religions for him is like living in a city and owning a country house—you can switch religious practices just as easily as you would go for a weekend in the country.

"There is a big problem for a lot of Israelis in accepting foreigners as part of the community. It's part of being a Jew. I think the problem is not with me or Dao. We know where we stand," he points out, stroking Tzur's hair. "The problem is for the little one. He'll grow up in a house with a mixture of Judaism, Christianity and Chinese beliefs. And when he grows up, he'll have to decide which side he is taking. I just hope he will adopt all good things, because it doesn't matter which God you believe in, as long as you are a good man."

As we are leaving, and out of earshot of her husband, Dao confides to me that Rochvarger has had a temporary loss of faith since his father died a few months ago. She thinks he will eventually find God within himself. On which side of the Jewish-Christian divide he will eventually land, she's not sure.

—.—

"My earliest memory was watching mother come home from the balcony of our apartment in Afula," Mai Wong tells me as we lunch at a kibbutz-run restaurant by Tel Aviv's beachfront the next day. "I was so happy to see her. I was always home alone."

Dressed in a black turtleneck and jeans—it's her day off; she flies out the next morning—Mai exudes an almost childish charm that is different from her three older sisters. She was only two when her mother carried her off the KLM flight from Manila.

Mai is an Israeli through and through: her best language is Hebrew, her circle of friends is Jewish, and she doesn't want to live anywhere else. Rachel Silas—the owner of the Port Inn where we stay, and a family friend of the Wongs—tells me that Mai is the most Israeli of the four daughters.

"She has an Israeli temper, and when she quarrels with her father, she has to translate her own words from Hebrew to Chinese," Silas says with a laugh. "And I'm like a Jewish mother to her because her own parents wouldn't understand what she's going through."

Over salad, Mai reveals that her boyfriend is in the Israeli intelligence community. Aman? Mossad? Shin Bet? She won't say, nor would she tell me his name.

"Would your father object to you marrying him?"

She hesitates a little before answering. "No, I don't think he will object. Well, he won't say you can or cannot marry him . . . It's going to be like . . . like . . . whether I marry a Christian or not . . . Oh, it's not that easy here in Israel." Her voice tails off.

Everywhere in Israel, young people in uniform are a common sight. Serving in the military is part of growing up—Dao and her sister Mai enlisted even though, as immigrants, they were not required to serve.

Israelis take security seriously and matter-of-factly.

One night, our car is held up in the city's club district off Dizengoff Square while a bomb squad checks on a suspicious-looking package a block away. Everyone stops as if waiting for lights to change.

Our taste of Israeli security takes a more dramatic turn after we leave Mai. While executing a "drive-by shooting"—Kwoi and David each filming from his side of the car while I drive—a security agent jumps in front of us, slaps his badge on the windshield, and hauls me into the station demanding to check our camera tapes.

This is par for the course, the risks we all take as photographers and filmmakers. I can't remember how many times I've been hauled in by the authorities whenever they think I'm overstepping their boundaries through my viewfinder. And it's understandable, given the heightened Israeli-Palestinian tension—we were there in the middle of the Second Intifada, after all.

Once inside the station, the agent treats the whole episode as a run-of-the-mill stop and search. Perhaps he has seen this too many times. He copies our passports and reviews footage of smiling men and women in uniform waving to our cameras as they come out of what looks like a military compound. Photographing soldiers is fine, he tells me, but filming the communications towers on the rooftop of the IDF headquarters is forbidden. We get our passports back.

When I get back to the car, Kwoi and David are having a good laugh at my expense. Then I notice the army fatigues that Kwoi bought—with an IDF insignia—in the backseat, in plain sight, all this time.

Kwoi has a way of getting into interesting situations.

On a previous trip, when I had to leave Israel early and left him behind to pick up more shots in Jerusalem, he hooked up with an off-duty female soldier, still in uniform and carrying an Uzi, at a disco bar. ("Is that an Uzi in your pocket, or are you happy to see me?") They ended up frolicking the next two days away on the shores of the Dead Sea.

The peaceful pastures and quiet villages along our drive through Nazareth belie the political, religious and ethnic tensions of everyday life in Israel. At Tiberias, on the western shore of the Sea of Galilee, we turn south toward Jesus's baptismal site at the mouth of the Jordan River.

Nee Wong is at the visitor centre (the real site of the baptism is said to be farther south along the river) hauling bottles of sake that have been kosher certified by a rabbi back in Japan. She and her husband, Yom Wong, have recently taken over the centre's cafeteria, serving a Chinese-Italian buffet. In the evening, it becomes a kosher Mongolian grill for the locals.

After a quick lunch of braised beef brisket in tomatoes on rice (an Italian-style Hong Kong comfort food), we walk down to a sheltered part of the river mouth. Even though the country is in the midst of another wave of Palestinian attacks, thousands of tourists come every year. A handful of visitors from the US are being baptized in their rented ceremonial white robes while we watch and applaud.

"I didn't want to go to Israel," Nee, the second-born, says. "In my mind, Israel is an ancient country, something I read about in the Bible." She was sent to high school in Taiwan soon after the family arrived and could have stayed there after graduation, but she chose to return to Israel to be with her family.

Yom and his family came with the third batch of Vietnamese refugees in late 1979. The couple met at the Crimson Flower, his parents' restaurant in Tiberias where Nee found work after returning from Taiwan. Soon after they married, they opened their own Panda Restaurant in the same city, which they still run. Wong has always said that Nee is the most entrepreneurial of his children.

Nee confides that she is also more Chinese than her sisters. She and her husband would like to spend more time with their children and bring them up in a Chinese culture, but they are hampered by long hours in the restaurant. When I ask her about safety for their children, she assures me it's very safe in Israel—it's just that "the media tends to depict a more horrible truth than what's going on here."

Haifa turns quiet late Friday afternoon. It's the start of Shabbat. Shutters are drawn, people hurry home.

Friday service at Kien Wong's Haifa Chinese Alliance Church is held at a rented space in a building on Jaffa Street that housed his first Yan Yan Restaurant. Li Hong Gang, one of Wong's most avid converts, is preparing for the service by laying out hymn books on folding chairs and checking the sound system.

Li is a lean and muscular man with an angular face, dressed in a dark suit and sporting a deep blue polka-dot tie. He is particularly philosophical tonight. There's a spiritual emptiness in China, he says, and he too was once spiritually empty. Now he sees the light—all the earthly troubles he faced have disappeared—and he is determined to "save the souls" of tens of thousands of Chinese expatriates languishing in Europe and the Middle East.

He ran a business in Shanghai before landing in the Czech Republic in 1992 on a commercial visa. Caught up in a turf war between two regional factions of Chinese migrants, he came to Israel in 1996 on a tourist visa.

"It's God's will," he says, thinking back. "When you have money in Czech, you just gamble it away. I had no inner peace and was always looking."

Three years later, while working as a cook in a Haifa hotel, he met Kien Wong and began helping out at Yan Yan and at the church (Wong initially used his restaurant as a makeshift place of worship).

Li has not returned to China—"I don't have a working visa here, so I can't come back"—and is separated from his wife. They have a twelve-year-old daughter who stays with his in-laws, and he would like to bring her out of China "to show her different parts of the world."

Tonight's service is unusually long, with two visiting pastors from Shanghai giving the sermon instead of Wong. To my surprise, Mei Wong, who is normally quiet and reticent, steps up to the podium to lead the hymns—a loud and hearty singing for the fifty or so who gathered in the room. Afterwards, helpers haul over large pots of Cantonese-style braised beef brisket and rice that Cee's husband has prepared at the restaurant— enough comfort food for the congregation.

The next day, we drive to Upper Galilee. There's snow by the roadside—we are on the same road that leads to Mount Hermon, Israel's ski resort in the Golan Heights.

In the car, Wong tells the story of Abraham and his two sons, Ishmael and Isaac, and how Arabs and Jews are practically cousins, having descended from the two half-brothers: "A fight between these two half-brothers led to a family tragedy that's now mankind's tragedy."

A dozen migrant Chinese workers meet us at the Arab Christian town of Jish and take us to an unfinished house they rent from an Arab contractor. It is more like a concrete bunker, with no doors or hot water. Twenty workers, five or six to a room, sleep on castaway mattresses in sleeping bags.

In what would be the living room, Wong begins his sermon with the story of Abraham and his two sons. His congregation sits on the mattresses, listening intently. Wong is animated, peppering homilies with practical advice he hopes the workers will take away. They sing hymns from song sheets.

Then Wong leads them in singing "My Chinese Heart," a patriotic song that was popular in the 1980s. Some consider it propaganda. The song is about Chinese identity and culture and has become the de facto anthem of the mainland Chinese diaspora.

> The rivers and mountains of home exist only in my dreams
> My motherland has been in turmoil for years
> No matter what, nothing can change
> My Chinese heart.

There are 12,000 Chinese workers in Israel on two-year visas, modern-day indentured labourers exported and exploited by Chinese state-owned companies. They work at jobs that Israelis would not do—and would not give to the Palestinians. These Chinese workers earn US dollars for their families at home, which is why many go underground after their visas expire.

"These Chinese are lonely and helpless. They can't speak the language. They are abused by their employers. Sometimes they don't even get paid," Wong says on our drive home. This is the first time I've seen him so emotional and agitated. "They can't communicate with the doctor when they are sick. We feel that we need to help these people. If I don't help them, who will?"

Wong's family has been twice displaced. His father left China for Vietnam in the 1930s, working for Nationalist China's railway ministry. Wong was born near the Chinese border. The family moved to Saigon when he was two. After Mao Zedong came to power in 1949, Wong's father decided not to return. Thirty years later, Wong and many of his generation of Chinese Vietnamese fled Vietnam when Ho Chi Minh became victorious.

I can't help but think that this sense of displacement feeds Wong's passion to help other Chinese expatriates. He has never been to his ancestral homeland, yet he tirelessly instills in these migrant workers a love for *their* homeland.

As members of the Chinese diaspora, we each have multiple nationalities and allegiances, speak multiple languages, and live multiple cultures. Like chameleons, we become fluid in our identities, always adapting to our environment.

While driving through Afula and its apple orchards on our way back to Haifa, I turn the question back to Wong and ask him who he really is.

"First of all . . . I'm sixty, I have three nationalities: Chinese, Vietnamese, Israeli," he says. "Who am I? I'm still Chinese, no matter which nationality I have. I am Chinese."

CHAPTER 3

Feelin' de Vibe

SAN FERNANDO, TRINIDAD AND TOBAGO

This is J'ouvert morning I just want to dance and sing
Everybody gather 'round when music start playing
People going crazy when the big truck start moving
Music fill the atmosphere and people start jumping.

Ah feelin' some ole time calypso
Ah feelin' the vibes of the rapso
Ah feelin' the drum and the bass so
Ah try to make you, make you move and you rock so.

CARNIVAL TUESDAY. THE SUN HAS NOT YET RISEN, BUT THE PARTY IS ALREADY in full swing. Thumping soca music is everywhere on San Fernando Hill.

Kwoi and I arrived in Trinidad and Tobago the night before. We'll have had only four hours of sleep when Anna Soong and her husband, John Johnston, pick us up at our hotel. They are taking us to Port of Spain for the annual extravaganza known as Carnival.

Trinidad's Carnival is the largest in the Caribbean—one wild, week-long national party. It's said that if Trinis—what Trinidadians call themselves—aren't celebrating Carnival, they are preparing for the next one while reminiscing about the last one.

The first parties start Sunday evening and end at 4 a.m. Monday, when J'ouvert begins—a day of street parades where partygoers smear paint, mud or oil on their bodies. It's an annual excuse to go wild.

Carnival Tuesday is the climax of the festival, when costumed masquerade (mas) bands parade all over the island. The biggest and grandest parade is in the capital, Port of Spain. Festivities continue until early morning Ash Wednesday, when the entire island shuts down and everyone hits the beach to cool off their collective Carnival fever.

Today we are going to play mas.

Anna and John are meeting up with their friend Lawrence Low in his house, nestled in a lush valley just outside Port of Spain. Banyan trees sway in the wind, birds chirp in the slowly lifting mist and the sweet smell of morning fills the air.

Lawrence is a second-generation Chinese Trinidadian who owns five Café Caribbean fast-food stalls in shopping malls. He and his Italian Canadian wife, Carmen, met in Toronto. Along with Anna and John, they are joining Carnival veteran Edmund Hart's mas band, one of the largest of the festival and a favourite of Chinese Trinidadians. Today, it gathers about 5,000 players, divided into different coloured sections based on this year's theme: Hell of a Life.

My new-found friends are donning Aztec-themed turquoise costumes: bikinis, feathered headgear and decorative beads for the women; loincloths over bikini shorts, along with gold-coloured breastplates, for the men.

Johnston has played mas since he was a child—there are Kiddie Mas shows for the children "as soon as they can walk and swing." Even though she was born in Trinidad, Anna never played until she met John.

At eight o'clock, with last-minute costume fixes and the filling-up of hip flasks with rum, we're ready to head out to the public grounds that serve as centre stage for Carnival.

There is a large Trinidadian community in Toronto. A majority of them—or their parents—immigrated to Canada in the late 1970s, along with immigrants from other islands in the Caribbean.

Ever since I moved to Canada in 1976, I have known and worked with many Trinis. Many of them are of ethnic Chinese origin.

When Heather De Peza, one of my staff at the not-for-profit Harmony Movement, visited her extended family in Port of Spain, I asked her to look for a Chinese restaurant owner who would have an interesting story to tell. She came back and told me that everyone she talked to on the island said Soong's Great Wall in San Fernando served the best Chinese food in the Caribbean and that their Wednesday-night buffet was legendary.

I got in touch with Maurice and Brenda Soong in Toronto on one of their frequent sojourns to Canada. It turns out that the Soongs immigrated in the 1970s so that their children could get a Canadian education but continued to go back to Trinidad to help with the restaurant, though their daughter Anna now runs it.

They invited me to come visit them during Carnival. Which is how I ended up in the biggest street party of my life—and we are talking about an entire island.

—•—

Soong's Great Wall is housed in a two-storey building inside a walled compound with a fish pond, rock garden, miniature pagoda and garden waterfall. At night, with flashing neon lights and elevator music playing from outdoor speakers, the place looks every bit like a Chinese fantasyland in the dark hills of San Fernando.

And it is a gem.

When the Chinese Trinidadian entrepreneur launched the Great Wall with much fanfare in 1981, it was front-page news. The restaurant is a place to see and be seen. Guests have included prime ministers, presidents, ambassadors and Hollywood stars—even Miss Universe contestants from Asia who craved Chinese food. Displays of framed newspaper clippings and autographed photos cover one wall and the grand piano in the dining room. One of them shows Maurice dancing with the prime minister's wife.

"Chinese food is very difficult, not like English food," Maurice Soong explains after our buffet lunch. "Chinese menu has hundreds of items. Customers will say, 'I'd like to have some shrimp, I'd like to have some roast duck and some steamed fish.' And you'll have to serve the right mix of dishes."

The Cantonese food here is authentic. Maurice serves the most delicious roast duck this side of the Pacific, prepared by chefs hired directly from his native district in China, and barbecued in a Chinese rotisserie imported from Miami.

But the dim sum is simply out of this world.

Thousands of kilometres away from Hong Kong, I find one of the best dim sums that I have ever tasted. The har gow wrappings are translucent, showing off the shrimp inside; the BBQ pork buns are spongy and steaming hot; the skin on the chicken feet in black bean sauce is fatty and succulent; while the beef balls are delicately spiced, and most important of all, loose enough to break apart in your mouth.

But the pièce de résistance is daufufa (soy milk pudding)—smooth and silky, made every morning in a traditional wooden tub and served warm with a generous serving of rock sugar syrup. I have never eaten something as good as this outside of Hong Kong.

It's to die for.

Maurice is also justifiably proud of his kitchen—one of the cleanest Chinese kitchens that I've seen. A long prep table runs down the length of the kitchen and divides the room. On one side are four built-in woks and a steamer where bamboo steamer baskets are stacked five high. On the other, a bank of refrigerators and pantries. Spotless, well stocked and orderly. When I walk in, a Chinese cook in chef's whites is polishing the stainless-steel service area, while an Indian maître d' carefully wipes sauces from the edges of plates before they go out.

Needless to say, the service is top class. The Great Wall's staff is professional, smartly uniformed in black and white and trained in proper food service. So it's no surprise the restaurant is a training ground for restaurant management in Trinidad.

Priya Choo-Ying is on her knees, polishing the glass of a French door. Just out of school and in her first waitressing job, grateful for the opportunity to train at the Great Wall. Her paternal grandparents are Chinese, and her mother has Indian and African heritage. She was raised with that cultural mix and dreams of going to China.

"Their parents love it that we train their kids," Maurice says. "It gives them a good foundation in life."

Maurice Soong's father, William Soong, arrived in Trinidad in 1937. In his early thirties and educated, having learned English in Hong Kong, he was sponsored by a distant uncle from his village of Lung Kong, near Hong Kong. Like many Chinese of his generation, he left his young family in China to seek a better life in the Americas.

The elder Soong was part of the third wave of Chinese migration to Trinidad, between the 1920s and 1940s.

Even though he wired money home, his family in China was very poor and barely survived the Sino-Japanese War. They often had to flee to the hills to evade bandits and Japanese invaders, and Maurice's mother would go down to the village in the morning to beg for food for her family of five. (Maurice has three sisters.)

Ten years after he arrived in Trinidad, William sent for his only son, who was twelve.

It took Maurice twenty days at sea on an American President Lines ship from Hong Kong to San Francisco, and another two days by plane, to reach Port of Spain. He remembers meeting his father for the first time at the airport: "I didn't know it was him. We came face to face, and he said, 'Son, I'm your father.' I didn't know my father because he'd left China when I was only two years old."

Maurice helped out at his father's small general store in the village of Hermitage, not far from San Fernando. William, known as a bon vivant, was "always well dressed with a white shirt, driving around in a fancy sports car." He soon left his young son in charge of the store.

Maurice's mother came to Trinidad five years after him, adopting a Christian name, Lucy. It is at Maurice and Brenda's modest home, after Maurice cooked a dinner that included the Hakka classic of braised pork belly with preserved mustard greens, that I broach the subject of his parents living apart all these years.

"Brenda told me you were very close to your mother."

Maurice chokes up when I raise the topic. "Mother sacrificed a lot for us. I didn't know my father until I came to Trinidad. I'm very close to my mother. So naturally I was very happy when she came."

It was not unusual for a Chinese man far from home to have other families in the New World. I am curious about it and ask him whether his father had another family here. He is evasive at first, but eventually admits his father did.

"Did your mother know your father had another woman?"

"Yeah, she knew. That other woman would come to our shop sometimes, but the lady was very good."

"How many children did your father have with this woman?"

"He claimed he had one son, whom I know also. He claimed that was his son, but I never . . ." At this point, he looks away, trying to hold back his tears.

Young men from China have joined their fathers and uncles in the Caribbean since the late nineteenth century. When they were old enough, they were sent back to China to find wives who would bear them children. These women stayed in China to raise the family while their husbands returned to the Americas. This separation of family—and perhaps having a second family elsewhere in the world—has left profound scars in many immigrant families in the New World.

It was Maurice's mother, Lucy, having lived apart from her husband for fifteen years, who held the family together as Maurice transformed from a humble shopkeeper to a successful restaurateur.

Maurice Soong also gives a lot of credit for his success to Miss Noëlle, his first teacher in Trinidad. She is of mixed French, African and Indian heritage and from the neighbouring island of Barbados—her grandfather was French Creole and from St. Lucia. Noëlle was twenty-four when Maurice showed up, not speaking a word of English. She took him under her wing.

It's late afternoon when Noëlle, Maurice and I arrive at Cipero Roman Catholic School. The modest school, with about five to six open classrooms, is housed in a single-storey brick building with concrete lattice windows and a corrugated roof. Nothing much has changed since Maurice was a boy.

The school is empty today. Roosters are crowing in the yard. An Indian caretaker, recognizing Noëlle, opens the doors to let us in. They chat about the old days and remember acquaintances.

Maurice is sentimental about his first days in Trinidad, recalling them as he sits at a school desk in the front row, facing the blackboard, just as he did more than fifty years ago. "I would always sit close to her in class."

"Well, you see, because . . . It was only so I'd be able to talk with him and explain to him, and not with all the other children," says Noëlle, enunciating like the English teacher that she was. "Then I would go to his home and help him in the evening, so I could give him my personal attention. And we had good times. We used to play cricket in the shop area. Remember?"

She gives him a tug under the arm.

According to her, Maurice has always shown gratitude and respect for all those who helped him. "No show-offs or anything, not any kind of boasting. It takes humility and honesty to maintain and keep up a decent and clean business."

On our way back, we stop at the Hermitage store where Maurice grew up. It is now a family home. After a few loud knocks, a young man opens the door. When we explain why we came, he gladly produces some old photos from that time, including one of his own father standing with William Soong.

"When I came from China in 1948, it was a wooden structure," Maurice explains as we do a walk-around. "We used to sell everything you can find. We had a licence to sell liquor, scotch, rum, wine, foodstuffs, clothing, needles and thread, bicycle parts, everything."

All over the Caribbean, in every village and town, there's always a "Chinese shop." Like running restaurants and laundries, opening a small general store that sells anything and everything is a way for immigrants to survive and integrate into the new country.

When the Chinese first arrived in the mid-nineteenth century to these islands, they worked as indentured labourers on sugar plantations. In the early 1900s, they came as free labour—merchants and shopkeepers—while larger numbers of Indians, who had also been brought to the country as indentured labourers, became farmers.

Maurice later takes me to the hustle and bustle of Charlotte Street, Port of Spain's Chinatown, so I can see for myself how Chinese Trinidadians have progressed from running general stores and mini-markets to food emporiums and supermarket chains.

We visit the Wing Sing General Store, which supplies most of the Great Wall's Chinese ingredients. The place is a beehive of activity, with customers lining up three deep at the front counter. At the back of the store, he introduces me to the owner, Ti Leung Wong.

"We're like a family here; we help each other out," says Wong.

Charlotte Street is also where the Chinese congregate and where their associations are located. Maurice points out the Fui Toong On Society, an association for those with Hakka heritage like his.

Most of the Chinese diaspora in the Caribbean are Hakka, a subgroup within the ethnic Han Chinese. Hakka are often referred to as the Jews of China. For two millennia, they migrated from the central plains, absorbing various cultures and cuisines along the way, before putting down roots in southeastern China.

After Trinidad and Tobago's independence in 1962, there was a modest increase in social acceptability for the Chinese, who numbered about 10,000 in the 1970s. But after that their numbers decreased, as many of the next generation felt insecure in a post-colonial society and immigrated to Canada and the US.

But for those who have not left, Charlotte Street is an anchor and haven—a comforting place where they can come from all over the island to meet, shop, eat and trade.

—————

I am taken to the outlook point at the top of San Fernando Hill, where, on a clear day, you can see Venezuela. Maurice Soong and Brenda Law are strolling—and holding hands as if they are on a first date—under the golden hue of the late-afternoon sun.

Brenda grew up in the same Chinese village as Maurice during the war, when her family sought refuge there. They attended the same primary school, and their mothers knew each other. After the war, Brenda's family moved back to Hong Kong, and her godfather—who had immigrated to Trinidad years earlier—suggested the match to her parents.

"It was the late fifties, and there was no future in Hong Kong anyway," Brenda points out. "My family was poor, and I didn't want to become a bar hostess like some of my classmates."

Her parents encouraged her to take a trip to Trinidad, hopeful she would like Maurice, marry him and settle there. But Brenda didn't even know where San Fernando was and, on the way over, wondered why she wasn't getting off her Pan Am flight on the stopover in *San Francisco*.

"When I met her at the airport, she surprised me. I remembered her in grade one—she had a chubby, cute face," Maurice says. "But she was all grown up, so beautiful."

They dated a few times—going out for ice cream in his car—and married in 1958. The contrast between them is remarkable. He, a shy country boy, speaks softly in his Hakka dialect. She, a city girl, is more outgoing and engaging. Like a social butterfly, according to her daughter Debbie. And Brenda speaks the more modern Hong Kong version of Cantonese.

At first, Brenda didn't like Trinidad, finding it even poorer and more backward than the British colony. "Hong Kong may be underdeveloped, but at least we had television," she says.

At one point, she told Maurice that for $15,000, she'd call off the marriage and return home. He didn't have that kind of money. But it was her future mother-in-law who won her over, welcoming Brenda with open arms. Lucy was eager to see her son find a good spouse. Brenda had an emotional bond with her mother-in-law and has shed many tears since she passed away in the late 1970s.

"She was very good to me, kind and gracious," says Brenda. "And later on, she would babysit my kids while I worked in the restaurant. I loved my mother-in-law more than I loved my mother."

After running Chinese shops for almost two decades—first for his father, then on his own—Maurice wanted to open a restaurant. He had always been a good cook, having learned from his father from the age of twelve. (His daughter Patsy says he's a natural cook, with a knack for duplicating whatever he tastes.) Brenda persuaded her husband to move to San Fernando, located on the southwestern part of Trinidad—an industrial centre of steel mills and refineries, and the second-largest city on the island.

In 1968, with money from his father and a staff of six, Maurice opened Soong's Snackette on the ground floor of the Lucky Building on Coffee Street. His lone Chinese cook made chicken and chips (an all-time Trini favourite), hamburgers and some Chinese food. Maurice didn't draw a salary.

A few years later, Soong's Cherry Blossom opened upstairs. It was the first Chinese restaurant in Trinidad that was fully carpeted and centrally air-conditioned, with eighteen staff and seating for one hundred.

"I never expected to see this in San Fernando," the mayor said at the time. Even San Fernando–born Patrick Manning—future prime minister, then leader of the opposition—held his wedding reception at the Cherry Blossom.

As the two restaurants shared a kitchen, the couple ran up and down the stairs all day, managing both while raising four children: Anna, Johnny, Debbie and Patsy.

As many Caribbean Chinese did in the early seventies, Maurice and Brenda successfully applied for citizenship in Canada, another Commonwealth country, as insurance against political uncertainty. Brenda moved with the children to Toronto, where they attended high school and university. Maurice stayed only for a few months. He believed that if he returned to Trinidad and worked hard, the people would support him and he would be successful.

In 1981, he opened the Great Wall, with a $3 million investment and a staff of fifty. Debbie took a year off university in Canada to help her father launch the restaurant. A little later, son Johnny also returned to train the staff there.

But it was Anna, the eldest, who moved back from Canada to help run Soong's Great Wall.

—•—

Queen's Park Savannah is a huge patch of public green space in the middle of Port of Spain. Dozens of colonial heritage buildings border the west side, including the residences of Anglican and Roman Catholic archbishops and a grand, early-twentieth-century home that resembles Balmoral Castle. The Royal Botanical Gardens sits to the north. There used to be a racetrack here, part of the country's British legacy.

This is centre stage for Carnival.

Every year, a bandstand is erected at the south end for viewing and judging. There are multiple other stops around the city—mas bands go through judging stations to collect points for the competition—but all must pass through the grandstand. Each band decides on a route that allows it to march past as many stations as possible.

Soca ("Soul of Calypso") is the upbeat, electronic party music that is a successor to calypso. Over the last decades, it has become the mainstay of Carnival, replacing traditional steelpan music and the gentler singsong social commentary of calypso. Thumping music booms through the streets from sound trucks propelling the bands as they weave through the city. There are players of all races and ages, dressed in costumes of all colours and shapes, jumping and gyrating.

A controlled chaos.

Unlike carnivals in Brazil—where samba schools rehearse for months on end—Trinidad's carnivals are informal. There's no regimented parade formation—just a massive flow of humanity moving forward. As I watch from the footbridge by the grandstand, above the parade route, a river of colour flows under me like an Impressionist painting.

It's a perfect reflection of the country's diverse society and culture.

I wait patiently for Hell of a Life to come through on this hot day. But with many prolonged stops of swinging-in-place, their progress is slow. Five other groups pass before Hart's band arrives, and it takes another half-hour for all its players to parade through.

Entering the crowd below, I see Chinese faces everywhere. A lot of Trini expats from Toronto flew in with us Monday evening. Anna and her friends come through briefly, before they are pushed on by a river of humanity. An impromptu conga line erupts. People are everywhere. It's so hard to talk through the noise that I barely say hello.

Anna told me her brother Johnny Soong would be in the gold section behind her. I have no idea what he looks like, so when that section comes through, I keep asking every Chinese male whether he's Johnny.

Johnny finally shows up, dressed like a Roman soldier in gold and black, his long-time girlfriend Lydia Lagall in red and gold. I introduce myself over the music.

Meanwhile, Kwoi is in his element, chasing down dancers in the crowd with his tracking shots. His camerawork is nimble and fluid. It's all in the footwork, he says. He does tai chi. So do I. And I know what our *sifu* ("master") always tells us: keep your centre of gravity low, direct all your *qi* ("vital energy") to the abdomen, plant your feet firmly on the ground (connecting with the Earth), and move with stealth just using your lower body.

The day is getting hotter, and the camera backpack I'm carrying for Kwoi feels heavier than before. Three hours into the parade, we dodge down a side street to pick up curried-goat roti from a food stall. As we sit on the curb cooling down with Carib beer, smaller bands march past.

These are "people's bands," sometimes no more than twenty people, at the fringe of the carnival, with no elaborate costumes. They're not competing— just having fun, making their share of noise and music from makeshift sound carts and portable boomboxes. And they are just as entertaining as the rest.

Trinidadians and Tobagonians equate their nationality with citizenship rather than ethnicity. The country Trinidad and Tobago is an artificial construct. The two islands couldn't be more different, in people and temperament. And they call themselves Trinidadians or Tobagonians depending which island they come from.

The mixed ethnicity today came from indigenous Amerindians, African slaves, Chinese shopkeepers and indentured Indian labourers, as well as a succession of European colonizers: Spanish, French and English. To the mix, blend in Arabs from Lebanon and Syria, and Jews who came with European expeditions in the late sixteenth century.

Anna's husband, John Johnston, is a fourth-generation Trinidadian of mixed Chinese, French, Spanish and African heritage. He attended high school in Canada and college in the US before he and Anna met (when he was servicing a broken cash register at Soong's Great Wall).

Everybody in Trinidad is a Trini. There's no hyphenation. No adjective in front of nationality. Many, like John, have long lost their links to any ancestral heritage. In running the Great Wall with his wife, he is, in some sense, discovering his Chinese heritage.

"Mr. Soong worked so hard to bring it to where it is," he says as we sit down after the restaurant is closed, around midnight. "It's been well laid out, well organized. Our job has pretty much been done for us."

"Restaurant work is hard, round-the-clock work," Anna, sitting next to her husband, says. "But I've seen my parents do it, and if they can do it, I think we can do it, because we're the young blood now."

But there's a language barrier for John: "The cooks don't speak much English, and I don't speak any Chinese, so communication between the cooks and me is difficult."

Not so much for Anna, who has some proficiency in Hakka from her father and Cantonese from her mother. She also worked in Hong Kong for a year after graduating from university.

"We can make them proud of us because this restaurant is like a baby to my parents, especially my dad," she says. "I don't think he would ever retire. But he's a little bit laid back now, and he wants us to follow in his footsteps."

———

Nothing else in this whole world could make me feel this way
No pretty mas' could ever pass with the vibe of my J'ouvert
It's a special feeling when the night turns into day
Pitch oil pan and a good steel band is the order of the day

The feeling is the vibe . . . Jump-up
The feeling is the vibe . . . Jump-up
The feeling is the vibe . . . Jump-up
The feeling is the vibe . . . Jump-up

"Feelin' de Vibe" is on the air as I walk into Johnny Soong's radio station, 96.1 WEFM. The soca song—by Chinese Laundry, aka Anthony Chow Lin On, a second-generation Chinese Trinidadian—is one of the Road March contenders. The Road March title is given to the song that has been played most during the two days of Carnival parades.

After helping his father launch Great Wall, Johnny staked out an even more lucrative career as impresario of the island's music and entertainment industry. He's now part-owner of the top-rated FM station that plays urban Caribbean music, as well as two popular nightclubs, Zen and Club Coconut.

The radio station is directly across the street from the Queen's Park Oval, the hallowed cricket ground where Trinidad's own superstar Brian Lara plays.

"He's a friend of mine," Johnny tells me as I look at a picture of him with the test cricketer, which is hanging on the wall.

Johnny is forty years old, unassuming and surprisingly shy, not at all like the flamboyant music impresario I expected him to be. He's also a lot more Chinese that I thought. He speaks Hakka and is in tune with Chinese culture, even though when he lived in Canada—and to the consternation of his mother—he hung out only with fellow Trinis. (Brenda was hoping her son would settle down with a young woman from Hong Kong.)

The impresario is visibly distraught this afternoon. Somebody broke into Club Coconut early this morning. It doesn't seem like a good time to talk, but he agrees to give me a tour and talk about his father's fame.

"I think that my father being very famous in Trinidad is a plus, but you're always trying to live up to the standards he has set. If I'm able to accomplish 50 per cent of what he has in terms of humility and the respect that he gets from people, I'll have done a good job."

Maurice helped financially, but Johnny picked up on his father's entrepreneurial savvy to build up his own business. "I'm a little bit more aggressive in the business world. Which means not everybody is going to like you as much."

"Will you get back to the restaurant business?"

"One day I might come full circle," he says. "But it's not an easy business; you have to really make up your mind to go back into the food business."

"Any thoughts of moving back to Canada?"

"There's no place in the world I would rather be than here. This is paradise to me. Trinidad is paradise."

—•—

There's a food stall by the airport parking lot that is famous for its doubles, a traditional curried chickpea sandwich on flatbread. It's a ritual for expats to have one last bite of Trinidad before departing.

Maurice Soong and I are eating our doubles by the stall when he tells me, "Next time you come through the airport, tell them that you're coming to see Mr. Soong. You'll get special treatment. They all know me."

A lot of people wanted Maurice to open a restaurant in Port of Spain. People he trained—cooks, managers, maître d's—opened restaurants after they left Great Wall. But he doesn't want to compete with them because "they're still part of the family."

"I don't think I'll ever retire. This restaurant is like my last child. Even if I have nothing to do, I come and stay for half an hour, look at my goldfish, and go into the kitchen to make sure everything is all right. Sometimes I come inside and greet the customers. They're just like my family."

Like others in the diaspora, Maurice espouses many of the traditional Chinese values: humility, hard work, respect for the family and sacrificing for the next generation. As our time together comes to a close, I come back to my continuing question: Are we defined by our nationality or our ethnicity? I want to know if he has ever left China, spiritually.

"I'm Chinese," he replies. "I came here when I was twelve. But I'm a naturalized Trinidadian. I'm a Trinidadian now."

A wok fire at the kitchen of Hotel Valentino
in Darjeeling.

ABOVE: Luís Yong demonstrating the art of chifa with La Chola Energía on Cable Express, Lima. BELOW: Kwoi shooting the taping of the *Cosas de la Vida* show, Lima.

ABOVE: Colette Li Piang Nam making poisson sauce tomate at Chez Manuel, Mauritius.
BELOW: Chow Fong and Noisy Jim at the New Outlook Cafe with new owner Ruby Lee looking on, Outlook, Saskatchewan.

ABOVE: With Anna Soong and friends at Carnival, Trinidad. BELOW: Interviewing Luís Chung at the Havana Chinese Cemetery. Mark Valino with boom mic, Kwoi at camera, Valeria Mau Chu interpreting.

Scenes from Carnival 2000, Port of Spain. Lydia Lagall and Johnny Soong in the first photo.

Cantonese egg tarts and roast suckling pig in São Paulo. Fresh crab in Mumbai.

ABOVE: Mai Wong reviewing her performance on camera, Tel Aviv. BELOW: Kwoi tracking a shot in Kolkata.

TOP: A day in the life at Lille Buddha, Tromsø: Uncle Chung at the wok, Michael Wong scooping rice, Kine Nylund serving. BOTTOM: Relaxing with a view of the Dome of the Rock on the rooftop of Jaffa Gate Hotel in Jerusalem.

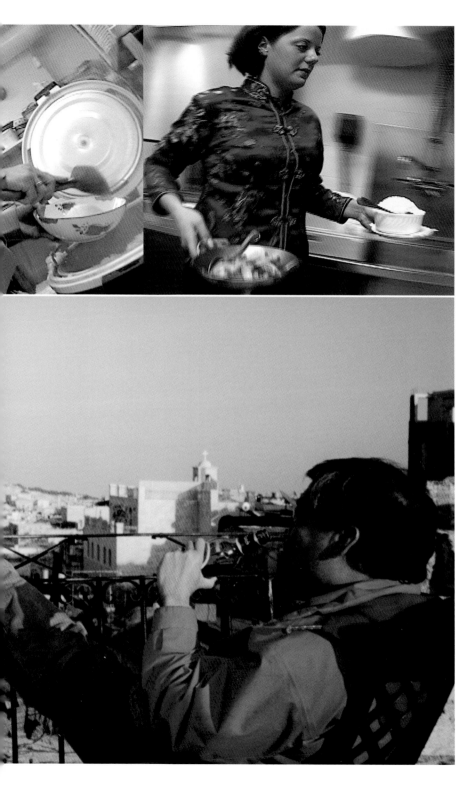

TOP: Stephen Yeh cooking Indo-Hakka in the New Embassy kitchen, Kolkata. CENTER: Checking the sun before a shot in La Boca, Buenos Aires. BOTTOM: David Szu waiting for the midnight sun in Tromsø.

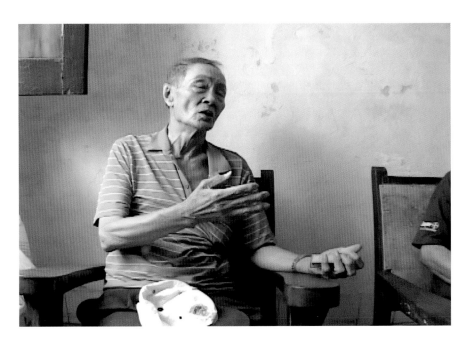

ABOVE: Fermin Huey-Ley crooning *Ilusión china* in Havana. BELOW: Fatima Ma at China Restaurant with Aya Sofia in the background, Istanbul.

Writing beautiful Chinese characters at Tamatave Chinese School.

Liu Yung Yer serving up bootleg at Épicerie Liu, Tamatave.

Nini Ling shopping at Sassoon Docks Fish Market, Mumbai.

Johnny Chi, ambassador-at-large, Ling's Pavilion, Mumbai.

Jack Sun with a fishmonger at Mercado Central, Manaus.

Kien Wong sermonizing with Old Jaffa in the background, Tel Aviv.

Samuel Yeh on the rooftop of Hotel Valentino, Darjeeling. The world's third highest peak, Kangchenjunga, was nowhere to be seen.

Luis Lee (in Seleção blue) and Jun Watanabe (in Brazil yellow and green) celebrating Brazil's World Cup victory, São Paulo.

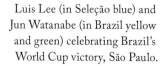

ABOVE: Maylee Ying and mother Onkuen at the southern tip of the African continent, Cape Point. BELOW: Yet more Malbecs at the parrilla, Buenos Aires. From left around the table: Chia-Ying Chiang and father Foo-Ching, me, Kwoi, Luz Algranti and Sarada Ramaseshan. Ajay Noronha took the picture.

ABOVE: Celebrating Kwoi's birthday with Ajay Noronha at a Bengali restaurant in Kolkata. BELOW: Interviewing Foo-Ching Chiang at La Boca, Buenos Aires. Kwoi with camera, Ajay Noronha with boom mic, Luz Algranti interpreting.

Saying goodbye to Foo-Ching Chiang in San Telmo, Buenos Aires.

CHAPTER 4

No Money, No Island

MOMBASA, KENYA

THE MAN SITTING NEXT TO ME HAS A BANDAGED CHEST WOUND, BLOOD DRIP-
ping on his white pants.

I'm in a police station in Mombasa. In the dimly lit room with peeling
blue and white paint, a lone ceiling fan is whooshing furiously to keep the
air cool on this equatorial night. Five of us are waiting to report to the officer
on duty, who is sitting at one of two desks, trying her best to cope. A young
man walks in with a bandaged head. More blood. No doubt he will be ahead
of me too.

No big deal, I'm not hurt. I'm just reporting a robbery.

Earlier in the evening, I was walking down Moi Avenue—named after
Daniel Moi, the second and longest-serving Kenyan president—on my way
to a Chinese restaurant where I'd dined twenty years earlier. There were few
cars and the sidewalk was unlit. I passed a Barclays Bank.

All of a sudden, I heard footsteps behind me. There must have been
four, maybe five youths in their late teens. One accosted me, brandishing a
machete; another yanked away my shoulder bag. A third reached into my
back pocket, and my wallet vanished. It was over in three seconds. They scur-
ried into the dark alleys of a shantytown across the street. I'd just lost my

cameras, my money, my traveller's cheques, my credit cards and my Canadian identity. All the while, two turbaned security guards at the bank watched with indifference.

"They've been following you," one of the Sikhs said.

"It's the Somalis," added the other, not showing any sympathy. Refugees from the Somali Civil War had been flooding into Kenya.

I was appalled: "You were watching all this and you didn't even come to my rescue?"

The taller one was kind enough to call the police from a phone box while I sat at the curb waiting for what seemed like an eternity for the inspector to show up.

It takes over an hour for my turn to come up at the police station. The officer fills in a form, in triplicate. When she's finished, she tells me to wait outside for the inspector to take me back to the hotel. Two policemen are smoking outside the station.

"The inspector will be back shortly," one of them says between puffs. "He's on another call."

"Where're you from?" the other asks. "Were you at the beaches in Malindi?"

I am in no mood for small talk and just want to get back to the hotel. I don't know how long it will take to get a new passport in Nairobi, and I have a flight to Mauritius in four days.

Back in the hotel, I spend the little cash I have left on a last-call dinner of tandoori chicken at the rooftop bar. Luckily, I left my airline tickets in the room: a round trip to Lamu up the coast, the return ticket to Nairobi and one for an onward flight to Mauritius and my return to Toronto three weeks later.

The night air is cool. Two people sitting across from me, under a potted tree, are flirting. They are enjoying themselves. I am not. And I don't have any money left to drown my sorrows. I just want to go to bed.

It's past midnight, November 21, 2000. I doze off to breaking news on CNN. Al Gore is fighting for his political life in the Florida recount. I'm just dealing with a minor inconvenience.

—··—

My first foray into the continent was two decades earlier. I was working in Nigeria and took the opportunity to visit other countries before returning home to Montreal: Kenya, Egypt and Morocco—with a side trip from Cairo to Jerusalem, crossing at a Sinai checkpoint.

Nairobi was an oasis of calm in the 1980s, with distinctive colonial charm: pillar postboxes, roundabouts and red double-decker buses. There was also the New Stanley Hotel, where I took afternoon tea. The hotel was named after Sir Henry Morton Stanley, who famously asked "Dr. Livingstone, I presume?" when he found the missionary and explorer David Livingstone languishing "in the wilds of Africa" while searching for the source of the Nile.

This was the British East Africa that I'd heard so much about. Swahili Coast. Serengeti. Victoria Falls.

I happened to be on assignment for an image bank in Japan and went to Lake Nakuru to photograph the spectacle of more than a million pink flamingos feeding on its shores. On the way back, I drove through a small town just south of the equator, lit up by thousands of oil lamps, as in a dreamscape. I had come upon the Hindu festival of lights, Diwali. Members of the Indian diaspora were celebrating, the women resplendent in their best saris.

Back in Nairobi, craving Chinese food, I went to the middle of an office complex to dine at a Chinese restaurant. I don't remember what I ate, nor much about the place. But I recall befriending the owner and hitching a ride with him the next day to Mombasa.

I don't remember his name, either, or much about our eight-hour drive. He was an African-born Chinese, medium-built and tanned, in his late twenties, driving a white Mercedes. In Mombasa, he dropped me off at the hotel and asked that I come by his second restaurant, located in Mombasa, for lunch the next day.

The Hong Kong Restaurant was situated in a white-walled compound, in a large bungalow with patio seating and a grand view of the Indian Ocean. My friend greeted me and recommended the stir-fried beef with watermelon and the double-boiled papaya chicken soup.

It is not unusual for Chinese restaurants around the world to marry local ingredients with traditional Chinese cooking techniques to create what is today considered hybrid cuisine.

But that double-boiled soup in Africa? That divine experience still lingers with me today.

Double-boiling is a Cantonese cooking technique characterized by submerging a sealed ceramic pot into a larger pot of boiling water. This slow-cooking technique not only coaxes out the delicate flavours of the ingredients but seals and preserves all the nutrients—especially important when cooking with expensive ingredients such as shark fin and bird's nest. But a double-boiled soup can take up to five hours, taxing the patience of most kitchens.

Which brings me to my favourite: the double-boiled winter melon soup often found at Chinese banquets. The soup is cooked in a whole melon, with its pulp and seeds removed—the melon becomes the inner pot. It often elicits oohs and ahs from diners, especially when the melon is beautifully hand-carved on the outside with dragons and phoenixes, or with the Chinese characters for longevity and fortune.

And who can forget the delectable snow fungus dessert soups my mother made? Snow fungus sounds more poetic in Chinese, literally "snow ears." These double-boiled sweet soups can be made with various combinations of papaya, pear, dried longan (a cousin of lychee), lotus seeds, dried red and black dates, dried apricot, and north and south almonds.

"They make for healthy desserts," my mother used to say. It was her way of coaxing me to enjoy them. Snow fungus—like bird's nest, but cheaper—provides the lubricants and nourishment the body needs in the fall and winter, when the air is dry and chilly.

I became even more impressed when I walked through the kitchen and saw only Kenyan cooks. Who could believe that, in continental Africa, I would enjoy a sublime Chinese meal, prepared without any help from Hong Kong?

A few blocks from the restaurant, I came across Fort Jesus. The Portuguese fortification was built in the 1590s to guard the port of Mombasa, and it is often viewed as a testament to the first successful attempt by a Western power to establish influence over the Indian Ocean trade.

A billboard enticed me to visit the exhibition of sunken treasures at the archaeological museum. My curiosity was piqued. Lost treasures from Atlantis? Instead, on display were Ming dynasty artifacts that included porcelain and ironwork recovered from sunken ships off the coast. In the centre of the room sat a replica of a fifteenth-century East African dhow with a rudder design that, according to the guide, could only be found on Chinese ships of that era.

In a Eurocentric view of world history, China's cultural influence in the Indian Ocean and the east coast of Africa is often minimized. Even not mentioned. But China has had a connection with Africa since antiquity. Maritime trade routes through the Arabian Peninsula were well established as early as the Han dynasty, around the first century BC. In 1320, a Song dynasty cartographer charted southern Africa, and around 1418, a Ming fleet commanded by Admiral Zheng He reached Malindi on the Swahili Coast—a full eighty years before Portuguese explorer Vasco da Gama rounded the Cape of Good Hope to get there. On the fleet's return voyage, the Sultan of Malindi sent a personal envoy, along with a giraffe as a gift to the Chinese emperor.

The next day, I made a two-hour trip—hitchhiking on top of a lorry part of the way—up the coast, to visit Malindi and its white sand beaches. Once rivalled only by Mombasa for dominance in this part of Africa, Malindi traditionally has been a port city and a stopover for European explorers en route to India.

I found the Vasco da Gama Pillar, a monument erected by the Portuguese explorer in 1498 as a navigation aid, on an oceanside cliff. But there is no trace that the Chinese had ever landed here.

—•—

Zheng He was born in 1371 to a Muslim family in southwestern China's Yunnan province, when the area was still under Mongol rule (Yuan dynasty,

1279–1368). During the Ming conquest of Yunnan, he was taken prisoner as a child, castrated—as was common with prisoners at that time—and placed in the service of the household of Prince Zhu Di, who eventually became Ming Emperor Yongle.

The future admiral was a brilliant and tenacious boy who grew up to be physically imposing, and he advanced through a brilliant military career to become an Imperial Court eunuch. It was Emperor Yongle who commissioned Zheng He as commander of the fleet that would make seven far-reaching maritime expeditions to the South China Sea and the Indian Ocean between 1405 and 1433.

The first three of these voyages reached Calicut on India's Malabar Coast. By the time the fleet arrived, Calicut was well established as a vibrant commercial hub on the Indian Ocean. The admiral would have seen Arabs, Indians, Chinese, Somalis and Venetians trading in precious goods and spices, and cartographers exchanging maps. He would also have noticed *cheena vala*, Chinese fishing nets, introduced by traders from the court of Kublai Khan during the preceding dynasty.

On its fourth voyage, the fleet stopped at the Maldives, en route to Hormuz in the Persian Gulf. On the fifth voyage, the fleet sailed from Hormuz to Aden, Mogadishu, and down the East African coast to Malindi in present-day Kenya.

Ming China was a pre-eminent naval power and employed navigational techniques and naval architecture that were far ahead of their time.

Zheng He's maiden voyage in 1405 included more than 300 ships carrying 28,000 people, an armada not matched by the West until the First World War. There were sixty-two *baochuan*, treasure ships, for the commander of the fleet and his deputies. Each one measured 127 metres long, with nine masts and four decks, housing a crew of 500 to 600 men.

By comparison, Columbus's *Santa María*, which sailed ninety years later, was five times smaller, carrying only fifty-two men. Some 180 years later, the Spanish Armada had only 130 ships, and its largest galleons were only 55 metres long.

The Ming fleets were heavily militarized (they included troop and equine transport ships) and carried great treasures (silk, porcelain and lacquerware), which served to project Chinese power and wealth to the known world. There were cartographers, astrologers, astronomers, pharmacologists—even protocol officers to help organize official receptions—on board as well.

On return trips, they brought back precious stones, ivory, spices and exotic animals such as ostriches and zebras—as well as envoys, whose kings and rulers were willing to declare themselves tributaries of China.

For me, these maritime feats were significant in affecting the dispersal of Chinese people and culture worldwide. It has always been known that Chinese settled in Nanyang ("south ocean") as far back as the Tang dynasty, but it was these Ming expeditions five centuries later that led directly to a surge of Chinese migration to Southeast Asia.

To the Chinese in these communities, Zheng He is a folk hero—venerated, immortalized and deified, and he is worshipped in many Chinese temples named after him. As a child in Singapore, I read about the legends of Sam Bo Tai Gam, the Three-Jewelled Court Eunuch, and devoured booklets of serial graphic novels about his exotic adventures.

There is also a bit of believe-it-or-not folklore that has the admiral urinating on a durian tree, thus giving the fruit its characteristic foul smell. (Known as the "king of fruits" in Southeast Asia, durian is an acquired taste, with a stink like Burgundy's Époisses cheese.)

But more importantly, I learned that Zheng He was a Muslim. The admiral played an important role in establishing relationships between China and the Islamic world. He personally saw to the building of mosques in Southeast Asia and is said to have sent a squadron up the Red Sea to make a pilgrimage to Mecca before his death on the seventh voyage.

—·—

It was Nicholas Kristof's article, entitled "1492: The Prequel," in the June 6, 1999, issue of the *New York Times Magazine* that tipped me off to Pate Island.

Kristof was trying to track down a legend of an ancient Chinese ship-wreck that had led to a settlement on the African coast. And he found them on Pate Island, a boat ride away from the town of Lamu, a UNESCO World Heritage Site located a five-hour drive north from Malindi.

In the article, Kristof wrote about an encounter with a tribe on the island who heard from their elders that they were the descendants of Ming sailors shipwrecked off the coast of Africa. He discovered that these inhabitants had Chinese facial features (light skin, narrow eyes), possessed artifacts from China (porcelain and ceramics), as well as customs and practices (drumming style, basket-weaving pattern, silk-making, graves) closely linked to those of ancient China but very different from those of the African continent just ten kilometres away.

International trade and migration were prevalent in Ming China. The city of Quanzhou in the south—the starting point of the maritime Silk Road and a major stopping point for Zheng He en route to India and beyond—was home to 200,000 foreign residents: Arabs, Persians, Malays, Indians, Africans and Turks.

The Chinese knew more about the outside world than people give them credit for.

Why didn't the Chinese colonize Southeast Asia and Africa like the Europeans? Kristof offered several reasons: the insular nature of Chinese empires, the distrust that emperors had for merchants and traders, and the fact that Chinese simply didn't care about colonizing new territories. They just wanted to project their power to distant lands.

After Zheng He's seventh voyage in 1431, the successor to Emperor Yongle ordered the fleet destroyed and the maps and plans burned. The advancement in naval architecture and navigation was lost. China turned inward.

Pate Island intrigued me. And this is why I came to Kenya: hoping to tie my search for Chinese restaurants to the existence of Chinese settlement on the island.

—·—

Ever since that meal in Mombasa, I had become determined to find Hong Kong Restaurant again. By chance, I came to know Raymond Yeo, a neighbour of the parents of a friend of mine in the suburbs of Toronto.

Yeo is a lanky, seventy-year-old Chinese South African who moved to Kenya in 1961. He spent almost thirty years running the Mandarin Restaurant in Nairobi before immigrating to Canada. When I asked about Hong Kong Restaurant in Mombasa, he immediately confirmed that he knew the owner, Richard Lau, and his family. The Lau family was also from South Africa, he told me. Richard was only a child when they moved to Kenya. And he drove a white Mercedes.

I ask Yeo why he left South Africa.

"I'm a South African, but I'm a coloured South African. I didn't want to live in apartheid, and that's probably the same reason why Richard's family left as well."

And why Kenya?

"It was a British colony, orderly, calm and peaceful, sort of like paradise," he reminisced. "We thought for sure that we would be able to live as equals. There were only a handful of Chinese there. Most were like us, from South Africa, running restaurants. In those days, there were the big three in Nairobi: Pagoda, Hong Kong and Mandarin."

I knew I had, twenty years later, found my connection back to Kenya.

———

When I walk out of the hotel the morning after the robbery, Kamau is waiting in his taxi, ready to take me back to Mombasa Airport for my flight to Lamu. I had taken his taxi on arrival a day earlier, and we became friends on the short ride to my hotel.

I break the news that I was robbed the previous night and am no longer going to Pate Island. Could he take me around to the Ministry of Interior to file a lost-passport report? And after that, I would have to get back to Nairobi on the next flight out.

"No money, no island," he says with a smile.

"And I've no money to pay you," I tell him.

"No problem. You send me a postal money order when you get there."

I've always had good luck running into good-natured and helpful taxi drivers. Like the time in Isfahan when my driver helped negotiate a touchy situation with what seemed like an agent from SAVAK, the internal security service under the shah of Iran. Or the time I visited the Taj Mahal and became very sick in the middle of the night, and my cabbie drove me all around Agra looking for a pharmacy that was still open.

Kamau takes me on a two-hour runaround to different ministry locations, filling forms in triplicate—a British legacy. (At one point, the typist runs out of typewriter ribbon, and we have to wait until she finds one somewhere else.) He doesn't seem to mind. He knows the routine, including when to cut in front of the line. Then he drops me at the airport, just in time for the next short hop back to Nairobi.

Back at the Nairobi airport, I find Margaret at the travel counter. Little more than twenty-four hours earlier, on my arrival from London, she had arranged my tickets to Mombasa and Lamu and booked the Nairobi Hilton for my return stay. On hearing my plight, she quickly asks one of her staff to take me to the Canadian High Commission, the HSBC Bank and American Express (no, you can't leave home without it).

I spend the next two days watching cricket on television in my hotel room, too paranoid to go out. The robbery has made me apprehensive—I was fearful of another attack, fearful of being robbed.

There's nothing to do but to wait.

I receive my new passport on the third day and venture out to City Market to wire the money I promised to Kamau, and to visit the Hong Kong Restaurant (Nairobi branch), where I first met Richard Lau.

Lau is as I envisioned after all these years—a youthful face, with just a hint of grey hair. He remembers giving me a ride. I tell him I found him through Yeo. He remembers Uncle Raymond.

"It's so long ago—both of us were so much younger then," he says with a laugh. He is forty-eight, two years younger than me.

"I remember you were driving a white Mercedes."

"It's silver-white," he corrects me.

Lau doesn't remember much of Pretoria, where he was born. His family moved from South Africa in 1959 and started the Hong Kong Restaurant in Mombasa two years later, then this branch in Nairobi. Lau's elder sister now runs it, while another sister owns the city's Dragon Pearl.

"Have you thought about emigrating?"

"No, never. I'm 100 per cent Kenyan. I love Africa."

The Mombasa I remember, I tell him, exists no more.

"Kenya has gone downhill since you were here in the eighties," he says. "There's no water, the phone doesn't work. And there're a lot of carjacking and violent crimes."

"I was robbed walking to the Hong Kong," I finally tell him.

"You have to be more careful," he says, with nary a hint of sympathy. "When you go out, you have to constantly watch your back."

"My guard was down. I thought I was still in the eighties."

I reveal the reason why I wanted to track him down after all these years: to make a documentary film about his life and his restaurant. He's not warm to the idea. In fact, he seems secretive and evasive, but he promises to think about it. He asks me to come back for lunch the next day. After dinner, he drops me back at the Hilton. He's going to a friend's party but doesn't ask me to come along.

Lau has no time for me the next day. He's busy in a meeting at the back of the restaurant while I eat by myself. Then he has to leave in a hurry, to take his cousin to the airport—the cousin who runs the Mombasa branch of the Hong Kong that I was on my way to when I was robbed. There is no time to talk, but he promises to stay in touch. With that, he is gone.

I'm leaving the next morning for Mauritius and will have to abandon my search.

My last night in the country I spend at the Thorn Tree Cafe in the New Stanley Hotel, listening to an East African jazz band, savouring a Tusker lager and wishing for a gentler Kenya.

CHAPTER 5

A Very

Ferocious People

SAINT JULIEN, MAURITIUS

"I HEARD YOU'RE LOOKING FOR CHINESE CREOLE FOOD."

A dignified and bespectacled Chinese man in his early sixties approaches me, speaking in French. It's early afternoon. The stranger has sought me out at Le Saint Georges. People at the reception seem to know him.

"Chez Manuel has the best food on the island. Go check it out before you leave this evening," he says as he hands me his card, which reads "Joseph Tsang Mang Kin / Former Minister of Arts and Culture."

News travels fast. I'm leaving in the evening for Paris, concluding a three-week journey to look for Chinese restaurants among African countries touching the Indian Ocean. If I find what I'm looking for, I'll be back to this part of the world with my crew.

How did he know that I was looking for Chinese Creole food? He said he heard through a former employee at the Mauritius Film Development Corporation, with whom I'd just met in the morning.

"Why don't you drop by my house in Floréal on your way to the airport tonight?" And with that Joseph was gone.

With the tip in hand, I summon Raj, whose taxi is always parked in front of the hotel. Raj picked me up at the airport when I first arrived several days earlier and has since become another one of my helpful guides and friends.

"I know where it is; I've taken customers there," he says. "Why don't you pack up and check out. We can go to the airport from there."

The taxi speeds along the narrow spiderweb of roads around the island, passing Indian grocery stores and Chinese bakeries, cutting through lush green sugarcane fields lit by the afternoon sun. Even with no traffic in sight, Raj honks constantly.

"It's my wife, Colette, you want to speak to," Manuel Li Piang Nam greets me as I walk in. A mild-mannered man in his late fifties, despite his tough-as-nail looks, he's been expecting me: his brother-in-law Joseph called to tell him I would be coming.

Why was the former minister so sure I would make the trip?

At this time, Colette Li Piang Nam emerges from the kitchen. She is fifty-five years old, with a charming, cherubic, ever-smiling face, addressing me in French with the familiar *tu*, rather than the more formal *vous*. We are speaking in French since I don't speak the Hakka dialect, and they don't speak English particularly well.

"*As-tu déjà mangé?*"

Have you already eaten? As happens so often, she greets me with the colloquial Chinese saying akin to "How are you?" It's way past lunch service; the kitchen must be closed. I hardly have a chance to reply before Colette offers to make me "*la spécialité de la maison*."

"Oh no, you don't have to," I lie.

To tell you the truth, this is why I came. In any case, it's disrespectful in Chinese culture to refuse food from a host, no matter the time of day, no matter how full you are.

I follow her to the kitchen to watch the making of poisson sauce tomate, fish in tomato sauce. First, she pan-fries pieces of garoupa filets. Then the wok is fired up to brown onions, garlic, chili and thyme. Diced tomatoes go in next. All the while, she dabs the sauce on her palm, licking it, to make sure it tastes just right. Good chefs do that, tasting every step of the way. After a few minutes of simmering, tapioca flour is added as a thickener. The fish goes in last, for about thirty seconds. *Et voilà!*

Raj and I devour the dish, along with a side of stir-fried Chinese greens and copious amounts of rice. I tell her I love the garlicky fragrance and the heat from the red chili.

"This is my Sino-Creole invention." Colette beams. "All my customers love it. Sometimes, for my Indian customers, I add a bit of curry to give it even more heat."

"What about your native Hakka cuisine?"

"Oh, I do that too. But you know, Creole food is actually a unique combination of African, French, Chinese and Indian. So, you have all this cuisine melting together on this island."

"*Comme un* melting pot," I say, not knowing the proper French word to describe this merging of cultures and cuisines.

"*Oui, tout mélangé*," she says with a laugh. It's all mixed up, like this country.

Sitting down, Colette tells the story of how she came from a poor Hakka family to become a restaurateur. I am impressed by her cooking already, and her fascinating life story seals the deal.

"I created this restaurant," she says, using the French verb *créer*. She also single-handedly innovated a complete Sino-Mauritian menu. Colette promises to make other Sino-Mauritian specialties next time I come, like ourite safrané, saffron octopus. (*Ourite* is Mauritian Creole for "octopus.")

"But I can't share the recipe with you—it's my secret. They can try to make this dish, but it will never taste the same as mine."

My four-day search for Sino-Mauritian food on the island had been fruitless, but mere hours before leaving Africa, I had found my restaurant story.

———

I've always known about the vibrant Chinese community in Mauritius.

When I was a year old, my father moved the family from Hong Kong to Singapore to run a commodity trading firm. He dealt in sugar, rubber and palm oil, and had frequent contact with his Chinese counterparts in Mauritius. As a young collector, I used to snap up colourful Mauritius stamps from his correspondence with these traders.

For that initial trip to Mauritius, I was armed with leads from Sino-Mauritian friends in Toronto—a family member here, an old friend there—eager to share their connections with the community. Through these contacts, a group of community leaders was hastily assembled—heads of associations and business chambers, managing directors of trading firms, as well as the chairman of the telecom company Mauritel—to welcome me with a dim sum lunch at the First Restaurant on Rue Royale, at the entrance to Chinatown. They spoke enthusiastically about the 30,000-strong, close-knit Hakka Chinese community.

Hakka, which means "guest families," is a cultural and linguistic subgroup of ethnic Han Chinese that traces its lineage back more than 2,000 years. They migrated in successive centuries from the central plains of China to predominantly settle, around the sixteenth century, in several counties of Guangdong and Fujian provinces.

The Hakka are perhaps the most diasporic of all Chinese subgroups.

From southeastern China, they fanned out across the globe during the second half of the nineteenth century and early twentieth century: to India and the Indian Ocean, the Caribbean, the Americas, as well as the South Pacific. A majority of the Chinese in Mauritius trace their Hakka roots to one county in Guangdong province: Meixian, literally Plum County, or Moiyen in the Hakka dialect.

—•—

Four months after I first visited Chez Manuel, on the day after St. Patrick's Day, Kwoi, David Szu and I eagerly stepped off the plane onto this sunny, tropical island in the middle of the Indian Ocean, twelve hours away from the pubs of a cold and misty London where we transited.

The film shoot is my favourite part of the project. The research is done, and the anxiety about finding the right place is over. It's time to relax and immerse myself in the joy of telling the story.

Mauritius reminds me a lot of Singapore. Both are small multi-racial island nations, entrepôts, and former British colonies with the former empire's legacies—such as driving on the left side of the road. The capital, Port Louis, has a tropical colonial feel that is familiar from my youth: balmy days, palm trees swaying in the breeze, stately colonial buildings, British banks and the racetrack.

Chinese merchants and traders first arrived in Mauritius during the mid-nineteenth century. The island was a transit hub for Chinese settlers on their way to Réunion Island, the Seychelles, Madagascar, Mozambique and South Africa. Many of these merchants and traders settled along Rue Royale, transforming the area into a vibrant Chinatown.

Spread out over four city blocks, the resemblance to Singapore's Chinatown in the sixties is striking. I feel as though I'm walking in my old neighbourhood—among colourfully painted shopfronts, arcaded walkways and Chinese signs engraved on concrete columns. Even the open storm gutters that run along the street are familiar.

Tonight, the crew eats its first meal, appropriately, at the First Restaurant, self-advertised as serving "authentic Hakka cuisine." Proprietor Mike Ng, who works as an infield bookie at the Champ de Mars Racecourse, remembers me from my lunch with the Chinese community during my previous trip, which was followed by a trip to the races.

We have beef ball soup, salt-baked chicken, steamed tofu with minced pork, and bitter gourd stuffed with fish and shrimp paste. All Hakka standards.

I don't eat bitter gourd because it's a "cold" food. My Chinese herbalist always reminds me to maintain a hot-and-cold, heating-and-cooling balance in my body. I have a "cold" constitution, he advised, and should not ingest any "cold" food, such as bananas and fresh mustard greens. David, who has no problem with his constitution, is having the time of his life, eating his way around the world.

Kwoi and I grew up in a Hong Kong that welcomed Hakka people and enjoyed the food. Early in the twentieth century, many Hakka crossed the porous border between the British Crown Colony and Guangdong province.

"This is so Taiwan!" David exclaims as we walk out of a restaurant that has the same kind of decor, has the same feel, and serves the same Hakka food that he grew up eating. There was a significant Hakka migration during the mid-seventeenth century from Fujian province, just across the Taiwan Strait. Hakka food is prominent in Taiwanese cooking. And the sultry night reminds him of lazy summer days in southern Taiwan.

"This is so Wong Kar-wai!" says Kwoi who, by this time, is going full-throttle on nostalgia. The mood and atmosphere on Rue Royale bring back memories of Hong Kong in the sixties—as portrayed in many of the Hong Kong director's films.

It's comforting to work with Kwoi and David because we come from the same cultural background; more than shared language and customs, settings like this evoke a common mood and sensibility in all of us.

—-—

The village of Saint Julien, in the municipality of Flacq, is forty minutes from Port Louis on a road that leads to the beaches on the east coast. Raj is my driver again.

Chez Manuel is in an unpretentious but spacious walled compound nestled in fields of sugarcane. The restaurant is a one-storey building with a pagoda-style roof. There is a Chinese garden with miniature pagodas and waterwheels, and a bamboo grove.

"So you brought your crew this time?" Colette greets me, asks a waiter to set up a table for us and quickly dashes into the kitchen to prepare yet another memorable meal of curried fish and steamed pork belly in preserved mustard greens.

Because the Hakka are a nomadic people, their cuisine borrows heavily upon, and draws inspiration from, myriad regions where they have lived. Hakka cooking is known for its use of preserved meats and tofu, particularly in stewed and braised dishes. The skill lies in the ability to cook meat thoroughly, keeping it tender and naturally bringing out its umami.

According to Linda Anusasananan, author of *The Hakka Cookbook*, Hakka cooking is "honest, earthy and rustic—the simple, comforting soul food of the peasant."

Hakka pork belly is my favourite comfort food. The belly is first cooked in an elaborate sequence of simmering and frying to soften the rind and loosen the fat, then braised for hours in a sauce made with preserved mustard greens, dark soy, sugar and five-spice powder. The softened meat has a melt-in-your-mouth, you-can-cut-with-your-chopsticks quality, and the fat moistens the accompanying preserved vegetables, giving the dish a strong aroma and rich, heart-warming flavour.

I have never tasted a better rendition of this dish, not in Hong Kong, not in Taiwan.

"The pork belly was made yesterday," Colette notes. My mother always said that braised dishes taste better the day after, when the flavour is more infused and more intense.

After lunch, I wander with Colette in the garden and talk to her about the restaurant and her approach to the cuisine. The afternoon is hot and humid, the bugs buzzing around us. David can't hold his boom microphone still as he keeps slapping his arms and legs to get rid of them.

Colette learned Hakka dishes from her father but created everything else on her own. Her curried fish is a combination of Creole and Indian cooking. "You know, we've a lot of Indian customers; we've always lived side by side with Indians," she says. "Do you know my father spoke Indian? Because our store customers were Indians, eventually, he spoke Indian fluently. Don't you find it funny? An Indian-speaking Chinese?"

In 1970, fed up with working and living at her father-in-law's store, and serving a dominating and demanding mother-in-law, Colette struck out on her own—leaving the family business to start a noodle shack for plantation workers in Saint Julien, selling noodles with oyster, tomato and curry for 25 cents a plate.

"This is the beginning of Chez Manuel," she recalls. "Slowly, slowly, like a bird building its nest, the business started to grow, and people from every corner of the island came to Saint Julien to try my noodles, my oyster curry and other Mauritian dishes."

She would often work deep into the night, making fresh noodles to meet the demand. One night, her right arm was caught in the flour mixer. Her doctor told her it would take at least two years to heal.

"After that, I don't know how I got the energy to continue working. I could only use one hand," she says, trying to keep her emotions in check. "I was working so hard that I would cry because I could not keep up."

It was good to have a lot of customers, around 100 to 150 people a day, she says, "but I was all by myself." She healed within three months, but with a very visible scar on her forearm.

When Cyclone Gervaise completely destroyed her shack in 1975, Colette was determined to build a proper restaurant *en béton*, in concrete. Chez Manuel opened without fanfare, and she was able to use her larger kitchen to integrate the various cultures of Mauritius into her cuisine—Creole, Indian and her native Hakka. Business grew. But after six years, she was tired of repeating the same menu.

Colette said to herself, "Forget about the Hakka cuisine, I want to learn something high class, the real Cantonese cuisine from China."

She closed the restaurant for two months to attend culinary school in Hong Kong. "I learned how to make different sauces like black bean and barbecue. I learned Chinese roasting technique and started to make char siu and *canard laqué*," BBQ pork and roast duck.

On her return, Colette invited the prime minister to the restaurant's reopening. "*C'était une grande affaire*," she says as she shows off the certificate from Hong Kong now framed and placed in a prominent place behind the bar. She continues to improve, returning annually to Hong Kong to learn new dishes.

Even though Chez Manuel is a success story, Colette still cooks every day: "I take pleasure in cooking, but sometimes I need helpers. When the restaurant is busy, the helpers don't care, they cook in a hurry. Then I get complaints."

Her husband, Manuel, on the other hand, seems to be a gentleman of leisure. Even though the restaurant is named after him, he isn't involved. He doesn't cook, and Colette says he only does dishes at home. This is in line with what I have heard about Hakka families, whether in China or overseas: they are matriarchal—women tend the fields, run the households and make all the decisions.

During one of our visits, Colette fires a kitchen helper. As she marches the worker out the door, Manuel takes me to the garden for a tour of the tropical plants and flowers he cultivates. "This is a cythère tree. Here, have you ever tried its fruit?" Cythère (ambarella) fruit has a juicy, golden flesh with a pineapple-mango flavour. It is used in various cuisines, turned into preserves, made into juice or tossed into salads.

Maybe Manuel doesn't run the restaurant, but he contributes in a small way by tending the garden, which supplies vegetables that Colette needs for her kitchen.

Mauritius is a crucible of multiple cultures and races: Hindus, Muslims, Buddhists and Roman Catholics live side by side, speaking French, Creole, English, Tamil and Hindi, as well as Hakka, Cantonese and Mandarin. They live in villages and towns with French names like Bon Accueil, Beau Champ and Grand Baie.

First discovered by Arabs, the island was uninhabited when the Portuguese found it during their early voyages in the beginning of the sixteenth century. A hundred years later, the Dutch arrived and named it after their Prince Maurits van Nassau. Dutch, French and British colonialists turned the island into a plantation, harnessing slaves from Madagascar and continental Africa.

There has been a small Chinese presence in Mauritius since the 1600s, when the Dutch introduced indentured labourers from Java, but the first big wave of Chinese immigrants took place during the 1780s under French rule. When slavery was fully abolished in 1835, the British brought indentured workers from India to the island. Their descendants now make up 70 per cent of the population.

Interracial marriage between French colonials and African slaves created the Creole culture, with its unique traditions and distinctive language. Creole is the lingua franca, the mother tongue of 85 per cent of the population.

While the French still control most of the industries and sugar plantations, Indians dominate local politics. The Chinese, at less than 3 per cent of the country's 1.2 million population, are disproportionately represented in professional services such as accounting, engineering, law and medicine, and many of them are educated abroad. They are also business people, with a virtual monopoly on retail trade.

Napoleon ceded Mauritius to the British after the Napoleonic Wars and made them promise to preserve the French culture. Today, although English is the language of administration, French remains the first language taught in schools. To my surprise, there are no English dailies on the island—French newspapers carry government notices in English. Signage is in English, in French or in both languages, without any of the language sensitivities one finds in Quebec. Perhaps when an entire society is functionally bilingual, it doesn't worry about which language dominates.

Most Mauritians are thoroughly trilingual, switching effortlessly among Creole, French and English, as well as their native languages and dialects. The petite Chinese woman at the Atom Travel Agency, where I booked my flights to continental Africa, switches seamlessly between the three languages: local singsong Creole on the phone, French with another caller, and Mauritian-accented English with me. She also would have spoken Hakka, too, if I understood the dialect.

When Colette's Hakka parents came to Mauritius in the late 1920s, her father first worked as a cook for a wealthy family, then opened a small general store. As in the Caribbean, Chinese general stores dot the island. Some go upscale and expand into supermarket chains. Colette's father's general store still operates on its original site, at a busy intersection in Bel Air, a small town by the east coast, about a half-hour drive from her restaurant.

"I have ten sisters and brothers, and we all helped in the store. I remember selling rice, fabrics and doing the laundry when I was seven," Colette says as she gives me a tour of the family store. This whole setting is very familiar to me. As a child in Singapore, I frequently visited some of my classmates' homes, often in a loft above an old-style Chinese store like this one, with a woody and dusty feel, and furniture from the forties.

She started cooking at nine. Her first dish was fish cooked in yellow Hakka rice wine, quintessentially Hakka. Her family loved it. "I was so proud that my father chose me to be his helper. That's how I ended up being in the kitchen now."

At twelve, her father asked her to quit school to help out in the store. At fifteen, a family friend came calling, suggesting marriage. The friend told her father that Manuel was a good boy, he didn't smoke, he didn't gamble, he didn't go to the casino, and he worked in their store.

"A business type just like my father," Colette says with a nod. "So, there was no problem with my father." She and Manuel were married the following year, and she began to work in her father-in-law's store. Their son, Paul, was born a year later.

But Colette's life with her in-laws was not happy. "I was a very obedient girl. I always obeyed my parents. They told me all the time that if I got married one day, I'd have to listen to my husband, my father-in-law and my mother-in-law."

Surtout ta belle-mère, especially the mother-in-law.

"You know the type, they would take advantage of their daughters-in-law. It's always like that in Mauritius, even among the Indians. But I did whatever she asked. She was bossy. I had to agree to everything she told me. She treated me like a slave, but I told myself, it doesn't matter. I would often cry by myself. It wasn't easy to live with such a mother-in-law."

When Colette's father died in 1970, the shop was passed on to her eldest brother. When *he* died in 1990, it went to his son George. George, his wife and their two young children now live in the quarters behind the store, where Colette's family once lived. That's the traditional Chinese way, even more so for a Hakka family.

It is dusk when we leave Colette's family store in Bel Air. The muezzin's calls to prayer can be heard as we walk a couple of blocks toward a snack bar that Colette's second brother runs. He sells Chinese and Indian snacks, including curried noodles, over a wooden counter. Rows of wine and liquor are lined up to the ceiling on the aluminum racks behind him.

"He's not as ambitious as me," Colette says of her brother as we approach the snack bar. She doesn't understand why her brother can't be more like her, continually improving himself, going on to bigger and better things. She knows she is more ambitious than her siblings, having moved up in life and escaped the poverty she experienced as a child.

—•—

> Our history dwells in us
> and vibrates in the air.
> The memory of the Hans
> Breathes deep in our genes.
>
> From the dreams of the past
> to the shores of today.
> We carried our own ways
> as well as our language.

So writes Joseph Tsang Mang Kin in his epic poem *Le Grand Chant Hakka* (*The Hakka Epic*). He wrote the poem when he was in his late forties, after a trip to his ancestral homeland to meet his father's family for the first time. It is an ode to the Hakka people and the longing that has kept their 2,000-year-old traditions alive.

Joseph—the man who originally told me about Chez Manuel—is a poet, writer, historian, diplomat and philosopher. A cultured and gregarious man, he was born in Port Louis's Chinatown to a family of twelve, with an immigrant father from Meixian and a second-generation Sino-Mauritian mother from the town of Pamplemousses.

I stop by his home in Floréal on this trip again to interview him in his cluttered study. Lined with bookshelves, it befits a learned man.

"Hakka people actually came from the State of Wei situated in the Yellow River basin," he tells me. Wei is one of the seven major states of the Warring

States Period. The First Emperor, from the State of Qin, eventually conquered them all to unify China in 221 BC. (He went on to build the Great Wall.)

The Hakka people, not willing to submit to the First Emperor, became nomads, sojourners and settlers. For two millennia, they meandered from the Yellow River basin, rarely hesitating to pull up stakes and move on to another destination.

"So we're the real Han Chinese," he says with a rather serious tone.

To the world at large, to be Chinese is to be Han. But there are fifty-five other groups officially classified as ethnic minorities: Uyghurs, Tibetans, Zhuangs, Miaos and even Huis, who are Chinese Muslims of Han ethnicity. These minorities comprise only 8 per cent of the population. But that's still 100 million people.

Hakka are known to be conservative, hard-working and traditional. Children are strongly encouraged to marry within the group. The Hakka I meet in Mauritius are no different, tenaciously preserving their language, culture and traditions, even in the modern, post-colonial cultural melting pot they now call home.

"We are also known to be an assertive and a stubborn bunch," Joseph goes on to say. "We are a quiet people, a pleasant people, but when provoked we can be very bad because we're not a submissive race. We're fighters, and once we get the opportunity to rebel against the Manchu government or to change the system, then all our fighting abilities come out."

He draws a direct parallel between Hakka and Xiongnu, a tribal confederation of nomadic peoples who inhabited the eastern Eurasian Steppes from the third century BC to the late first century AD. (Xiongnu are to Chinese what the Huns are to Europeans.)

I've frequently heard that Hakka women are particularly strong, resilient and assertive, often the ruling matriarchs in large families. While women in China were conditioned to accept foot-binding in the late thirteenth century—which, like the wearing of high heels in the West, was a symbol of eroticism—Hakka women never submitted to this custom.

I ask why.

"While the males were fighting, if they were killed, who was going to look after the family? The women!" he points out. "The men were running away, running for their lives, or they were killed. So, responsibilities fell on the women who had to look after the household."

"And more importantly, to work in the fields," I add. I am reminded of the enduring image of Hakka women wearing Hakka wide-brim hats to shield them from the sun while working in the fields.

"Right. If you have bound feet, how are you going to plough the fields?" he continues. "So, this is one of the reasons why the Hakka Chinese never accepted the practice of having the feet of their women bound."

Perhaps this explains Colette Li Piang Nam's fighting spirit. She is fierce and ambitious, determined to define her life through perseverance and hard work.

—·—

Colette's mother-in-law's ashes are kept in a Buddhist temple on a small hill overlooking Port Louis. When we visit, Colette lights incense to pay her respects and to express filial piety to a woman with whom she finally reconciled, just before the elder woman died.

"I took care of my mother-in-law all those years, and during her last moments, she told me she loved me very much. I harboured no hate in my heart. It's what she said that made up for everything: 'You're like my mother, and I need you.'"

Colette's father-in-law was a smoker, an alcoholic and a happy-go-lucky man. He never worked and was considered the troublemaker in the family. It was her mother-in-law who ran the store and carried the burden of raising the family. At this time, I can't help but recall that Manuel is also not the one in charge of the restaurant—but, rather, sits behind the bar and chats with customers.

"So, why Chez Manuel, why not Chez Colette?" I am curious.

"I'm a very humble woman," she says with a smile. "I don't like to show off."

"You have a very loyal customer base."

"I'm close to all my customers, even after they leave for Australia, South Africa or France. They always come to my restaurant when they return to Mauritius. There's always friendship and loyalty. I keep in contact with all of them."

"What about the future?"

"I cook with love. I feel like I can work for another ten years. I'm in good health. There's no reason for me to stop now. If I did, what would I do?"

CHAPTER 6

Love in the Time of Apartheid

CAPE TOWN, SOUTH AFRICA

"I WANT TO BE MORE CHINESE."

A month before my trip to Cape Town, Edna Ying called to tell me that she has stopped using her Christian name. "From now on, I want to be known as Onkuen. I have a very strong feeling that I should be called by my Chinese name."

Sixty-six-year-old Onkuen has lived in Cape Town all her life, and she's never been anywhere outside the city. She wants to more fully embrace her Chinese heritage in the post-apartheid era.

"I was prevented from becoming Chinese by apartheid," she adds.

Onkuen is her given name, romanized in her family's Hakka dialect. She started studying Mandarin Chinese just a few years ago and now speaks and writes it rudimentarily. During my initial visit, scouting locations, she wrote her name for me in Chinese characters.

"Ugly English words," she said of her Christian name. "Dark period of South Africa."

"I'm such a terrible cook . . . I screen myself from all visitors because everybody says to me: *tai luan la, tai luan la.*" Way too messy.

Onkuen Ying is stir-frying a beef-and-bean-sprout noodle dish in a wok in the corner of the tiny kitchen. Her long, unbridled hair flies as she scoops the noodles into takeaway containers.

"You shouldn't be filming in here on your first day in town," she protests.

Kwoi, David Szu and I arrived late last night from Mauritius, staying not far from Onkuen's restaurant in Sea Point, an upscale waterfront neighbourhood of Cape Town.

Walking into the restaurant just before dinner service, I bypassed the empty dining room and headed straight into the kitchen. Unlike the romantic, chicly decorated front of house, with candlelight and white tablecloths, the kitchen is indeed unkempt.

It's March 21, 2001, the International Day for the Elimination of Racial Discrimination, a public holiday in South Africa. On this day in 1960, South African police shot and killed at least sixty-nine Black protesters in the township of Sharpeville, 75 kilometres from Johannesburg. The Sharpeville massacre drew the world's attention to apartheid.

Having been involved in anti-racism work for over two decades, I am happy to be in this country on this day.

"You know, my father was very specific in how he cooked," Onkuen explains when she has a chance to sit down. "And my sister and my brother will know exactly—you must use one cup of so-and-so and cut to that size, it must be long enough and it must look like this. But I wasn't given a format. It's just totally instinctive."

Golden Dragon is the oldest operating Chinese restaurant in Cape Town. It opened in 1960 on Bree Street, on a block that could be loosely considered Chinatown. It moved once before, then again fifteen years ago to its current location on Main Street, sitting in a row of single-storey businesses with a wooden-fenced sidewalk patio out front.

Onkuen took over running the restaurant in 1992 when her husband, Lam Al Ying, died. She switched from a traditional Cantonese menu to northern Chinese fare—partly because immigrants and businessmen now came from China, and partly because local tastes changed. Several years ago, she redecorated with the help of two designer friends, whom she lovingly refers to as "the two gays," and launched a new marketing campaign.

There are now many Chinese restaurants in the city, including Mr. Chan just down the street—which serves a delicious dish of ostrich meat stir-fried in fermented black bean sauce—but the Golden Dragon retains its loyal customers.

"I think this is the root of our survival. And the way I've kept it up is to give them a variety," she says with a touch of pride in her voice. "And I tailor the food to a specific customer. Maylee will say, 'There's a group of Chinese, they look like they come from Jo'burg,' then I'll tailor to their taste. Or she will say, 'Those Indians, they look like they come from Durban,' then I will know."

Maylee Ying, Onkuen's daughter, manages the dining room with a service staff of primarily visa students from China. The lone exception is Peter Van Wyk, an Afrikaner with epilepsy who walked in one day looking for a job. Onkuen gave him a chance when nobody else would.

When I ask how she's found working in the restaurant, Maylee says, "It has been challenging and stressful. For several years after my father was incapacitated by an accident, my mother and I struggled with running the business."

The restaurant is filling up. Maylee is busy dashing in and out of the kitchen helping out her staff while keeping a watchful eye over the customers—occasionally giving pointers on how to use the chopsticks.

"People say we have a good team now. My mom's in the kitchen, and I'm outside. It's a difficult trade to run. But we do enjoy the people side of things. I suppose if my mom didn't cook, I would have to get somebody in to help or learn the way she cooks."

Her two older brothers did not want to get into the business, and I'm aware her generation is not inclined to take over their parents' restaurants. Will she be taking over the restaurant when her mother retires?

"For the short term, yeah. For the long term? I don't think it's a good environment to have if you want to have a family," she replies. "There's long hours, there's no patience, children can't settle down."

This is a dilemma that many Chinese restaurant kids face: their parents don't want them to stay in the family business but can't get—or won't trust—anyone else with it.

Wang Zhaohui is taking a break from his kitchen duties to share a beer with me on the sidewalk patio. A thirty-year-old from Shanghai here on a work visa, he was looking for any job that he could find. When he walked by the Golden Dragon one day and noticed the Chinese couplet at the entrance—the lines of the couplet begin with the characters "golden" and "dragon"—he thought he would be most comfortable working for a Chinese proprietor.

Having helped out in a kitchen before, and knowing a bit of cooking on his own, he was hired on the spot.

I tell him that his Shanghai-styled braised eggplant is exemplary. Stewed in Shaoxing wine, soy sauce, ginger, sugar, vinegar, garlic and chilies, the dish is a perfect combination of salty, sweet and savoury.

The night is cool. Dinner service is over. Onkuen joins us outside, warmly greeting many long-time customers as they leave. There is a sense of accomplishment. Business has not been as good as she had hoped, but the restaurant survives. Besides, having staff from China has gifted her with even more of a link to her Chinese heritage than changing her name.

—•—

Cape Town was home to South Africa's first Chinese settlement. From the mid-seventeenth century to the end of the eighteenth century, Dutch settlers brought in exiled Chinese from Batavia (present-day Java) as craftsmen and gardeners. There was a need to repair Dutch East India Company ships plying the spice trade and to supply the ships with fresh fruits and vegetables to fight scurvy.

In 1740, a dozen Chinese restaurants were opened to serve the locals.

During the second half of the nineteenth century, the British brought thousands more Chinese migrants to various parts of South Africa to serve as farmers, servants and shopkeepers. Many more came as independent immigrants in the 1870s, before the passage of the Chinese Exclusion Act in 1904. (It was repealed in 1933.)

That same year, almost 65,000 indentured Chinese workers arrived to work at Transvaal gold mines—there was a labour shortage because Black miners were frequently on strike. Chinese contract miners were credited with increasing gold production and reviving the South African economy. But the whites were afraid the Chinese would take away jobs, and these workers were repatriated in 1911, the same year that China's dynastic rule ended.

By that time, Chinese were well established in many trades, particularly in running "Kaffir eating-houses." Kaffir—the K-word—is a racial slur loosely used for Black people or Natives.

The Chinese population in Cape Town remained small, despite an influx elsewhere: in Port Elizabeth, East London and Durban, as well as Johannesburg and Transvaal. But all over the country, they lived on the racial edge of apartheid: not white enough to be white, not Black enough to be Black. And not "coloured" either, a term normally reserved for people of Indian and mixed-race origin.

Unofficially, the Chinese were regarded as white because the term Asian was reserved for Indians, who experienced more discrimination because of the darker colour of their skin. Still, Chinese had to sit in separate sections on buses and in public places; but they were allowed to live in white districts because they provided an essential service: they ran grocery stores. However, their businesses and homes had to be 51 per cent owned by a white nominee.

"The Japanese were honorary whites," Maylee tells me. "They were one grade higher than us."

—·—

Lam Al Ying's father brought him to South Africa in 1917, at age nine, to work at his uncle's grocery store. He landed in the city of East London with one suitcase. Immigration officials registered his family name as Ying—again, because that's where Anglo-Saxons put their family names: last.

When he was sixteen, Ying moved to Cape Town to work on the docks. Before long, he opened a grocery store and a tea shop and had his own trading company, LA Ying & Co. In 1947, a year before apartheid officially began, Ying opened his first restaurant, Nanking, on Marine Drive in Paarden Eiland, an industrial area by the city docks.

At heart, Ying was a social justice activist. He was prominent in Cape Town's Chinese community, raising wartime relief funds for China, founding the Chinese Seaman's Association and the Chinese school, and acting as secretary of the Cape Town Chinese Association—all of which is documented in Melanie Yap and Dianne Leong Man's book *Colour, Confusion and Concessions: The History of the Chinese in South Africa.*

He was outspoken while other Chinese were docile, Onkuen says of her husband. Because he could speak English, he skillfully navigated between the whites and the Chinese—interpreting, negotiating and sometimes rescuing his contemporaries from legal trouble.

Ying also was well known for his campaigns against apartheid. One time, he convinced the local railroad station to take down a sign reading "No Kaffirs, No Chinese, No Dogs." He argued the Chinese have thousands of years of civilization, so why would they want to exclude such a superior culture? In an era of much apathy, this defiance echoed a Gandhi-led protest in 1906, when 1,000 Chinese joined Indians to march against laws that barred Asians in the Transvaal Colony from purchasing land.

But foremost, Ying was an entrepreneur and marketer. He had many ideas, producing and marketing Chinese snacks, ingredients and condiments, including canned abalone, lap cheong (Chinese sausage), shrimp crackers, soy sauce, five-spice powder and MSG. He even produced a *Chinese Cooking* record with step-by-step instructions on how to cook Chinese food, narrating eleven recipes that included sweet and sour pork, crayfish omelet, almond chicken and, in a bit of self-promotion, braised abalone. The ingredients are listed on the LP's back cover.

Onkuen is not sure how many of her husband's ventures were successful but says, "He was so clever. Didn't have much schooling, but he was amazingly perceptive. He could figure things out, work things out. He could do so much."

She was born to an immigrant Hakka family that ran a grocery store in a white neighbourhood. In 1960, at age twenty, she started her first job at Ying's first Golden Dragon. They were married two years later. Ying was fifty-five.

The age difference never bothered Onkuen. Instead, she says, he gave her total freedom. "That freedom was my bondage; it was the freedom that gave me the limits as well. Because I would say 'Can I go?' and he would say, 'It's up to you,' and that put the onus on me to be responsible." For Onkuen, that freedom built up into the strength she has used to continue running the restaurant for all of these years.

—·—

The weather is beautiful at this time of the year—Capetonians say rain always comes after Easter. On the restaurant's day off, I take Onkuen and Maylee on an excursion to Bo-Kaap, formerly known as the Malay Quarter, the oldest surviving residential neighbourhood in Cape Town.

Adjacent to the central business district, Bo-Kaap is known for its colourful early-nineteenth-century homes and steep cobblestone streets. Many of the Muslim Batavian slaves, brought over by the Dutch in the seventeenth century, settled here, alongside exiled imams from there who had challenged Dutch colonial rule. Their descendants, known as Cape Malays, still live here and have, by and large, kept the community's identity intact. There are seven mosques in the area, including the first mosque of the Cape, built in 1804.

Onkuen has never explored this part of the city. It is all new to her.

"The Cape was a melting pot," says Firied Bassier, manager of the Bo-Kaap Museum, as he gives us a tour of the exhibits and points out that the Turkish fez, a traditional felt headdress, has been adopted by local Muslim Malays.

"Somehow the word *Malay* is used to describe all sorts of people who don't belong to the purely white, Black or Asian groups," he says. "They could have Middle Eastern, Indonesian and Arab origins, or be people of mixed heritage from these races."

When the Group Areas Act was enacted in 1950, residents were forcibly relocated from this Muslim-only area to Cape Flats and dispossessed of their homes. But people appealed to the government to preserve the old mosques and historical places, even though they were not allowed to live there anymore.

Some stood their ground.

Yosef Ahmed was born in the house where he still lives. He recalls his family's resistance: "My mother told them, 'Fine, you take the house, but I'll squat here with my children. We're not going anywhere.'" The family was able to stay.

Post-apartheid, the Malay community rejuvenated the neighbourhood. The restoration is striking. Historic houses, representative of Cape Dutch architecture, were renovated and painted in vivid colours: deep purple, burgundy, dark red, bright yellow and baby blue.

Though it's now a tourist destination, the area remains poor. "We were lucky to preserve our heritage, but 95 per cent of the people that used to live here, they lost it," Ahmed laments. "And the soul of the city is gone."

Ghaniema Johnson, a physiotherapist whose office is upstairs in one of the houses, is positive about the post-apartheid changes. "People are here because of the unique culture that we have. The majority of them are Muslim. But we also have Christianity, Judaism, Hinduism, and we have the African people, who also have their own cultures and beliefs.

"So, we're a rainbow nation, we really are," she assures me.

—·—

Noon Gun Tearoom is perched on top of Signal Hill, a steep climb from the Bo-Kaap—not easy with a manual shift. The tearoom is in the family home of Sherine Habib, an anti-apartheid activist I met on my previous trip to Cape Town.

I bring Onkuen with me to meet Habib, hoping the two women will share stories of their lives under apartheid. Habib's mother has prepared a sumptuous lunch for us, which we enjoy on the verandah with a breathtaking view of Table Mountain, Cape Town's landmark.

The cuisine is Cape Malay, an Indonesian-Dutch fusion. Among the dishes is koe'sister, a spicy, cake-like fried dumpling sprinkled with coconut flakes. Tradition has it that Afrikaans and Malay women would get together every Sunday to make this pastry, cooking together in sisterhood.

"We as a community identify ourselves as Cape Malay, more so than the generations before us," Habib points out. "This fusion of foods and cuisine is like many cultures coming together. So, Cape Town has merged in cuisine far quicker than it has merged in race."

Habib was active in the 1980s with the United Democratic Front (UDF), a loose federation of anti-apartheid movements linked ideologically to the African National Congress (ANC). In the last city council election, she ran as an ANC candidate but lost to a candidate from the Democratic Alliance, a right-wing party. Her campaign flyer shows her wearing a hijab.

"My stories include people who had just left my home, and I wouldn't see them in the evening because they were shot down by the police," she says, almost in tears. "Friends died on a daily basis."

I break cinematic rules by having Habib speak directly to the camera: "There were many, many bad things happening in the townships before Mr. Mandela was released. Now and then the schools would protest and the police would shoot and we would have children dying, screaming and shouting. There was a lot of torture and trauma. My role with the UDF at that time was to hide all these activists in my home at Cape Flats."

Cape Flats is an expansive, low-lying area southeast of the central business district. During the apartheid era, race-based legislation such as the Group Areas Act forced non-white people out of more central urban areas, designated for whites, into government-built townships on the Flats.

We come to the definition of race. Habib says, "I don't know what picture they had of people who are Black in this country. Because 'Black' included African, Malay, Indian, people from Saint Helena island who were coloured, the Bushmen's descendants, Khoikhoi . . . And they were very confused when the Japanese came. Because they didn't know whether they should make them Black or white, or what. This was a big issue, you know. I remember that we were laughing so much at this."

South Africa is in transition. How do you transform a nation that has awakened from fifty years of apartheid, when five out of six people were disenfranchised and herded like cattle into townships and ghettos, and the best lands were reserved for whites? How long can a period of transition last before people become impatient?

"The white people in this country must learn to share, then everything will go right. We first have to feed the people properly. They say *zakat* starts at home." Habib uses the Islamic term for almsgiving. "The government needs to give people the means to rise."

"The country is still going through a maturation process." Onkuen is more cautious. "It will take people time for all the new-found knowledge to sink in."

"People are happier now; they have some freedoms, but it's still hard to survive. Young people don't want to wait it out. I was like that. I left the country many, many times and came back here because I couldn't see any Table Mountain or any sea."

"You're so cosmopolitan. You've been everywhere. I've only been in one place: Cape Town."

"For me, Cape Town is still the best place."

"Yes, still the best place to be." Onkuen stares out the window toward Table Mountain.

———

Apartheid drew a stark line between Black and white, segregating the races and plunging the country into bloodshed and violence.

Chinese people, who had been in South Africa for more than 350 years, suddenly found themselves in no-man's land. The community all but disappeared during the apartheid struggle. They kept to themselves, kept quiet and kept working.

Living with uncertainty, insecurity and confusion, they became deeply divided. Some, like Lam Al Ying, did all they could to put up passive resistance. Many others focused on their own community's concerns and remained distant from the struggle, if not wholly complicit with the apartheid regime.

Today, many are still reluctant to talk about this period of their lives. When I met Onkuen for the first time, four months earlier, two of her friends counselled her to not talk to me. They were afraid the community's shameful history of complicity would be revealed.

It took some time for her to open up. Only toward the last day of the trip, after an Italian dinner with her Jewish friend—Jews have had their own ambivalence about living under apartheid—did she take me into her home to reveal a sad reminder of that period of her own life.

She begins by bringing out a mahjong set and starts to tell her story about growing up in a white area. "There were three other Chinese families, all running grocery stores within a two- to three-kilometre radius. We had no sports to bring us together. So, we bonded by going to each other's house for birthday parties, and every Sunday, when our mothers played mahjong."

Then she brings out the wedding album.

Onkuen is elegant in bridal white, and Ying is wearing a dark suit with a boutonniere. The ceremony was held in a Catholic church, and the reception at a club.

"My husband was considered a *white* Chinese because he immigrated here; and I was a native, a *Black* Chinese. We were actually breaking the law to get married and had to obtain special permission to do that. At the reception the Chinese had to be divided—you couldn't mix socially. The local-born Chinese weren't supposed to mix with the whites, who were some of our clients, and, of course, the older generation of Chinese born in China."

I ask about the dancing.

"They had the whites sitting on one side and the Chinese sitting on the other side. After a dance, all the white people went back to one side, and all the Chinese people went back to their side. We had a big laugh about that."

Both Onkuen and Maylee identify more as Chinese than South African. When asked to identify her race on the government forms, where the choice was always coloured, Asian, Black, or white, Maylee would never tick any of them but just write down "Chinese."

What about marrying a Chinese?

"I always believe that Chinese would be the best choice," Maylee says. "So basically, South African Chinese, because we come from the same background. At the end of the day, it's not really the colour of their skin. I would prefer somebody who's honest and true inside."

More Chinese immigrants and students are coming into South Africa since the country established diplomatic ties with the People's Republic of China in 1998. While out dancing the night before, I sensed that Maylee and Wang Zhaohui from the kitchen had become a couple.

—-—

Francis Liang and a couple of other men are cooking up generous cuts of meat on fired-up grills, each with a bottle of Castle Lager in hand. It seems like all 200 local Chinese families show up for the Western Province Chinese Association's Sunday potluck *braai*, Afrikaans barbecue.

The Chinese association and community centre are located in an old observatory bought through a community trust. There's a basketball court—a pick-up game is in progress—as well as classrooms and activity rooms upstairs. Tables have been set up in the courtyard for today's potluck.

"The main focus of the association is to have a sense of Chinese unity, a place for the Chinese to interact socially and to preserve the Chinese identity, especially amongst the youngsters," Francis explains as we sit down at his mezzanine office with a view of the basketball court. He's a director of the association and, in his early fifties, considers himself an elder in the community.

Francis grew up in Queenstown, Eastern Cape. As he was not allowed to attend public school in those days, his father, Lionel, arranged a ministerial permit for him to study in a white school in East London while boarding with his aunt.

Lionel is native Chinese South African, and Francis's mother, Juliette, is Sino-Mauritian. They ran a food distribution business in Queenstown (now Komani), located between two Black homelands, Ciskei and Transkei.

"Our customers were 100 per cent Black because the Blacks came to us; they didn't trust the whites," Lionel tells me when I visit his home. But the family kept a low profile, minded their own business and "didn't tread on anyone's toes."

Francis, who still speaks the Hakka dialect with his parents, tells me why his community is so united, even to this day: "There's very little inter-racial marriage, and we stick together. I'm second generation, I can speak Chinese. But you'll find the younger generation, the children, are not really interested in speaking any Chinese. However, I believe once you get older, you will actually try to retain a Chinese identity and be proud of that."

He is hopeful about the future of his country. He has always felt it was wrong to discriminate against someone and deprive them of opportunities merely because of the colour of their skin.

"People who are five or ten years older than myself probably have certain feelings of resentment and maybe bitterness toward the country because of what they went through," he continues. "People who are seven or eight years younger than myself, they were all allowed to go to public schools, so they would have a more positive sentiment."

Many have emigrated elsewhere, but Francis believes those who stayed are very united. He has no intention of emigrating, but should things turn in a way that he finds unbearable, he probably would.

"I see myself as Chinese, as a Chinese South African, definitely I am a South African."

—·—

I've always been fascinated by tales of the Portuguese explorer Vasco da Gama rounding the Cape of Good Hope looking for the spice route to India. I'm surprised to learn that Onkuen has never been to Cape Point, only an hour and half away from where she has lived her entire life.

When I visit Cape Point National Park, I invite Onkuen and Maylee. Our car hugs the eastern coastline, passing through quintessential English towns with Dutch names like Muizenberg and Fish Hoek.

At Cape Point, the most southwestern point of the African continent, the Flying Dutchman Funicular hoists us up to the Old Lighthouse. The view from the top of the cliff is spectacular, overlooking the meeting of two oceans. The sun basks us with a brilliant haze, rendering the sea and land mystical.

Cape of Good Hope, which can be seen from the cable car, is just north of Cape Point. And the southernmost point of the continent is at Cape Agulhas, about 150 kilometres to the east.

I explain to Onkuen my fascination with the Cape and its place in the history of the European colonization of Asia. She listens intently and offers her view of European settlement and its legacy in South Africa.

"There's no national pride here," she says. "We always thought we were sojourning here. The place actually belonged to the whites; we were just encroaching on their space. It was never meant for us to claim."

"Have you ever claimed this country as your own?" I ask.

"Never claimed it. Not emotionally . . . not at all. How do you put it? We regarded it as a paradise that we were sharing, but not ours to have."

"What about now?"

"Now the Blacks say: 'Let go, let your grasp go.' It's said with energy and fervour. 'Let go! You don't belong here. If you don't like it here, go!'"

"Is that how you feel?"

"That's how I feel now. I feel that's the message."

Like many Chinese South Africans, Onkuen would like to immigrate to Canada. (Two of her sisters live in Toronto.) But that seems unlikely at the moment. Her hesitation is palpable—she has her husband's legacy to contend with.

I have spent more than a week trying to draw Onkuen out from her physical and emotional cocoon. But all I get from her is an undercurrent of ambivalence and resignation, about her place in the new South Africa.

CHAPTER 7

Soupe Chinoise

TAMATAVE, MADAGASCAR

I WAS IN A PLACE SURROUNDED BY SPIRITS—THE SPIRITS OF PEOPLE WHO DIED in faraway lands but returned to this Chinese temple to rest in peace. It's common in China to set aside space in a temple for spirits of the deceased to return to the land of their birth. To be remembered.

But I was not in China. I was in Madagascar, half a world away.

In the Hall of the Forefathers in Tamatave's Chinese temple, I lit three sticks of incense and bowed three times at a red altar, surrounded by faded black-and-white photographs of the dead.

It was late November 2000. I was scouting for my *Chinese Restaurants* documentary series when I found myself in this temple that adjoins Congrégation Chinoise de Tamatave, the local Chinese association.

"These people have moved far away from here: Paris, Montreal, Melbourne," Shum Ying Hung, the part-time caretaker, pointed out. "But their families would place their photos here when they die."

Shum was born to a Malagasy mother and a Chinese father. They sent him to China after the Second World War, at the age of thirteen, to further his education—as was customary in the local Chinese community at that time, even for those who were of mixed descent. When Mao Zedong's Communists were victorious in 1949, Shum went to live with relatives in Hong Kong and did not return to Madagascar until he was thirty.

Back in Tamatave, Shum taught in the Chinese school and, with his wife from Hong Kong, raised seven children. When she died in 1973, he married a Malagasy woman and fathered seven more children.

Despite the many years he has spent in Madagascar, his link to China was still strong. His father was from Nanhai county—where my grandfather came from—and he still has cousins in nearby Guangzhou (Canton).

"Do you see yourself as Chinese?" I asked.

"Of course I'm Chinese," he said with conviction. "That's why I went back to study in China after the war."

Shum was retired, but he still taught part-time and helped out at the Chinese school. He planned to return soon to Vatomandry, where his family lives, about 180 kilometres south along the east coast: "I'm going home to the mountains."

Earlier that morning, I'd flown in from the capital, Antananarivo—which the French call Tananarive, Tana for short—to Tamatave, the port city by the Indian Ocean. I'd come to the city to look for a Chinese restaurant. It was Chris Lee Sin Cheong of Mauritius—a friend of the sister-in-law of my Sino-Mauritian office neighbour in Toronto—who suggested that his brother Paul Lin Sin Cheong, living in Antananarivo, could connect me with the Chinese community here. Paul told me, when I stopped over at the capital the night before, that a business friend of his would greet me at the airport.

I was greeted by Catherine Deneuve—well, a look-alike anyway—blonde and tanned in an all-white cotton dress and a white wide-brim hat like she'd just walked onto the rubber plantation set of *Indochine*.

Except that we were in Africa, and everything was dripping wet from a morning downpour. Catherine—I don't remember her name anymore—led me to her Suzuki 4x4, all the while stepping around potholes, puddles, pebbles and cracks like she was on a catwalk. Nothing sullied her white pumps.

"*Mon mari est métissé*," she said as we pulled away. My husband is mixed-race. (In French, the word "métis" means mixed race.) "He's not the one you want to talk to. I'll introduce you to *Chinese* people in town."

To my utter astonishment, I learned that the Chinese had settled in Madagascar for more than five generations. Many of them hailed from my ancestral Nanhai county in southeastern China's Guangdong province. One even went to the same high school as my father in Hong Kong.

Three days later, I returned to Antananarivo on a tortuous eight-hour car ride—my return flight had been cancelled, and I desperately needed to get to Tana early the next morning for my outbound flight to Mauritius. By that time, I had come down with a stomach flu, and I was still wearing the same clothes that I had been wearing for four days—my luggage was somewhere in the African continent.

Here I was, lying on the backseat half-delirious, and what did I see flashing by? A three-storey building with columns engraved with the Chinese characters for the Nan Shun Association.

In the most unexpected of places, in the city of Moramanga, in the middle of the mountains, in the dark of the night, I came across an association for Cantonese people from the counties of Nanhai and Shunde—the same association I used to live next to during my childhood in Singapore, in a building like the one I just saw.

Life had come full circle. Though separated by geography and history, I felt a palpable tie to the Chinese people in Madagascar—like we are all one extended family from the same village.

—•—

"Restaurant Cantonais."

"Soupe Chinoise."

These words are painted in red on a wooden board, nailed above the blue door of a wooden shack with a corrugated roof at the far end of Boulevard Joffre. Inside, it's dark. Rays of mid-morning sun pierce through the cracks of the wall boards. A wonton broth bubbles in a huge pot in the unkempt open kitchen. About a dozen customers are seated on benches having their mid-morning snack, soupe chinoise.

Soupe chinoise is wonton soup, an adopted national dish, just as the Brits regard chicken tikka masala as *their* national dish. Along with the pousse-pousse (Chinese rickshaw)—found all over Madagascar and still the best mode of transportation around town—soupe chinoise is a cultural import by the Chinese immigrants of the late 1890s.

In France, "Chinese soup" refers to any Chinese noodle soup, no matter what meat or vegetable it contains. In Madagascar, soupe chinoise is almost always wonton soup, without noodles.

I fell in love with Cantonese Restaurant when I first set foot in it four months earlier. It was like a Western saloon—cue the tumbleweeds.

Chan Suk Ting's immigrant parents came from Shunde, a neighbouring county to my ancestral Nanhai. She was born in a small mountain village in the north. The family moved to Tamatave, and she attended Chinese school. She took over the restaurant six years ago from her late mother, who opened it in 1972.

On that trip, I had a hard time convincing her to be in my film. She was reluctant and kept insisting that she was "no good at talking." Later the same day, I found her playing mahjong with three other elderly Chinese women in a recreational club. They were cheerfully chatting in Cantonese, each with a cell phone on the table.

So I tried again. She remained non-committal: "Why do you want an old woman like me?"

Now I've returned to Madagascar with my crew, Kwoi and David Szu, hopeful that Suk Ting will talk to us. I am determined to tell the story of one of the most interesting Chinese restaurants I have come across in my world travels.

"You're back from Canada?" the diminutive seventy-year-old Suk Ting asks.

"I'm here to tell your story," I remind her.

She shoves us away, "I don't want my ugly place on TV. I've got nothing to say. Put your camera away. You should go talk to the other Madame Chan at Jade. She's much more presentable, and her restaurant is nicer and bigger."

Restaurant Le Jade, on Rue de Lattre de Tassigny, is indeed nicer and bigger. It's in a two-storey white house with a green-and-white awning over a front patio. Inside, the white walls are decorated with paintings of scenes from the South Seas—beach sunsets and coconut trees.

I can sense good Chinese food when I walk into a place. This is confirmed as soon as I scan the menu, written in French and Chinese: crab stir-fried in black bean sauce, salt-and-pepper fried squid, sautéed scampi in garlic and steamed whole red snapper in ginger and scallion. All classical Cantonese cooking *de la mer*, from the sea.

My taste buds are aroused.

I order red snapper, scampi and some locally grown Chinese greens. I look over to the large crab at the next table, dripping in a tantalizing black bean sauce. Oh ya, I'll have what they're having, too.

Madame Chan then suggests the *plat du jour*, crevettes bouillies. Despite its unappetizing name in Chinese, "white boiled shrimp," it is one of my favourite Cantonese dishes. The shrimps are cooked in their shells just long enough to turn pink, and then finger-dipped in a soy sauce sprinkled with chopped red chili peppers.

"They just came in this morning," she says, tilting her head toward the kitchen, notepad in hand.

In Hong Kong, seafood restaurants typically fetch the shrimp from a display tank and bring it to the table for customer approval. Here, they jump out of the Indian Ocean, two blocks away.

When the food appears, I am speechless. Not only is it the freshest seafood I've ever tasted, but the cooking is impeccable—to the perfect doneness, that is, slightly undercooked. Cantonese have a saying that you need to "see red" in a steamed fish, meaning pink in the bones.

It's Kwoi's forty-fifth birthday, and the meal befits the occasion. David also bought a birthday cake that cost just 20,000 Malagasy francs (about US$3). We ask for a candle.

Sixty-year-old Miday Chan is a second-generation Chinese Malagasy born in the town of Brickaville, about 100 kilometres to the south. She graduated from Tamatave's Chinese school, and her Cantonese is flawless, though tinged with her parents' native Shunde accent. She even taught at her alma mater for three years before opening this restaurant a decade ago.

None of Miday's kitchen help is Chinese, but the food they prepare is truly exquisite. Citing the freshness of her seafood and the subtlety of the seasonings—two key elements in Cantonese cuisine—I tell her she can give the best Hong Kong kitchens a run for their money. But I'm shocked to hear that she has never been to China or Hong Kong.

"I learned from my father. He likes to cook," she says. "I watched and learned. I also studied cookbooks from Hong Kong, especially those of Mrs. Fong's."

Mrs. Fong, aka Lisa Yam, was a popular TV chef in Hong Kong who produced practical, easy-to-use cookbooks and magazines in the 1980s.

The restaurant's kitchen is a bare room with home kitchen equipment. Six people hustle and bustle along with steamers, woks and clay pots, while Miday supervises, teaches and re-teaches, and checks each dish before it is brought out. What impresses me most is watching a helper roll out rice flour dough to make translucent skin for steamed dumplings.

"They've never eaten authentic Chinese food, so they haven't acquired the taste that is necessary to cook well," she says. "Some of the smarter ones pick it up quickly in two or three months. There's really no formal way—they just watch me. I teach them how to prep, how to stir-fry, and the order in which the ingredients go into the wok."

At the back of the kitchen, in the open air and within sight of the sea, two other workers are descaling a giant red snapper, which will be used in another distinctive Chinese dish: sweet and sour fish filets.

Le Jade's customers are primarily "people with money." The restaurant caters to many Chinese expatriates. ("They order only the freshest!" says Miday.) They may be traders from China, businessmen from Hong Kong or investors from nearby Mauritius. Many come during the holidays from as far away as Antananarivo.

I point to a dish at the next table, chicken sautéed with pineapple served in a half shell. Is this some sort of hybrid?

"I created that myself. I made it for the customers, and they liked it, so I put it on the menu," Miday tells me. As an aside, I mention that Shunde people are known to be good cooks.

"I didn't intend to open a formal restaurant. Just one to make enough money to survive. It's a tough life," she demurs.

I am just about to ask her about her family when she puts her hand over the lens. "Okay, enough from me. It's time to put your camera away."

Big Island, as Madagascar is lovingly called, is 400 kilometres off the east coast of Africa and the fourth-largest island of the world. It is also one of the most multicultural, peopled over two millennia by Africans, Arabs, Malayo-Indonesians, Europeans, Indians and Chinese.

Human settlement on the Big Island began as early as 350 BC, when Malayo-Indonesians arrived on outrigger canoes from Indonesia. Africans crossed the Mozambique Channel around the ninth century. Arabs came mid-twelfth century, followed by Indians, Chinese and Europeans.

Amazingly, half of the inhabitants of Madagascar have genetic lineages derived from settlers from the region of Borneo, and the other half from East Africa. The Malagasy language can be traced back to Indonesia, where it most closely resembles modern Malayo-Polynesian. This Indonesian heritage can be seen everywhere, in peoples' facial features and in the stretches of wet rice fields.

The first documented Chinese settlement in Tamatave was in the early 1860s, before French colonization, coming mostly from the islands of Mauritius, Réunion and the Seychelles. At the end of the nineteenth century, the French colonial administration recruited 3,000 Cantonese labourers from Shunde county to work on excavation, road and bridge building, and the Tamatave–Tananarive railway. Indentured Indian labourers came around the same time. (Both Chinese and Indians were easier to train than local Malayo-Indonesians, and they demanded lower wages than European and Creole workers.)

Chinese fanned out from the east coast of Madagascar, where they first settled, to villages in the highlands, or up the mountains into the jungles, where natural resources were more plentiful. They did what Europeans were reluctant to do: travel across the roadless countryside, working and living in the bush. They sold basics such as salt, sugar, soap, petrol and cloth to the farmers, in exchange for vanilla, coffee, pepper and cloves. Others ran coffee and vanilla plantations.

I am determined to dig up the history of Chinese settlements in Madagascar and have enlisted the help of Bruno Lao, who runs a taxi service. He was one of Miday's students at the Tamatave Chinese school.

"I'll take you up the mountains," Lao says in Cantonese. "To my hometown, Brickaville."

In Chinese culture, "up the mountains" has a mystical connotation— and it's not the first time I've heard the phrase in Madagascar. Taoist monks go up the mountains to seek herbs and plants for Chinese herbal medicine or to search for the elixir of life. Martial arts swordsmen go up the mountains to retire, to seek inner peace and enlightenment away from an earthly world. Even Shum Ying Hung, back at the temple, wanted to go home to the mountains.

Brickaville is a town of 20,000 along Route Nationale 2, the road that links Tamatave to the capital up in Central Highlands. It used to be home to a large Chinese community, but for generations they married local people, creating a new kind of Malagasy.

"*Ils sont tous métissés comme moi*," Lao says. They are all mixed race like me.

"There are only about 1,000 full-blooded Chinese left in the whole country, and only seven such families left in Brickaville," he tells me. "But there're lots of métissé Chinese, especially in the north, which creates a unique cultural mix. They're Malagasies, but their ancestors are Chinese."

The sun shines brightly on lush green valleys as we travel south, following the coastline and climbing for 100 kilometres before sharply turning west. Finally, we cross the Rianila River and make a sharp right to leave the national road and turn onto Brickaville's main street. One-storey brick houses with aluminum roofing line both sides, giving the town a frontier feel. This is a scene straight out of a Spaghetti Western. We half expect to find Clint Eastwood challenging us to a duel.

But the people are friendly and issue invitations to their homes for beer. It helps that Lao knows most of them. Miday Chan's younger brother Gilbert is one of four Chinese in town who own grocery stores.

At the last store, I notice an old Chinese woman pouring bottles of bootleg rum into a wooden barrel. The scene is eerily familiar; the woman looks very familiar, too. On closer look, I recognize her from the Hong Kong television program *Stories from Afar*, about Chinese immigrants around the world—and specifically the Madagascar episode that I just watched, two weeks prior to my arrival.

What serendipity.

The woman's husband, Lai Liang Ying, comes out from behind the store to greet me in Cantonese. "Welcome. I'm Lai from Shunde."

"I'm Kwan from Nanhai," I introduce myself as someone from a neighbouring district.

It is customary for China's older generation to introduce themselves by announcing their home county. It's a way to quickly make a connection, no matter how many generations away we are from our ancestral homeland.

Until the 1960s, 95 per cent of Chinese immigrants to Madagascar hailed from these two districts in southeastern Guangdong province, near Hong Kong.

Lai Liang Ying was thirteen when he arrived in Brickaville in 1920, and he never left. Now ninety-three, he is the oldest Chinese on the island. His wife, Tsang Ngan Sing, came in the 1940s as a mail-order bride. Together, they have been running Boulangerie Lai for more than fifty years. Despite its name, the store is not just a bakery. It retails and distributes grains and produce, imported canned goods and all kinds of liquor and beer.

In towns and cities across Madagascar, Chinese shopkeepers help maintain the island's social fabric. Their stores are meeting places—people drop by to chat, have a drink, listen to music and exchange gossip. They also serve as creditors, giving villagers loans against future harvests, playing a key role in the rural economy.

Lai and Tsang insist that I come to their nearby home for a beer, leaving their youngest to tend the store. Their two-storey home is like a warehouse and barn, spacious but unkempt, with furniture and decorations from the 1950s. But there are telltale signs of prosperity: they have two working refrigerators and two domestics—one is ironing as we walk in. The dining room and adjoining kitchen face the river.

Tsang urges me to try her homemade mooncake. I'm amazed at the Chinese traditions these immigrants in Madagascar preserve, so far from their native land. Mooncakes, filled with a sweetened lotus seed paste, and sometimes with a cooked salted egg yolk or two, normally are made to celebrate the Mid-Autumn Festival on the fifteenth day of the eighth month in the lunar calendar. Here, the boulangerie bakes them year-round.

After several bottles of Three Horses beer, we go upstairs to the living room where the couple show off their true claim to fame: their TV appearance. It was in the Madagascar episode of the Hong Kong television program, in which Lai reminisces about his journey from China as a young man.

After we've watched it, I pop the question, as I always do with older men: where does he want to be buried?

In China, he says. If that's not possible, he would like his photograph to be displayed in his ancestral temple in Shunde, to ensure his spirit returns to the village of his birth. But he concedes this is likely not possible either. China is no longer the place he once knew.

—·—

It takes me a few tries to find the apartment Marco Taochy shares with his mother, Miday Chan. Their fourth-floor balcony has a commanding view of the sea. An ocean breeze blows in.

Taochy is twenty-seven. Typical of his generation, he left Madagascar to finish his education in France. After completing his military service there, he worked at an American restaurant in Antibes for three years "to find out how life is outside of Madagascar."

He has just returned with his French wife, Viriane, and their eight-month-old son, Antoine, to help his mother at the restaurant. His brother is in France. His sister, who started the restaurant with his mother, just married.

"So, I'm the one who has to take care of the business." He gives out a laugh. "For now, I'll give myself five years. It's a really difficult career because I won't have a family life. We'll see what happens in the future."

What about culture shock?

"Yes, it was difficult at first. People here live differently. They take time to live. Now, things are better, I'm back into my routine. Madagascar is not like Europe. There's no social safety net; we'll have to depend on ourselves."

Viriane is a teacher at the local Lycée Français. It wasn't until she came to Madagascar that she realized her husband's family is Chinese. "He led a more European life in France. But the way his family and his mother live is different from mine. The cultures are different. Sometimes it's difficult because my mother-in-law and I don't have the same way of thinking."

I ask Taochy about discrimination, based on his heritage.

"There's discrimination and racism everywhere, but Chinese are well accepted and well integrated here," he says. "There's mutual respect between the locals and the Chinese. All Chinese speak Malagasy, but only about 20 per cent of the French do. This facilitates our relationship with the locals. We're in the middle, a go-between. The Chinese have always been traders and merchants. *C'est connu partout.*" It's well known.

Taochy feels he is a product of Chinese, French and Malagasy culture, but he remains very Chinese in his way of thinking.

He now opens up about the family history his mother tried to avoid. His maternal grandparents came from China, but his paternal grandparents were born in Madagascar. His father, the Chinese man I see working in the shadows behind the restaurant bar, is Miday's second husband, but they are divorced and no longer live together. His mother's first husband was a marine, Taochy says—and doesn't specify his ethnicity.

He clearly admires his mother's determination: "When she decides on something, it has to be done. This is how she has succeeded. This is important in the restaurant industry. Once you prepare a dish, you can't start over."

I raise the subject of soupe chinoise, which is such a staple here, and which everyone seems to love.

"It's really popular and tastes good. A lot of people have it for breakfast," he says. "But many of those who make soupe chinoise are métissés. And Chinese roots are everywhere in the restaurant industry. Everyone enjoys Chinese cuisine here."

Echoing what I had discovered at his mother's restaurant, he adds, "The *soupe* is almost our national dish."

—·—

Tamatave, the largest port in the country, is a relaxed, quiet city of about 150,000. Its shady boulevards exude a gracious French colonial ambiance. But at night the city comes alive. My guidebook tells me that this is when discos and nightclubs, restaurants and snack sellers, drug peddlers and prostitutes vie for customers. (There are complimentary condoms in our rooms at Hotel Neptune, the best hotel in town.)

Kwoi and David decide to hit the town after dinner. I'm usually too exhausted by the end of the day, being both director and fixer. (A fixer, usually a local hire who speaks the language, makes all the arrangements, however small and menial, at the shooting location.)

The duo returns to the hotel earlier than expected. There's talk about fleeing three skimpily dressed prostitutes at a roadside bar, and I hear words like G-strings, nipples and Black Mama. I don't want to know.

The next morning, we take two pousse-pousses to Épicerie Liu on Boulevard Joffre, Tamatave's main thoroughfare. There was a downpour overnight, and it's amazing what a monsoon-like outburst can do to a city with little or no road drainage.

The streets are flooded. The pousse-pousse has big wheels, so passengers sit high above the water, keeping dry. For the pullers? Not so much. They wade through knee-deep water trying to avoid the now-invisible potholes. And there are many. Yet they help each other when one of them is stuck.

Liu Yung Yer's general store sells just about everything: cigarettes, canned goods, candies, medicine, liquor and beer. He also bootlegs rum with alcohol content as high as 75 per cent. Moonshine is big business. In Madagascar, toaka gasy, literally "Malagasy alcohol," describes any rum produced by farmers, in sugar fields, without an official licence. It has a long history in the country—lengthy enough for the popular alcohol to have become the de facto "national drink."

The drinking at Épicerie Liu starts early—in late morning. People come in alone or in twos or threes, to talk and to share bottles of beer. But mostly they come for cheap illegal liquor, dispensed from the barrel at the back of the store into tin cups. Some bring their own bottles for refills.

Hong Kong–born Liu arrived in Madagascar when he was thirteen. He worked for a relative at a grocery store in Moramanga, which means "cheap mangoes." It's situated on the central plateau, 120 kilometres from the capital, surrounded by rainforests.

Ten years later, he opened his own store in the north, where he met and married Raymonde Chan, a third-generation Chinese Malagasy. When another relative from Tamatave offered Liu the opportunity to take over the present store in 1989, he agreed and moved here.

Raymonde and Liu have three children. The two elder daughters went to university in Taiwan, and one is now a teacher there. The other lives in Australia, married to a Frenchman. Their youngest son, James, works in the store.

For years, Chinese immigrants, even local-born with mixed heritage, have been denied citizenship in Madagascar. So they have held on to their original Republic of China citizenship, even though none of them has a connection to Taiwan. And when Madagascar established relations with China in 1972, the new Chinese embassy was only too happy to exchange those dark green Taiwan passports for red ones issued by the People's Republic.

Chinese business associations, schools and social and cultural organizations were persuaded to switch their allegiance to the new Communist regime in China. And China's national flag—red with five yellow stars—was raised in many of these places in lieu of the flag of Taiwan (often referred to by its moniker "blue sky white sun").

This is part of China's United Front strategy to win the hearts and minds of overseas Chinese, to cultivate loyalty to a "new and stronger motherland." This morning, the headline of the *Madagascar Tribune* screamed "*La délégation taiwanaise expulsée,*" Taiwanese delegation expelled. The remnants of Taiwanese influence in Madagascar were finally gone.

There is no doubt where Liu's allegiance lies, however. He is staunchly pro-Kuomintang, the Nationalists who "lost" the mainland to the Communists and retreated to the island of Taiwan.

Liu is a meek and frail eighty-year-old with greyish hair and a couple of missing front teeth, and he speaks Cantonese laced with a heavy accent from his native Shunde county. We are sitting in a small patch of green in the middle of the city. The cicadas are noisy at this time of the year, and a cow someone left tied to a tree is mooing annoyingly at us.

I broach the subject of citizenship: "It seems like Madagascar doesn't want you to be a citizen here."

"It's not that you can't obtain citizenship, but you have to bribe," he says, his voice becoming weak.

"To get a passport?"

"Yes. It takes a bribe. It's corrupted here. You can't be too honest in this town. Otherwise, you're just ordinary, like me. I'm old and I don't take risks, not like the young people."

"And if you take risks?"

"Then you inevitably get into the business of corruption and bribery."

"Have you ever thought about going back to China?"

"We all have ancestral shrines in our homes. Chinese always think about where they came from; they don't forget the source. But how could I go back? If I could go, I would go now; I won't have to wait till I die."

After a pause, he adds, "Nobody wants to go back. China has become communist. We can't go home anymore. I haven't seen a single Chinese who wants to go back."

It's Independence Day. Shops are closed. Boulevard Joffre is eerily deserted. Leaves rustle in the wind. Cicadas sing. An occasional pousse-pousse goes by. We are in for a hot and lazy afternoon.

Two customers are sipping aperitifs on the verandah of Hôtel Joffre— the landmark hotel which was sold by a Frenchman to a local Chinese twenty years ago. Many of the grocery stores and businesses in Tamatave are also owned by Chinese Malagasy, including Disco Oh La La! on Rue du Commerce.

The hotel dining room offers a taste of French colonial decadence, the cuisine of a bygone era. A blackboard advertises a menu du jour that includes, as a first course, salade de fois gras. Ceiling fans whirl nosily, flapping the tablecloths.

A lone server, in a traditional French black-and-white waiter's uniform, remains discreet and unobtrusive. The dated decor and threadbare uniforms only add to the nostalgia.

I'm having lunch with Roger Leung, who runs an import-export business. As we talk, our waiter Claude ladles a cream of vegetable soup from a large tureen—classic French service—and wishes us bon appétit.

Over steak au poivre, served at the table from a silver tray, Leung points out that Madagascar was a paradise even after independence in 1960. But since 1972, when the country turned socialist and expelled foreigners, it has been stifled by corruption and has fallen into a long decline. He blames the French who, unlike the British, never left behind a strong civil service or infrastructure.

In 1947, there was a nationalist uprising against French rule that lasted for two years and killed 100,000. Many Chinese returned to China. Leung was one of them. When the Communists came to power in 1949, he wanted to return to his native Madagascar but was unable to leave.

He finally moved to Hong Kong in 1959, when China allowed foreign-born Chinese nationals to leave. He lived and worked there for eight years before coming back to Madagascar. He was away for more than twenty years.

"I was born here," he emphasizes. "This is my home."

Leung typifies many in the Malagasy Chinese community, even those who are métissés. Born and bred here, they nevertheless went back to China to continue their secondary education before returning to Madagascar as adults.

His entire family are Malagasy citizens, and the three grown daughters live in Antananarivo, Paris and Montreal. "I'm going to retire here. Hong Kong is too dense, too intense. Not suited for me."

———

I am surprised to discover that, in Madagascar, many descendants of Chinese immigrants, even third- and fourth-generation, still speak their Cantonese dialect.

For generations, Chinese Malagasy sent their children, even those of mixed race, back to China to get an education. When it became impossible during the Sino-Japanese War, the community established its own schools all over Madagascar. The bigger ones offered boarding for students from towns and villages.

Liu takes me to Collège de la Congrégation Chinoise, Chinese Association School. The school started life as Tamatave Chinese School in 1938, with instruction in Chinese in the morning and French in the afternoon. Chinese teachers and textbooks were brought in from the Republic of China. I am shown a 1975 yearbook that could have come straight out of a Taiwan high school.

At its peak, the school had 600 students. Now it's the only Chinese school left in the whole country. And Chinese in name only. It is a public school with instruction in French and Malagasy where Chinese language classes are offered only after school.

"It used to be that we needed to go back to China for our education," Liu says. "After China became communist, it's not any good anymore. People go to France now."

I'm introduced to the principal and teachers, all of them métissés. They are happy to give me a tour. In one class, a métissée girl in a blue-and-white school uniform is writing her name in Chinese characters on the blackboard. Her characters are impeccably formed, as if she's been practising calligraphy for years. I'm in awe at the penmanship, knowing my own pales in comparison.

In the playground, as I watch the schoolchildren run around, I note there are only a few ethnic Chinese. The rest are of mixed racial heritage. Just as wonton soup has been assimilated into the Malagasy cuisine, the Chinese, over generations, have become part of the cultural fabric of the Big Island.

Looking at the schoolchildren in the playground, I can't help but think that this is the direction in which the rest of the world should be heading: becoming a place where cultures and races have intermingled so completely that it doesn't matter where one's ancestors are from. What matters is the life we create for ourselves in the place we call home.

CHAPTER 8

The Man Who Walked from China

ISTANBUL, TURKEY

ISTANBUL. SUNDAY, OCTOBER 31, 1976.

On that day, I had dinner with Charles Chabanol at Çin Lokantasi, or China Restaurant. My diary says I had "mushroom chicken" and "beef vermicelli." I also ordered Chinese greens for good measure.

The 1976 *Let's Go Europe* guide lists this eatery—in the basement of No. 22 Lamartin Caddesi, a street that runs diagonally off Taksim Square—as the only Chinese restaurant in Turkey. It notes that the owner had "walked from China."

I met Chabanol, a charming Eurasian man, earlier that day at Sirkeci Station, terminus of the famed Orient Express. He was in his early thirties, handsome, tanned, with the physique—and the air—of a French Foreign Legionnaire who'd spent time in West Africa. He asked whether I was Japanese, an easy assumption to make at that time.

I had just flown in from Tehran on the legendary Pan Am Flight 001—the airline's westbound round-the-world service—on my own round-the-world journey. So here I was, at the crossroads of Asia and Europe, looking for a train to Bucharest, my next destination. Chabanol was going to be in town for a few days. "Perhaps we could have a meal together?" he asked.

The next evening, after our meal at the Chinese restaurant, we met again over döner kebabs at the Pudding Shop. The coffee house was a popular hangout in the sixties, where overland travellers between Europe and Asia shared rides and stories—and, legend has it, fell in love. In the late seventies, it became a haven for budget tourists in search of cheap eats.

Over baklava and Turkish coffee, Chabanol told me his life story. Born in Vietnam to a French father and a Vietnamese mother, he moved as a teenager to France, where he embarked on a life of crime and drugs. Having escaped from a French prison a few months earlier, he was hiding in Istanbul, wanted by Interpol.

"I've hurt a few people," Chabanol said.

Maybe I was naïve, maybe too trusting. Or fearless. I thought nothing of it.

After dinner, we had drinks at the top-floor bar at the Sheraton, on the southern edge of Taksim Square. The sweeping view was beautiful—glittering lights of the Bosphorus and Asian Istanbul on one side, the Golden Horn and Galata Bridge on the other. Chabanol showed me his *cahier* of poetry. We talked about Camus. He told me what it was like to grow up mixed-race in France, and the discrimination he faced.

"Look at her in the pink sweater," he nodded toward the elevator entrance behind me. I turned around for a quick look. And when I turned back, he smiled and said he could have drugged my drink.

"That's how I stole passports from three Malaysian diplomats last week."

By this time, I was completely mesmerized. Nothing he said would worry me. Maybe I knew, deep down, that my colonial British National Overseas passport was so useless—with no "right of abode" in the UK—it would be foolish for him to steal it.

We didn't meet again. Chabanol disappeared into the night, walking down one of the myriad narrow streets leading to the Galata Tower below the hill.

Istanbul has always been a mystery to me. A magical city. A city of intrigue. A city on edge. I can't decide whether it's modern or traditional, secular or Muslim. But it has always been beautiful. And, to a photographer, a city with beautiful light.

Years later, that visit to Istanbul still haunted me. I could have been one of Chabanol's victims. And I had no idea, so many years on, what happened to China Restaurant, much less the man "who walked from China."

By chance, I met Nina Karachi-Khaled at an anti-racism conference in Toronto. Upon learning that I'd just flown back that morning from Israel after making a documentary about a Chinese restaurant there, she told me the family of a childhood friend owned the oldest Chinese restaurant in Istanbul.

"They're Muslim Chinese," she added. Nina connected me to Manli Delitzsch in Mexico City, who put me in touch with her sister Rosey Ma.

"I believe if you ate at a Chinese restaurant in 1976, it must be ours," Rosey emailed from Kuala Lumpur a few days later. "My father Wang Zengshan opened the restaurant in 1957, but he had already passed away by the time you ate there."

Her family had fled from China, she added, and then she encouraged me to attend the annual family reunion in the summer in Istanbul. "I won't be there, but you will get to meet my mother and many of my siblings."

That's the reason why, two months later, Kwoi, David Szu and I landed in Istanbul. I wanted to tell the story of the man "who walked from China"—the tale that originally inspired me to make the film series.

China Restaurant is in a three-storey building at No. 17 Lamartin, diagonally across from its former basement location where I ate in 1976. Over the front entrance hang four red lanterns, each with a Chinese character that, together, form the name of the restaurant. The reception, anteroom and kitchen are on the ground floor, and the main dining room upstairs. Isa Wang, the second-eldest child of Wang Zengshan, and nominal owner of the restaurant, lives on the third floor with his wife, Engin, and daughter Mayling.

"Welcome!" Yakar Çakar comes out from the kitchen to give me a hearty handshake as I walk into the restaurant. The air conditioning hasn't been turned on, so we sit on stools outside to stay cool. A breeze blows by, fluttering two large Turkish flags, a welcome relief to what promises to be a very hot day.

Yakar is a short, balding man in his mid-sixties who is quite animated when he speaks—with a lot of hand gestures. He had walked into China Restaurant even before it officially opened and Wang had hired him on the spot. When the patriarch passed away four years later, leaving eight young children—the eldest, Makbule, only eighteen—and a grieving widow who could barely speak Turkish, he took care of the family. He made the children's lunches, took them to school and helped with their homework.

"He's like a member of our family. We regard him as one of our brothers or uncles," Makbule Wu, now in her late fifties, tells me. "Mom and I even helped him propose marriage to the daughter of a Turkish general." Yakar often takes care of the restaurant now, especially during the high season when Isa runs a branch at a resort hotel in Marmaris, the Turkish Riviera town by the Aegean Sea.

"I brought in 14 million customers," he boasts in Turkish. (I don't believe that figure; the math doesn't add up.) "They used to say, 'Let's go to Yakar's,' not China Restaurant . . . They were filming a Western in Istanbul with Mr. Reagan, Anthony Quinn, Yul Brynner . . . And people like Louis Armstrong. Very famous people and also Kennedy generation people. I took care of all of them and served them."

Fatima Ma, Wang Zengshan's dignified seventy-seven-year-old widow, arrives later in the morning with her husband, Dawood Yang, to take their usual seats at the corner table by the front window. The rest of the family, many here for the reunion, shows up around noon, including Saadet and Terence Sun and their two daughters; Manli Delitzsch and her twins from Mexico City; and Makbule, who had just flown in from Taipei.

The family conversation is smatterings of Turkish, Mandarin, English and French. There's a lot of catching up. Laid out on the luncheon table are stir-fried eggplant, braised mutton, shrimp fried rice, stir-fried Chinese cabbage with mushrooms and pan-fried beef dumplings.

Chinese meat dumplings—whether pan-fried, steamed, boiled or in a soup—are usually made with pork. When the menu has the character *rou* ("meat"), it is always pork, as in *xian rou jiao* ("fresh meat dumpling"). The most versatile meat in all Chinese cooking, pork has the "sweetness"— what the Cantonese call *wo mei* ("harmonizing taste")—that combines well with the greatest range of other ingredients. And it's got that yin-yang balance that eating Chinese is all about.

"We're Muslims—we don't serve pork or alcohol here," Fatima pulls me aside to explain. "A lot of our customers wanted pork. Turkish people are not so pure anymore. One time, a customer even brought canned pork. We took one look at it and threw it away. We lose a lot of customers because we don't serve pork dishes."

During lunch, Manli brings out an album of their childhood photos in Pakistan that she rescued from a house fire decades ago. A photo of Wang getting off an airplane in a light-coloured suit catches my eye. It brings back memories of my father in Singapore. He, too, flew around Southeast Asia in the fifties on propeller planes, wearing white summer suits.

I am of the same generation—and led the same diasporic life—as the Wang children. My family, uprooted from Hong Kong, settled in three countries before I turned eighteen. Every time we moved, I would be overcome with sadness—from nostalgia, from never seeing your friends again, and, worst of all, from having to adapt to a new language and a new culture all over again.

The same goes for Kwoi. He left Hong Kong at age nine, for Canada and a father he had never met, only to feel displaced and lost and be bullied by white kids in the neighbourhood. He always feels Western among other Chinese, and Asian among Westerners.

The halal lunch lasts three hours—there's more talking than eating. The meal is simple, home-cooked fare, albeit made from a professional kitchen. The kids from the Mexican and Turkish branches of the family have swept away the last remnants of food on the table, and now they are off to get an ice cream treat from a McDonald's nearby.

Ever since I ate at China Restaurant twenty-five years prior, I have always wanted to know about the history of the Wang family: Where are they from? How did they end up here? Now, I was finally beginning to piece that history together.

Wang Zengshan was born in 1903 to a Muslim Chinese family in Shandong province, eastern China. He was a learned man who spoke many languages and rose in the political ranks of Chiang Kai-shek's Kuomintang party, the Nationalists. (Dr. Sun Yat-sen led the Kuomintang to overthrow the Qing dynasty in 1911 to establish the Republic of China.)

When Japan invaded China in 1937, the charismatic Wang moved with his government to the wartime capital Chongqing, in southwestern Sichuan province. There, he took a second wife, Fatima Ma, daughter of a Muslim religious elder and twenty years his junior. After the war, Wang was posted to Urumqi as the civil governor of Xinjiang, a northwestern province of predominantly Muslim ethnic groups, including Uyghur, Kyrgyz, Uzbek and Kazakh.

China's civil war between Generalissimo Chiang's Nationalists and Mao Zedong–led Communist forces intensified after their common wartime enemy, the Japanese, surrendered in 1945. Chiang and his government retreated to the island of Taiwan in September 1949, when Mao's victory was imminent.

An entourage of thousands of Muslim Chinese loyal to the Kuomintang, including Wang, fled Xinjiang via the only route available to them—travelling westward along what is known today as the Karakoram Highway, over the Himalayas through the Khunjerab Pass, into refugee camps in Pakistan. Wang's extended family, including his first wife and their three children, eventually settled in Karachi, where he represented the Republic of China (Taiwan) as an overseas member of the legislature.

In a 1952 Islamic world conference in Lahore, Wang stood up to denounce the Communist regime in mainland China. Yet Pakistan was one of the first countries to recognize Mao's People's Republic of China. His denigration angered the host government, and he was pressured to leave. In 1954, he and his family took a boat to Basra, Iraq, and from there, a train to Ankara. By the time they moved to Turkey, three more children were born.

The refuge in Turkey was no coincidence. Wang had studied history at Istanbul University in the 1920s as an exchange student and later had visited Turkey as a member of a "people's diplomacy" delegation from China. His former professor invited him to establish a department of Chinese language and history at his alma mater.

After the birth of his eighth child, Saadet, Wang decided to open a Chinese restaurant to supplement his meagre teaching income. China Restaurant soon became a drop-in centre and a refuge, popular with visiting students and embassy people from Taiwan.

In 1961, while lecturing in class, Wang died of a heart attack. He was fifty-eight.

Though his time was cut short, Wang's story, and that of his family, makes up yet another amazing chapter in the history of the Chinese diaspora. And my guidebook from 1976 was right: Wang *had* "walked from China."

I knew little about Muslims in China, much less how Islam came to China. My discovery of the Wang family in Turkey opened my eyes to that part of Chinese history, which was never taught in schools. And with the help of Rosey Ma's research, I now have a better understanding of the community.

As far back as the sixth century, even before they became Muslims, Arabs traded with the Chinese in the ports of the southeastern provinces of Guangdong and Fujian. At the beginning of the Tang dynasty, in the mid-seventh century, the government encouraged trade in these port cities, with explicit orders to protect foreign merchants and settlements.

Islam was first introduced to China around that time by a Muslim Arab who arrived in the city of Quanzhou, in Fujian province—first preaching to his own people and later spreading the religion through local marriages and conversion. Around the same time, an emissary from Arabia, travelling via the Silk Road, came to pay his respects at the Tang royal court in Chang'an, present day Xi'an. His delegation was given the freedom to live and propagate their faith, and they established the first mosque of the capital.

Between the eleventh and fourteenth centuries, Quanzhou was one of the most modern ports in the world, and the starting point of the Maritime Silk Road. Traders from Arabia, Persia, Syria, India, Italy and Morocco settled there, in the city Marco Polo called "the most prosperous and glorious in the world."

The golden age of Islam was in fifteenth-century Ming. It's believed the first Ming emperor, Zhu Yuanzhang, was a Muslim. So was Zheng He, the admiral whose armada made seven sea voyages in the beginning of the fifteenth century to the east coast of Africa.

Muslim Chinese, or Hui people, are officially recognized as distinct from Han Chinese (which make up 92 per cent of China's 1.25 billion people). A fourteenth-century Ming emperor conferred ten surnames to the Hui—among them, Ma (Mohamad), Ha (Hassan) and Yu (Yusuf)—and they have achieved high administrative and military positions throughout Chinese history.

Chiang's Nationalist government entrusted Huis like Wang with important political and military posts. Wang was posted to Xinjiang precisely because he was a Muslim and understood the Uyghur language, which has Turkic roots. With the fall of the mainland into Communist hands, many Hui people working for the Nationalist government followed its retreat to Taiwan.

There are 50,000 Muslim Chinese in Taiwan, and half of the 20 million Muslims in China are of the Hui minority.

—·—

"No telegram yet! No telegram yet!" Makbule was six years old in 1949 and remembers her father coming home, every day, worried that Mao's Red Army was getting closer. But the order to abandon Xinjiang had not come.

"When it finally came, we just grabbed whatever we could and left in a hurry," Fatima recalls.

The Wang family joined the exodus out of northwestern China on a long and perilous journey. They travelled first in a military convoy for three weeks, then on camels, mules and sometimes on foot, to cross the Himalayas into Pakistan. Makbule, Isa and Halime, the oldest children, travelled in baskets dangled from the sides of the animals. Rosey, the youngest, had to be carried by family members.

Rosey claimed she was abandoned in the snow to die, when the family could no longer find milk to feed her. She said she was eventually rescued by a grand-uncle who went back on foot to look for her.

Makbule laughs when I tell her Rosey's story.

"How can Rosey remember all this? She wasn't even a year old. The truth of the matter is that the grand-uncle carrying Rosey got lost along the way and had to trek through the snow before rejoining the group."

Fatima describes the journey as overcoming four barriers—water, fire, sand and ice—using the word "mountain" metaphorically to describe challenges they faced along the way.

"Water Mountain"—consisting of rivers and rapids—wasn't a problem: "You can ride across it."

"Sand Mountain," made up of dunes and quicksand, was dangerous: "You get buried if you step into it."

"Fire Mountain" is a reference to the Flaming Mountains just outside the city of Turpan, on the edge of the Taklamakan Desert. They derive their name from the sixteenth-century novel *Journey to the West*. In this fantasy account, a Buddhist monk, accompanied by a Monkey King with magical powers, runs into a wall of flames on pilgrimage to India. Wang's entourage no doubt saw red sandstone "flaming" under the sun as they passed through.

"Ice Mountain" is the Himalayas.

"We couldn't ride in the mountains. We had to walk and hold on to the tails of the horses and let them drag us up," says Fatima, holding both her hands up to demonstrate how she grabbed on to horses' tails. "The mountain is steep, and if there's a small path, the animals will go along it. However, if they slid, they would fall off the mountain. Lots of camels and horses fell off the mountain. Lots of people fell off and died."

She continues while busily fanning herself in the heat. "We couldn't take care of everyone. If we looked after the children, we couldn't take care of the adults. If we took care of the adults, we couldn't look after the children."

The exodus to Pakistan took more than two months—nobody in the family remembers exactly how long—and an untold number of lives were lost.

—◦—

"I'm proud to be Chinese—I always wanted to marry a Chinese," Makbule tells me over dinner at one of the many fish restaurants nestled under the Galata Bridge. The sunset over the Golden Horn is stunning. "I never thought of marrying a Turk," she continues. "However, I never thought of going to China or Taiwan to find a boyfriend, either."

She was helping her mother at their Ankara restaurant when she met Hsin-Tung Wu, a Taiwanese student studying Turkish at Ankara University. They became classmates when she enrolled at the university a year later.

Wu decided to convert to Islam to marry Makbule and took the Islamic name Uğur. The couple has lived in Taiwan since 1975. Makbule, however, is not a practising Muslim. She doesn't pray, doesn't fast during Ramadan, and hasn't been on a pilgrimage to Mecca.

"But I tell people I'm a Muslim. I believe in Islam," Makbule says. "I think I'm a good person, and I'm willing to help people everywhere. What I believe is that every religion teaches us how to behave well."

Saadet is the youngest in the family and the only child born in Turkey. She was three when her father passed away. She attended the French school in Istanbul and went to university in Taiwan, where she met Terence Sun. He moved to Turkey and they wed, but he did not convert to Islam.

"My two daughters speak with their father in Mandarin and with me in Turkish," Saadet tells me when I visit her at home. "They speak to each other in English."

She identifies as Chinese but sees herself rooted in Turkey. She doesn't know what the future will bring, but with Turkey becoming part of the European Union, she is certain they will all feel more European that way.

"My children tell me they might become Christian when they grow up," she says. "I told them that no matter what they believe in, they should be a good person. Every religion is the same, and they have their right to find their own faith."

—•—

I'm meeting Fatima Ma and Dawood Yang at the Beşiktaş wet market on the European shore of the Bosphorus, also known as the Strait of Istanbul.

Fatima personally goes to the market for the restaurant. She gets a lot of respect from the vendors, and they save the freshest produce for her. She doesn't banter with them—it's just the straight business of picking what she needs for the week, with a bit of a bargaining. Dawood, playing a supporting role with his lanky frame, walks slowly behind her with his cane. At times, he veers off to another aisle, deep in his thoughts, but he catches up with her eventually.

Afterwards, another hired car takes us back to the restaurant. While Yakar and the Turkish cook help unload, Fatima goes into the kitchen to go over the day's menu with her Chinese chef.

By the time I catch up with Fatima again, it's late morning. She is sitting at her usual corner table in the anteroom, slowly peeling a basketful of beans while chatting in a low voice to Dawood. He sits across from her, listening intently and replying occasionally, while methodically numbering and stamping a receipt book, page by page.

When the stamping is done, he picks up his Chinese newspapers, air-mailed weekly from Taiwan. He stays on top of Taiwanese politics and is a firm advocate for the reunification of China. However, very little of his family remains in Beijing, and his ties to his ancestral home have long been lost.

All of the Wang children tell me that Uncle Yang has been around for as long as they can remember. Like Fatima, he is Muslim Chinese. He was part of Taiwan's diplomatic corps in Saudi Arabia before being stationed in the Turkish capital when Fatima ran the Ankara branch of China Restaurant in the late sixties.

"It was this Mr. Yang whom the embassy sent to spy on us," Fatima says, without a hint of irony. It wasn't unusual during the Cold War for Taiwan and China to compete for the loyalty of the Chinese diaspora. One of Yang's embassy jobs was to make sure that Chinese in the Middle East remained in the Nationalist camp. (Turkey did not recognize the new China until 1971.)

"They got married in Saudi Arabia when I was in high school," Saadet recalls. "And no one was against it."

"Let me tell you. I'm eighty-eight years old and can't move too well. Can't you see how I walk? Not without a cane," he says with a sigh. "My home is Istanbul. I've gotten used to the life here. It's comfortable living here."

Dawood, with his weathered and angular face, reminds me of my grandfather—a determined and well-meaning patriarch who will go all-out to protect his family. He embodies a sense of Chinese dynastic history and would be quite willing to spend all night telling you what he's been through.

"Every Chinese hopes China can be unified," he continues, pointing out the nationalistic wishes of two peoples separated by the Taiwan Strait. "However, it's not good to be unified under the leadership of the Chinese Communist Party. We need a democratic China."

He returns to his newspapers, still dreaming of taking back China from the Communists.

—·—

There is a magnificent view, over red rooftops, of the Bosphorus from Feride Wang's office. We are on the third floor of a building, perched on the hillside, just steps away from Hotel Marmara—formerly the Sheraton, where I had drinks with Chabanol in 1976.

"Sometimes I think I'm a Turk. Then among Chinese people I feel Chinese," says Feride. "I've no idea who I am. I played with the German kids at my German school, and I felt I was the same as them, too."

Feride was first in the family to be born outside China. She doesn't remember much about growing up in Lahore—just that she could speak Urdu before she could speak Chinese. She was eight when Wang passed away.

"I was the naughty one in the family, but Father protected me. I was crestfallen when he died. I still have emotional scars to this day," she says while wiping off her tears.

She was the first in the family to get married. Her older siblings didn't want her to marry a Turk, but she didn't listen. "Actually, I've no regrets. It's an experience. At least I have my two children." She looks over to her teenage son, Doğa, playing computer games on one of the office desktops.

Feride had never been to China until recently. But her facility in Mandarin serves her well. She has worked as a translator and tour guide for tourists from China and Taiwan. Now she is a China trade consultant.

Her story really resonates with Kwoi. He was married to an Irish Canadian, and, like Feride, doesn't feel he belongs in the place he immigrated to. He is also the first and only offspring to marry outside his culture, against his family's wishes. It was a long time ago, he tells me. Since I've known him, I have only seen him date Chinese women.

Before I leave, Feride tells me that her daughter Çise wants to meet with me. "Something about immigrating to Canada," she says.

I meet up with Çise Ertan at a noisy, crowded café on İstiklal Caddesi, Istanbul's Champs Elysées. It is a pedestrian-only street where trams run down the middle. People are shopping and snacking on Turkish delights bought from bakeries and coffee shops. The air is filled with the constant ding-ding of streetcar bells, calls from ice cream vendors, and jingling from water sellers in Ottoman-era costumes with ornate jars strapped to their backs.

Sezen Aksu, queen of Turkish pop, has just released her latest album. Her music is everywhere. An old woman beckons me from a dark alleyway, next to a brightly lit music store, offering me bootleg cassettes of the pop diva's latest. She wants 4,000 each. (That's 4,000,000 liras, or about three American dollars—in conversation, the Turks drop the last three zeroes.)

"It's like a little China in Istanbul," Çise says, in fluent Mandarin. She talks about growing up with Grandma Fatima while her parents studied in London: "There were newspapers in Chinese, videotapes in Chinese. They spoke Chinese. They cooked Chinese. My first language was Chinese. I only learned Turkish in the streets with the other children."

She has her mother's rebellious streak. When Feride disapproved of her musician boyfriend, she just moved out one day then called home to announce that she had married. You will regret it, Feride told her daughter; just as Fatima had once told Feride that she would regret marrying too young.

Çise works at the Christian Dior duty-free counter at the airport and asks about immigration to Canada. She's trying to find a way out of Turkish society, pointing to the conservatism of the nation's men. Speaking several languages, she believes she can support her husband abroad. She recently passed her exams in Polish.

Why Polish?

"I already know most of the Latin languages, plus Chinese and of course Turkish. I wanted something close to Russian so that I could speak to my Russian customers at the airport."

All of Wang's children are polyglots: Mandarin, Turkish and English to start; picking up a fourth or fifth language in school or while helping each other with homework: French, German or Italian. Wang even tried to make them study the Koran in Arabic.

"I think your language skills will be useful if you want to immigrate to Canada," I say, and I promise to help. She thanks me and rushes off to her next rendezvous just like any other twentysomething.

—·—

"I'm old now and can't do it any longer," Fatima tells me as I say goodbye to her on my last day in Istanbul. "I only come here and stay for a while at noon. I never come here at night."

Makbule thinks the restaurant should be shut down. Her brother Isa is managing the other restaurant, and there's just not enough income to sustain the operation.

"*Mama* always says she's tired," Feride counters. "However, she can't stay home and do nothing. She's gotten used to this sort of life. I've no idea what she would do without the restaurant."

It's dusk. Lamartin is quiet; only a distant rumble of traffic can be heard from Taksim Square two blocks away. Yakar is at his customary stool, chatting with neighbours. Others greet him as they walk by.

An American expat walks in. He's a regular and orders his usual steamed whole fish with ginger and scallions, eating quietly by the window upstairs. He'll be the lone customer tonight. The Chinese and Taiwanese tour groups have come and gone.

Only Chef Pan and a young Turkish waiter are left in the kitchen.

Four years ago, thirty-five-year-old Pan Wenhui paid 30,000 yuan for "snakeheads" (human-trafficking Chinese gangs) to bring him to Turkey. The labour export agreement between China and Turkey allowed him an initial three-month visa to work at Isa's kitchen in Marmaris.

Isa also arranged for him to marry a Turkish woman.

"There was no time for wedding ceremony," he says with a laugh. "Turkey is a very secular state, and there is no pressure from my wife's side of the family to convert."

Pan belongs to China's new generation. He hasn't been taught in school about the Kuomintang's retreat to Taiwan and has little appreciation of the Wang family's exile from Xinjiang. Or the fact that China Restaurant is a haven for a whole generation of the Muslim Chinese diaspora in Turkey.

For Wang's grandchildren, too. It's their home away from home. Many were brought up in Grandma's household when their parents were away or unavailable. It's also their canteen.

Yesterday, Taysun, Isa's son from his first marriage, came by for dinner. Tonight, it's Doğa's turn while waiting for his mother to pick him up for last-minute, start-of-school shopping. The chef makes him a bowl of beef and vegetables on rice, which he eats heartily with chopsticks, washing it down with a Coke.

As the last customer leaves, Yakar turns off the lights, locks the front door, and walks down Lamartin, bathed in yellow streetlights. A cat saunters across the street behind him.

———

Three days after 9/11, I take a shuttle from Singapore to meet up with Rosey Ma in Kuala Lumpur.

Rosey lives with her husband, Nasir Ma, a Chinese Malaysian commercial airline pilot, in a two-storey house in a quiet, leafy neighbourhood. When the couple decided to get married in 1973, Nasir went to Istanbul to woo his future mother-in-law. Fatima was overjoyed to find out that he was a Muslim.

Part-time French teacher, historian and anthropologist, Rosey is the documentarian of her father's life. Most of her childhood memories are filled in from meticulous diaries that Wang kept during his refugee days in Pakistan and subsequent exile in Turkey. She recalls how her father was generous to a fault in welcoming visitors and students from Taiwan.

His passing triggered great emotions in his fourth-born.

"I can't remember how we buried Father," she tells me in her study, where Wang's archive is kept. "What gave me the deepest impression is that Mother wanted to jump into the grave, shouting that Father had cheated her."

Fatima wasn't even forty and was alone in a foreign country with eight children. She didn't even speak Turkish until after Wang died. Rosey remembers, "There was no furniture in the house. Mother insisted that we would all return to China in a few years anyway, so 'What would we do with all the furniture?'"

For the longest time, Rosey never accepted that her father was really gone—she thought he was probably working for the government, hiding somewhere in Taiwan. All that changed when she finished near the top of her class, studying at a university in Taiwan, in a language that she could barely read or write when she first got there.

"I'd never thought I could do that well. That night I cried for my father for several hours. I thought, this was what my father wanted to see. That's when I came to terms that Father was dead. After that, I no longer had any illusion."

This is an emotion that all Chinese children can understand—the overwhelming desire to prove to your parents that you can exceed their expectations. I remember when I was promoted, I called my father right away even though I had been living away from home, on another continent, for more than a decade. And I was not just being promoted, but promoted at a relatively young age, at a large corporation. That overachievement is always expected of you.

"The greatest advantage in life that Father gave us is that he enrolled us in different international schools," says Rosey, who attended a French school. "But our common language is Turkish. Each one of us speaks Turkish better than the language we learned at school. If you didn't see our faces you would think that we are Turks."

Then she adds, "I'm Turkish. And my children are Malaysian and Chinese. In today's world, it's best to be global. It doesn't work if we only confine ourselves to our own circle."

Rosey's internationalism and fluid identities resonate with me. Hers is a story of Chinese diaspora, the second generation. It is my story as well.

CHAPTER 9

Like a
John Woo Movie

TROMSØ, NORWAY

"I LOVE IT HERE," A FORTYISH MICHAEL WONG TELLS ME AS HE TAKES ANOTHER sip of Rioja. "It's a long trek out here. Do you know how many miles this red has to be trucked in from Spain?"

"Very different from Mong Kok." I mention Hong Kong's bustling and triad-infested district where he grew up.

"Heaven and hell. I came to Europe as a teenager and spent the better part of my life in Germany, Spain, Sweden and now Norway. I've found peace here."

We are in a Chinese restaurant in Tromsø, 350 kilometres inside the Arctic Circle. It's past midnight. The last customers have left; the waitresses, having eaten on the job, have gone home. Wong brings out more bottles of Spanish and Portuguese reds.

From his apartment upstairs, Chef Chung hauls out his private stash of harder stuff—including the potent mao tai, named China's national liquor in 1951, right after the founding of the People's Republic. Chung would not tell me his name: "Just call me Uncle Chung like everyone else here."

Wong's partner, Chung Ting Lee, whom everyone calls Ting, comes out of the kitchen to join us. As do my film crew Kwoi and David Szu. Assistant cook Lin Bin and kitchen helper and dishwasher Kim Tai pop in and out from kitchen-cleaning duties to gulp down some beer. As neither of them speaks Cantonese, they soon head home.

After a few rounds, everybody is warmed up. The bantering—in colloquial Cantonese peppered with colourful slang and mobster lingo—is irreverent and comical. And Cantonese is notoriously sweary.

We're in a party mood. And there's some serious drinking ahead.

The previously introspective Wong opens up. He trades friendly insults with Uncle Chung, using the honorific "uncle" to show respect for his age—Chung is fifteen years older than Wong, and a generation older than the rest of the kitchen staff.

"Don't you think Ting looks like Shu Qi?" Uncle Chung muses. Shu Qi is a Taiwanese model-turned–award-winning actress who debuted some years ago in Hong Kong Category III (x-rated) movies. We all agree that there's a resemblance. They both have pouty lips.

"But I'm not as well endowed," Ting fires back and empties her glass of wine. *Skål!* She can hold her own with the boys, and her liquor as well.

Cantonese slang is famously vulgar. Kwoi grew up in the same kind of rough neighbourhoods as Wong, so he's seen it all. Coming from an upper-middle-class family in Hong Kong, I have only seen it in movies.

By this time, I'm on to my second glass of scotch on the rocks, planning a switch to the cognac staring at me. I need something to cut the chill, even though it's the middle of the summer. I'm not a drinker—just the occasional wine or beer—but I can get into a drinking mood easily when the occasion calls for it.

Seriously, we're in a John Woo movie.

An hour into the drinking, I kick myself for not bringing our cameras. There's a Hong Kong gangster film to be made here. But I'm meeting Wong for the first time, and I don't know how he would have reacted to a Canadian crew descending on his restaurant. I usually try to build a rapport with my subjects before any filming begins.

It's 5 a.m. by the time we stagger out of the restaurant.

Wong and Ting head off to get a few hours' sleep before their day starts again. Uncle Chung, by this time very drunk, can barely climb the two flights of stairs to his attic apartment at the back of the restaurant. The three of us managed to find our way back to the hotel, two blocks behind the restaurant, fronting the inner harbour.

The streets are now empty. Several off-duty sailors from the Royal Norwegian Navy are staggering outside a closed bar. An Ethiopian immigrant makes his newspaper rounds. Seagulls hover low overhead, diving occasionally to the ground. It's got that eerie Hitchcock feel. Maybe I should be making *The Birds* instead.

The edge of the sky is bright, but the sun is nowhere to be seen, hiding behind low-hanging clouds. It doesn't look like we'll see the midnight sun this week.

Some years ago, a Hong Kong cinematographer told me he had eaten in the world's northernmost Chinese restaurant while filming near the Finnish-Russian border. It's run by Hongkongers, he said. I always wondered why people from semi-tropical southern China would move there to run a restaurant, with harsh wintry conditions and depression-inducing sunless days.

A friend of mine, Ying Duan Lei, had just moved back to Toronto after a two-year stay in Tromsø—her husband had conducted Arctic atmospheric research at an institute there. She told me they had frequented a Chinese restaurant run by a couple from Hong Kong and handed me a business card that read "Michael Wong, Cuisine Orientale."

Wong was rather abrupt when I called from Canada. They were busy renovating, getting ready to open for the high season. But you're welcome to come and film, he said. For the first time I decided to plunge into a shoot without first visiting the place or interviewing the owner—the Arctic was just too far to go for an advance scouting trip.

A week after summer solstice, my film crew and I land in Tromsø, having flown all day—transiting through London and Oslo—from 30°C Istanbul with a population of 11 million to a chilly city with 50,000 inhabitants. The entire country of Norway has just 4.5 million.

It's 9 p.m. The air is cold, and a heavy mist engulfs the airport. Lucky me, I'm wearing a leather jacket I'd bought from Istanbul's Grand Bazaar just days before. Kwoi and David both regret not doing the same. An hour later, our taxi drops us off at the hotel that Wong has booked for us.

But I am itching to go to the restaurant and say hello.

When you walk into Lille Buddha, meaning "Little Buddha," you are greeted by a smiling golden Sitting Buddha. The restaurant is in a two-storey heritage building on Sjøgata. It's tastefully decorated in chinoiserie—faux Qing dynasty vases, framed Chinese calligraphy and imperial Chinese robes mounted in shadow-boxes hanging on mauve walls—all halogen-lit. The waitresses, too, are dressed attractively in slim black pants and Chinese blouses embroidered with flowers—gold on indigo blue, or crimson on black.

"Atmosphere is very important," Michael Wong explains when I note the art gallery feel of the place. "It brings people in. The decor and the location must be good. The food doesn't have to be top notch, but it has to be acceptable. If you can have all these, you'll have a very successful restaurant."

We are sitting in one corner of the dining room—there are still two tables of lingering customers with their after-dinner drinks. Ting sits down, having finished her work in the kitchen.

Wong takes another sip of wine and adds, "There are only seven Chinese families here in town. Our customers are mostly Norwegians. We have Chinese tour groups during the summertime. After the summer season, they're all locals."

"But Japanese do come in the winter to see the Northern Lights," Ting chimes in.

"The local tastes are not as sophisticated as those in Hong Kong," Wong reminds me.

"People here are quite the country bumpkins when it comes to eating. When Michael was working here five years ago, a customer ordered shrimp cocktail and asked if he could drive afterwards."

"Cocktail . . . shrimp cocktail . . . That's just cooked shrimp with a Thousand Island dressing."

Ting can't help but inject a bit of drama. "We almost fainted."

"But in recent years, more and more people have visited Thailand or China. They now know how to order."

"A lot more people are ordering Peking duck these days."

"A Hong Kong guide once told us that our twice-cooked pork is as good as he's eaten in Hong Kong," Wong says.

As the name implies, the pork belly in this Sichuan dish is first simmered in water with spices such as ginger, cloves and anise; then it is stir-fried over high heat with cabbage, bell peppers, scallions and onions, adding Shaoxing wine, soy sauce, chili bean paste and tianmianjiang. What makes this dish distinctive is the latter condiment, a slightly sweet wheat-bean paste often used in northeastern Chinese, as well as Korean Chinese, cooking.

"At least we have a real chef here," Wong says of Uncle Chung, who is from Oslo. "He's really good if he puts his heart in it. But he's getting old. He's over sixty."

It is not easy to run a restaurant so far up north. Everything has to be shipped or trucked in from Oslo, 1,700 kilometres away. Chinese ingredients and cooking utensils are incredibly hard to find. Fresh fruits and vegetables are flown in from even farther south, as far away as Manchester and Amsterdam.

It's also difficult to staff a Chinese kitchen here. Most Chinese in Scandinavia are reluctant to come so far up north to work solo, especially when their families are well established in the south. Those who are willing to come from China face a seven-year wait for a work permit.

"And if they're chefs, they'd prefer to open their own restaurants," Ting laments. "Chinese would rather be employers than employees. It's a big headache for us."

But what I really find strange is that in a country where fishing is so much a part of life, it's a challenge to find my favourite steamed whole fish with ginger and scallions. In this part of the world, most fish are cut up or salted right after they are caught.

I ask whether there's steamed whole fish for dinner.

"You're in luck," Wong announces as he comes back from the kitchen. "We've *dai ngan gai* bought this morning, off the docks in front of your hotel.

We're saving them for Chinese groups tomorrow, but I'll ask Uncle Chung to make one for you." He's referring to Norwegian haddock by its colloquial Cantonese name, "big-eyed chicken."

Wong writes his menu to cater to what's popular with Norwegians: a mix of Cantonese and Sichuanese dishes, with a dash of Shanghainese. (Both Chung and his assistant Lin are Shanghainese.)

As it's past closing time, we share our welcome dinner with the staff. Staff meal is a tradition—and highlight of the day—in Chinese kitchens. Eaten communally, cooks whip up leftover ingredients—and sometimes prime ingredients reserved for customers—into authentic dishes, knowing that they don't have to cater to anyone's taste but theirs.

In addition to the steamed fish, Chung serves up the aforementioned twice-cooked pork and Kung Pao shrimp, fresh from the harbour. Plus a huge serving of spinach cooked lightly in a chicken supreme stock—another indicator of sophisticated Hong Kong cooking technique. After travelling all day from Istanbul, I find this comfort food amazingly satisfying.

By the time we finish our dinner, it's past midnight. The night is just getting started. There's more drinking ahead.

—•—

Silij Siemens is a petite eighteen-year-old blonde who raises horses at her family farm while studying to be a veterinarian. This is her first restaurant job. But she's perky, fast and energetic and has the natural restaurant smarts so important to Wong.

I love watching her work.

Carrying a handful of dirty dishes to the kitchen, she briskly kicks open the swing door. Just as quickly, she shouts out new orders, scrapes off leftovers, throws dishes to the sink, and dashes off with newly prepared dishes for the next table. A quicker kick and a louder bang and she's on her way out. (There's a reason why steel plates are mounted at the bottom of kitchen swing doors.)

Wong likes her because he runs the restaurant with Hong Kong–style efficiency, and he likes his servers to be personable and on their toes. Silij picks things up very quickly. "That's just keeping your eyes on the ball," he says.

She is also valuable to him because she can just grab the keys to his jeep to deliver takeout. In between her stints in the dining room, Chung cooks her favourite dish, beef and mushrooms, which she gulps down with rice while standing next to the prep counter.

"Do you like Chinese food?" I sit down with Silij after her shift. I am exhausted from just watching her all evening.

"In the beginning I didn't like it. I didn't like the smell," she says with a laugh, looking over to Wong and Ting having their dinner. "Now I like it. I eat here every day. Free food. Michael's a good boss. The kitchen staff are nice to me. They ask me every day, 'Are you hungry? Are you okay?'"

Kine Nylund, the other local waitress, is nineteen and a third-year art history major. This is her first restaurant experience, too, but Wong complains that she's sloppy and slacks off too much.

Kine tells her side of the story: "Mr. Michael? He's a very efficient man. Working for him is very stressful. But I like him. He's nice. He wants me to understand him so that he can understand me. But he likes me to work fast, you know. I think Chinese people are very fast, they are very . . . *jah, jah, jah.*"

She doesn't eat everything on the menu. She will not touch the haddock on the table with its "bulging eyes looking at me and a bunch of grass on its body." I tell her that the "grass" is actually shredded scallions. She laughs but insists that Norwegians don't eat fish with bones anyway.

Kine's co-worker Heejin Kim laughs when I mention this to her. "I'm the more mature one here," says the thirty-year-old Korean. "I'm married and have a two-year-old at home."

Heejin met her future husband, a Tromsø native, when they both studied in Minnesota. They moved back to his hometown two years ago. She seems aloof at first, but her reticence soon gives way to an eagerness to talk to fellow Asians who can relate to her American experience. Kwoi and David spend an inordinate amount of time with her in bars and cafés in the middle of the night.

Or is it day? I can't tell anymore.

"Michael's fast, he's very quick and he's very smart. And I respect him for that because when he came here, he really didn't have much. He learned Norwegian or Swedish, whichever came first. And he started a very successful restaurant. But he's very hard on us, too. And gets mad at us, especially when it's busy."

Wong tells me that Heejin is trying her best, but it will take time. "She doesn't speak Norwegian. When I'm very busy, she can't take orders over the phone. The good thing is that she's personable and can communicate with customers just by smiling."

<hr>

I've come to the Land of Midnight Sun, but the sun is nowhere to be seen.

Last week, I'm told, the region had a full week of sunshine and warm weather. Everyone celebrated by picnicking on shrimp and white wine at two in the morning. This week, we have gloomy weather, as low clouds from the North Sea climb over the mountains to cover the inlet and its surrounding hills.

My friend Lei told me that she couldn't get used to the midnight sun, or eternal nights, when she was here. She would be depressed in the winter, when the city had only a few hours of dawn and dusk then plunged into complete darkness for two months. In the summer, she had difficulty falling asleep because the sun peeked through her bedroom curtains.

It's especially disorienting for us on this trip because the twenty-four-hour day is dull and grey. It doesn't help that we have been drinking till four in the morning and getting up at two in the afternoon. Night and day have flipped, and time has no meaning. We have become impervious to the clock. When I get up one afternoon, David has already gone off to Lille Buddha to wait on tables for a tour group from Taiwan. He is from Taiwan, so it will be fun for him.

<hr>

Even after shadowing him for three days, Michael Wong remains a mystery to me. He's slim and muscular and has the toughness of a kung fu fighter. His weathered face and tough demeanour make me wonder if he was in a street gang in his former life. But he also has the aura of a dandy. I ride shotgun as he delivers takeout wearing a pastel green wool jacket, gold chains and a gold Rolex watch.

Wong left Hong Kong in 1971 at age seventeen, when people in the British colony were weary of communist China, with its constant social and political upheavals. He landed in the Netherlands—an easy entry point for drug and human smuggling at that time—and crossed the German border ("it was quite loose back then") to stay with a distant relative in a small town.

For a teenager who wanted to be free, helping out in their Chinese restaurant and going out as a family was *not* exciting. "They were afraid if I got caught, they'd get into trouble. I spent a whole year like I was under house arrest."

After a while, Wong looked for black-market jobs in other parts of Germany: Baden, Bavaria, Munich. "I tried to get work in München," he uses Munich's German name, "but they said the laws were very strict there, 'Why don't you go to Spain?'"

Conditions in Spain were no better.

"It's really hard to make money there. Especially when you are an illegal." By chance, he met a Swede who helped him obtain a student visa to Sweden. "He was very nice to me. Just a stranger, but he invited me to stay with him in Stockholm."

But a student visa did not allow Wong to work, so he became an illegal in a kitchen while applying for a work permit. When it finally came through, Wong was hired by a popular restaurant called Beijing. He spent seven years in Sweden.

He first met Ting when they were both working at an Italian restaurant in Stockholm. She is eight years younger than Wong—she used to call him Uncle Michael. She had lived in Sweden since she was eleven, but she acts and speaks like she's just landed from Hong Kong. Ting's father worked in the entrepôt for a Swedish shipping line ("the one with three yellow crowns on their chimneys") when the family lived in Hong Kong. But when he was transferred to Sweden with an offer of residency, he decided to move his family of five there, to Gothenburg.

After high school, Ting studied hairdressing while working in the restaurant trade. When Norway's North Sea oil economy boomed in the mid-eighties, many young Chinese Swedes crossed the border to seek better opportunities, Wong and Ting among them.

"We became close when we were in Oslo," Wong tells me over another Rioja. "The Chinese always go to the same disco. We were both attached then. Her boyfriend had to go to the States, and after my divorce I travelled to Australia. When I came back, we started living together."

When their daughter Jenny, aka Ga Ga, was born eleven years ago, they needed a babysitter. Ting begged her mother to come help, promising to pay her whatever she was making in Gothenburg.

"I liked my job a lot and I didn't want to quit, but I did it for Ga Ga's sake. What could I do?" Ting's mother, Wai Ching Leung, recalls. "So, I moved to Oslo to take care of the child. There was no way they could have gotten up in the morning to send Ga Ga off to the nursery, or to pick her up in the afternoon. They needed two shifts to take care of the kid."

Tromsø has three other Chinese restaurants: Tang's, which faces Tromsø Cathedral (the world's northernmost Lutheran cathedral); Hong Kong, not far down the road from Lille Buddha; and Midnight Sun, a half-Chinese, half-seafood takeout by the docks, which is run by another Chinese family, good friends of Wong's.

"When I was working at Tang's, they had a one-million-krone business each month, so I thought the market could support another Chinese restaurant," Wong says. He was supposed to team up with another partner from Tang's to open a new restaurant. When the deal fell through, he decided to go it alone and opened Cuisine Orientale, moving Ting and their daughter from Oslo to Tromsø.

The move was epic.

Three people, including Wong's nineteen-year-old son from his earlier marriage and Ting's younger brother from Sweden, took turns driving two trucks loaded with kitchen equipment for the thirty-six-hour trip. Leung says the road was not for beginners: "On the one side were snowy mountains. On the other, the abyss." Another four flew up.

This is typical of family-run Chinese eateries. The whole extended family helps out, and the spouse is always central to the running of them.

But Wong and Ting never married.

"If we wanted to get married, we would've done so a long time ago," Wong says. He laughs as I ask if it's because they are Scandinavians. "Our kids are pretty grown up already. And to get married now seems a bit awkward, a bit too old-fashioned."

She nods. "My parents don't mind. We don't have many relatives here, just our own family. For them it doesn't matter whether we are married or not."

Lille Buddha's kitchen is typically Chinese. It's orderly chaos in a tight space. Uncle Chung spends most of his shift in front of the wok while his assistant Lin Bin scrambles to prepare the ingredients. Kim Tai helps with chopping and dishwashing. Ting fills in wherever she's needed, and Wong helps out his servers by scooping rice and bringing out the dishes.

"Look! The cream and strawberries fell off already," Ting is raising her voice at Lin while he tries to rebuild a collapsed sundae. "Put some new cream, then put the chocolate sauce on. *Aiyaa* . . . you'll have to make it again. It can't be served to the customers like that. It looks ugly!"

Wong comes in, impatient, and grabs the other sundae—the one that is still presentable. "They're waiting. I'll just take this out first."

Five years ago, thirty-year-old Lin left his wife and child in Shanghai to come to Norway. "I didn't have the papers and I felt the pressure," he recalls. "My bosses were Cantonese, and I didn't speak the dialect. I never worked in a kitchen before. I was miserable, I missed home so much, and the only entertainment after work was to call home."

Eventually Lin found himself in the Cuisine Orientale kitchen. He and Wong quickly became good friends, and Wong helped him apply for residency.

After working for a year, Lin returned to Shanghai to wait for his papers. He is now back for his second stint, legally.

"You had a good job back in Shanghai. Why did you bother to be an illegal here?" I ask.

"I know it's tough to work in other countries," he explains. "But since we already have to work so hard in China, why not try our luck somewhere else to make more?"

"Did you have to pay anyone to get out of China?"

"You can't come out if you don't pay some people off. Even though life in Norway is very monotonous and quiet, the country is very stable. Norwegians are friendly, kind and willing to help others."

"What's in your future?"

"My goal is to open my own restaurant. I hope my kid can come and study here, so that she can have a better life. My generation just wants to make an okay living. I don't know what I would've done if I had not come here."

Kim is an ethnic Korean from northeastern China. Ting doesn't want him on camera for fear that authorities will be alerted to the restaurant hiring illegal workers. I turn on the camera anyway.

"Why should I leave home?" he asks rhetorically. "I only came to make more money. Even though life is not easy here, at least I can make more money. My brother and my friends want to leave China but I tell them: 'Don't come.' You make more here, but life is easier back home. When you're here illegally, you feel restricted and uneasy."

"I can't be on camera." These are Uncle Chung's first words to me when I enter the kitchen, spoken half-jokingly. Chung is the elder of the kitchen staff, and the most colourful. His family moved from Shanghai to Hong Kong in the fifties, fleeing communism.

Chung worked as a cook for the Norwegian shipping company Wilhelmsen in the late sixties and early seventies. During that era, Hong Kong's Shanghainese community worked for Norwegian lines, while Cantonese worked for Swedish shipping companies. After the leftist-instigated 1967 Hong Kong riots, these shipping firms facilitated residency in their home countries for employees seeking a way out of the British territory. Shanghainese migrated to Norway, while Cantonese settled in Sweden.

I ask how often he gets to go home to his family in Oslo.

"At my age, what does it matter? If I like it, I can go for a month or two. My kids are old enough to take care of themselves. I prefer to be alone to do whatever I want and my wife can't bug me about it."

Being a bachelor affords him a lifestyle of drinking and "chasing after women." He gets calls from women friends and slips out as soon as his work is done. He still refuses to give me his name at the end of our chat.

———

Closing time. Another fourteen-hour day at the restaurant. Kwoi and David have gone off to their nocturnal bar-hopping. I'm exhausted. But Wong and Ting insist I go back to their house for drinks. How can I refuse? I am amazed by their stamina.

The couple live in a three-storey house on a fashionable hillside. No one is home. Grandma Leung has brought their children back to Gothenburg for the summer. There's a loving note from them, in Norwegian, reminding their parents to please feed their hamsters while they're at Grandma's.

"How about closing one day a week?" I ask, as Wong pours me another drink. It's 2 a.m. already.

"We don't have that luxury," Ting gently interrupts. "We only take two days off a year. Christmas Eve and Christmas Day. You know why? Because the locals don't go out for dinner on those days!"

"Even when we're off, there's nothing to do but sleep," he adds.

Ting insists that they would not want to pass down the restaurant business to the next generation. "It was never my dream to open a restaurant, but my generation had no choice. Their generation will have more opportunities."

Have they ever thought of retiring back in Hong Kong?

Wong is emphatic that he doesn't like Hong Kong. "It's too fast-paced for me now. I've been living in Europe much longer than I ever lived in Hong

Kong. It would be great to get a house in France . . . The ideal would be to open a fashion boutique . . . No, even that's not realistic. A more practical idea is to run a small restaurant."

In France?

"I would like it to be this way: a house in France for the winter," Wong says. "In Norway, I would have a house and a restaurant that opens for nine months a year. Six days a week, dinner only, enough to make a living. It's too early to retire. At least I can keep busy."

It's 3 a.m. when I leave. The sun is breaking through the clouds as if it's daybreak—a misnomer for two months of the summer here. And it becomes clear to me what Wong and Ting have been forced to give up. They, like so many other immigrants, have chosen to put their family life aside, at least for a while, to guarantee a bright future for their children.

CHAPTER 10

Fantasia Chinesca

HAVANA, CUBA

*Hell, I never thought
I'd find my dream in Cuba.
I always thought of Shanghai
with a Chinese girl by my side.
And after I began to dance
son with a nice Cuban girl
I felt a great emotion
for Cuba and the women there.*

A FRAIL-LOOKING EIGHTY-ONE-YEAR-OLD CHINESE MAN SITS IN A ROCKING chair in the corner of a senior home run by the Lung Kong Association in Havana's Barrio Chino, its Chinatown. Sunlight streams through the barred window, lighting up his face. Fermín Huey-Ley is crooning a Cuban ballad, "Ilusión China," accompanied by the dual guitars of Jorge and Frank—two *mariachis* I found singing for tourists at a bar nearby.

"This is a musical number from the thirties that belongs to Cuban musical folklore," Fermín says when the song ends, nodding with satisfaction. "It's *fantasía chinesca* about a Chinese man who falls in love with a Cuban woman."

Fermín's voice, velvety and childlike, reminds me of Ibrahim Ferrer from *Buena Vista Social Club*. The Wim Wenders documentary is what ignited my passion for Cuban music and led me to Havana.

"I can transform my voice to sing like a woman." He gives a slight smile. "I can sing in English, I can sing different genres. I learned as a child by singing along with the radio, and I've been dancing at Havana's Carnival since 1961. It's one of the biggest shows in Cuba, with over a million participants and spectators."

"I heard you're called *el chino del carnaval*." His reputation precedes him.

"Even though I was born here, it's better for me that people think I'm Chinese," he says with a smile. "People are curious to see a Chinese man dancing rumba, danzón, conga, and singing Cuban songs. So, they know me as 'the Chinese of the Carnival.' Even the dogs know me."

His parents came from Guangdong. His father arrived as a fourteen-year-old, in 1902. Fermín was born in a provincial town but was sent to study in a Chinese school in Havana when he was a teenager.

"Now I'm going to sing you an English song." He starts to sing the first verse of "Fascination," a song famously covered by Nat King Cole. Jorge and Frank scramble to find the right key. A few bars in, they are off and running. Everyone listens intently, including an elderly Chinese and his Spanish Cuban wife sitting next to Fermín, in a row of rocking chairs.

Fermín is animated as he sings: waving his hands, tapping his fingers and playing air violin. There is, however, a certain sadness to his voice, and his eyes are forlorn. At the end of the song, he grasps his throat, telling everyone that his vocal cords have not been used for a long time.

"And I can't dance anymore," he says, pointing to his cane.

"That's all right," I tell him. "I came here for the music. I came to hear you sing."

Music is indeed everywhere in Havana—in people's homes, in restaurants and bars, on street corners and in the plazas.

—・—

It's 2002, in the middle of the summer. Kwoi and I are in Havana, accompanied by sound recordist Mark Valino. Mark is a student at the film academy where Kwoi teaches.

It's our first morning in Havana. Our taxi drops us off at the entrance to Calle Cuchillo—a lane that runs from a wooden Chinese gate with hanging red lanterns to the dilapidated five-storey building that houses Restaurant Pacífico, a favourite of both Hemingway and Castro. On both sides are restaurants bedecked with faux Chinese decor. Greeters with menus stand outside, costumed in Chinese dresses, kung fu jackets and coolie hats.

Chinese first settled along Calle Zanja behind El Capitolio, the National Capitol Building, which resembles its counterpart in Washington, DC. They set up shops, grocery stores and restaurants, as well as clan, county and village associations.

In the 1930s, Havana had the largest and the most prosperous Chinatown in Latin America. The community even published several Chinese newspapers. *Kwong Wah Po*, founded in 1928, still publishes a four-page weekly, using moveable type with thousands of Chinese characters.

Today, Barrio Chino is a pale image of its former self. No more than 200 elderly Chinese—almost all men—remain. They continue to live in a neighbourhood that has since been turned into a tourist destination. After the Soviets pulled out in 1993, Chinese Cubans were given back, and put in charge of, Chinese restaurants—businesses that had previously been nationalized or were abandoned by those who fled Castro's Cuba.

I've always wanted to tell the stories of *Cubanos chinos*.

A year earlier, I found Miguel Chang-Lee sitting in front of his Cafetería Flamboyán. He was also president of Sociedad Chang Weng Chung Tong, the Chan Association, on the second floor of the restaurant. Miguel was an embittered man—complaining about life under Fidel Castro and referring to *el Presidente* in Chinese as the "bearded fellow."

I'd planned to feature Miguel in my documentary until his wife, Aimi, told me a week prior to my arrival that her husband was bedridden following a stroke. But the hotel and flights had been booked, and I had already arranged for my interpreter Valeria Mau Chu to fly in from Los Angeles with her family.

Valeria is a third-generation Chinese Peruvian and wife of my high school classmate Tom Chu, a second-generation Chinese from Japan. Tom and I attended international school together in Yokohama, with classmates of diverse ethnic and national backgrounds—many of them of mixed heritage with Japanese mothers.

I decided to take a chance anyway, and now Valeria and I are strolling through this Chinese fantasyland looking for another Chinese restaurateur.

Iliana Pacheco-Guerrero, a young white woman with blond hair, accosts us with the menu of Tung Po Lau, a restaurant named after Song dynasty poet and gourmand Su Dongpo. She's wearing a silk embroidered *cheongsam*—a traditional body-hugging, high-collar Chinese dress—imprinted with logos of Hong Kong's Hang Seng Bank. I am chatting with her when Samuel Chang from the restaurant next door walks up.

"I've known Samuel since I was a little girl, and he knows my mother from when she was a young woman," she says, introducing us. "Everyone wants to go work for him. The Chinese are very hard-working and enterprising; that's why they get ahead in life."

"I came to Cuba in 1949 at age seven to flee the Chinese Communist Revolution, only to come to another communist revolution," Samuel says as he takes me inside his restaurant, Luna de Oro, or Golden Moon.

It's still early. The restaurant is dark, empty and air-conditioned. The phrase "Welcome Chinese Overseas"—written in Spanish, Chinese and English—is splashed across a white wall, along with signatures of delegates to the World Conference on Overseas Chinese held at the University of Havana three years earlier. In the back room, four elderly men play mahjong, speaking Cantonese to each other. They barely notice us.

"My name is Luís Chung, I work in this restaurant almost every day," says a burly man in his late twenties with a husky voice. "I've lived in the *barrio* all of my life. I'm a *mulatto*, but everyone calls me *chino*. I only wish I was a *real* Chinese from China."

Luís is eager to be our tour guide. "The Chinese settled here in Cuba, but after the revolution, lots of them left for Miami or New York, or returned to China. There are very few of them left."

A foreign camera crew attracts attention anywhere. A young woman in a halter top, hot pants and fishnets confronts us while we are talking to Luís, saying we are on private property and can't talk to local residents without permission. She's from Grupo Promotor del Barrio Chino de La Habana, established in 1995 to develop and promote a rejuvenated Chinatown—like a theme park developer.

I'm not sure whether she is taking issue with our filming without a permit—we entered the country as tourists—or with the fact that we're speaking to Luís, considered an unsavoury hustler in their eyes. Valeria asks to see the head of the Grupo to clarify the matter, but the woman soon loses interest and walks away.

Luís now tells me that there's a *casa de los abuelos chinos* ("house of Chinese grandparents") that we should visit.

That's when his boss, Samuel, jumps in, speaking in Cantonese, "They're having a Father's Day luncheon for the elderlies at Lung Kong today. You should go. You're a Kwan—it's your association."

Lung Kong associations in Chinese communities around the world were formed to serve those from the family clans of Lau, Kwan, Cheung and Chiu—surnames of four protagonists from the Three Kingdom period in the third century AD, and dramatized in the fourteenth-century historical novel *Romance of the Three Kingdoms*.

Havana's Lung Kong has its own three-storey building on Calle Dragones. It runs a community centre on the ground floor with free meals for seniors. Thirty or so drop by to eat and socialize every day. The association's restaurant occupies the second floor while the third floor houses an assembly hall, a library and an altar room for the worship of Guan Di, the deified General Guan—Kwan in Cantonese—from the novel.

Today being Father's Day, there are more people than usual at the community centre—old men and women left behind by time, huddled around makeshift tables, eating rice and beans off aluminum cafeteria trays.

I had learned from my grandfather that many from his village of Gau Gong had migrated to Cuba in the early 1900s. I now come face to face, in the land of Chinese fantasy, with links to my ancestors.

"I'm a Kwan from Gau Gong," I shout out, eliciting a hearty round of introductions. We shake hands all around.

A man tugs at my elbow. "There're lots of Kwans here from Gau Gong. Look, look, that man there, he's also a Kwan from your village."

"And this one over here is also a Kwan," another beckons. "But he's from a neighbouring village."

As I'm introduced to these men, I can't help but feel a connection to China, even though I was born in Hong Kong and have never been to my ancestral village. My grandfather would have been proud to see me now.

Kwoi is strangely quiet and introspective during this commotion—just following me around with his camera as I greet one village elder after another.

"This is the first Father's Day since Dad died," he tells me when we have a moment to ourselves. His father, who worked in a Chinese restaurant in Toronto, had died a few months earlier. He did not have a good relationship with his son. Though not a meek man, he never stood up for Kwoi when he was bullied by white kids from the neighbourhood.

My cinematographer never forgave his father. It was only after he died that Kwoi made peace with him—by writing a letter to him and burning it at the gravesite, a Chinese ritual of delivering a message to the dead in the heavens above.

Upstairs, in the office next to the restaurant, a sturdy eighty-one-year-old manager of the association, Alejandro Chiu-Wong, is sitting at a table with two men—one of them his eldest son from his second marriage—counting wads of pesos and dollar bills, wearing an "I Survived Hong Kong" T-shirt and a green visor. A lamp with green shade swings lazily overhead. Just like in a heist movie.

"The main goal of the association is to run the restaurant as a business," he explains, as if to justify the cash on the table. "What we gain from the society, we put back for the benefit of the people." Spoken like a true communist.

In the years following Mao's Chinese Revolution in 1949, Hong Kong became a battleground for competing ideologies—left vs. right, communists vs. nationalists—presaging, in a sense, the territory's future. "Red China" was softly infiltrating into the British Crown Colony, sending agents to recruit sympathetic "hot-blooded" young men willing to serve the motherland. Two of my uncles succumbed to the call. They went back to China and were not able to leave again.

In 1953, Alejandro lost his job at an American-owned film studio in Hong Kong. He was blacklisted for his communist sympathies. It was the McCarthy era.

"Were you a communist?" I can't help but ask.

"When I was young, I had progressive ideals and I sympathized with the Chinese Communist Party," he replies. "But I'm not a communist."

Not allowed to join his father and uncles in the US, Alejandro paid bribes and travelled to Cuba instead. He could not speak Spanish ("I was like a deaf mute") and worked at odd jobs. Eventually he worked for the pre-revolution Batista regime collecting taxes from gambling houses.

"Were these casinos?" I am curious.

"No, just gambling joints in Chinatown with Chinese games like fan tan," he says, mentioning a popular Chinese game played with dice. "You know how the Chinese love to gamble."

Barrio Chino in the 1950s was a place for vice—opium and gambling dens, brothels, even live sex shows at the Shanghai Theatre (still standing)—but Alejandro started his own business. "If you knew how to speak the language, you could open your own business. Almost half of the people did that."

Clan and village associations helped. Members pooled their money to offer interest-free loans. In exchange, they expected business owners to "pay it forward." The Chiu clan in Havana banded together to get him started.

"Your people from Gau Gong also helped each other out," he remembers. "Gau Gong people were well educated and ran high-end businesses all over Cuba. Trading, jewelry and other high-end goods. They even ran a clinic."

Alejandro was already married with four children in his home village in Guangdong when he left for Hong Kong. It was a loveless arranged marriage—"a historical problem," he told his adult children years later, after they had immigrated to San Francisco with their mother. It's part of many Chinese immigrant stories: wives left behind, children they never knew, and second marriages in faraway lands.

While working at the film studio in Hong Kong, Alejandro had fallen in love with a starlet. When he left for Cuba, he promised to bring her over after he'd settled. A year later, the young woman wrote that she could no longer wait for him and was marrying someone else from New York.

"What could I do? I was still married with four kids, and I didn't have enough money to bring her here," he laments. "If you love someone, of course you want her to be happy. You shouldn't stand in the way. Whether I like it or not, it's the reality."

"Did you look her up again?" I'm hoping for a romantic ending.

"What's the use of contacting her after all these years?" He sighs with regret, but not bitterness. "She has her own family and I have mine. Let bygones be bygones, but at least I tasted love with her." He pulls out her photo from his desk drawer. It's a classic headshot—she is stylish and beautiful, posing like a movie star.

Alejandro eventually married an Afro-Cuban woman. They had three children together, but they soon divorced. According to him, their cultural differences were major impediments. Communication was a problem, too: "Back then I couldn't even speak Spanish well."

They were also on different sides politically. She was a communist and supported Cuba's misadventure in Angola—Cuba's Vietnam. Relations between Cuba and China were also tense at that time.

"I'm Chinese," he says. "I got stuck in the middle, and we argued over this all the time."

He is now married for the third time, to Niyia, a Spanish Cuban, who comes to the association from time to time to help out. She's devoted to him and has even learned to use chopsticks and cook Chinese food.

Alejandro is resigned to the fact that he will never find a perfect marriage. "I can't keep looking anymore because time passes. The person I was in love with got married and went to the States. I was heartbroken. What's the use? Then I married someone else. It was one mistake after another."

When Fidel Castro took power on January 1, 1959, Alejandro was already well established and didn't see the point of fleeing, as many in the Chinese community had. "The government took all the businesses away, but they left mine alone. I gave it to them voluntarily, and I worked for them until I retired."

In 1995, the Grupo asked Alejandro to come out of retirement to take over Lung Kong. He asked for a loan and bought back the association's building. "We searched for people from the Lau, Kwan, Cheung and Chiu clans to come and help out. Most of these people were born here—only about eight were originally from China. But we had to start somewhere. Some of these second-generation Chinese are well educated. They are doctors and soldiers . . . they want to give back to the community."

Bar Pekín has two swinging front doors painted with four golden Chinese characters: "Beijing" on the left, "Bar" on the right. They creak loudly as we enter, letting in streaks of blazing sunlight that cut through the cool, dark interior—lit only with red Chinese lanterns—while noisy air conditioners work overtime.

It doesn't seem to have changed since it first opened its doors.

It's noon, and the bar has just opened for the day. Two regulars perch on bar stools with bottles of Cristal. A table of European tourists wait for their mojitos. Maritza Cok-Carballo is making their drinks: "Sugar, mint, lime juice . . . soda water to make it fizzy, mix it with ice cubes . . . *Salud*." To your health.

"Sixty years ago, this was a popular bar where Chinese people from the barrio would come by for a drink," Maritza says. "Like my father, they all came from China—but now many are gone."

Her father came in 1959 and married a white Cuban. But Maritza looks more Chinese than her mixed ancestry suggests. She demonstrates her penmanship by writing out her name in Chinese characters, Cok Won Man. I tell her that her given names connote "music" and "literature" and evoke elegance—not at all the clichéd flowery names Chinese usually give to girls. Like Beautiful Lotus.

Abel Lam is a drop-dead-gorgeous Black man with only a faint trace of Chinese features. He comes out of the kitchen dressed in chef's whites bringing *maripositas*, fried wontons shaped like little butterflies.

"Everything Chinese I know is from my mother and my uncle. And my Cuban grandmother insisted that we follow the Chinese traditions of my grandfather," he says. "More so in terms of the food, how you eat it, and what you should eat."

Among Chinese Cubans, this rediscovery of Cuba's Chinese heritage is mixed with over-the-top admiration for all things Chinese—kung fu, the lion dance, Jackie Chan, calligraphy and *comida china*, Chinese food. Chinese Cubans are reverting to their Chinese heritage with enthusiasm, sometimes shamelessly so.

Abel goes only by his maternal Chinese surname, Lam. "When the bar reopened, the requirement was that everyone who works here has to be of Chinese descent," he says in all seriousness. "When people call here for *chino*, we have to ask which *chino* are they referring to? We're all Chinese here."

—————

People in the barrio tell me that I can find Roberto Vargas-Lee at a courtyard called Martial Arts Square every afternoon at four. Roberto is a *wushu sifu*, martial arts master. His young students have won numerous gold medals from international martial arts competitions held in China.

Several of them are leading a tai chi class when we arrive at the courtyard. Roberto takes me to the second floor of the Lam Association building nearby that also serves as a martial arts practice hall. "It's quieter here."

His maternal grandfather Lee came from China, and Roberto grew up in Barrio Chino learning "things Chinese." He began studying karate at the age of twelve—the same age his mother was when she started studying Cantonese opera. She is one of three surviving female Cantonese opera singers known collectively as *las tres divas*, the three divas. Unable to read Chinese, they learned to sing in Cantonese from phonetically transliterated lyrics.

Cantonese opera thrived in Cuba in the middle of the nineteenth century, when four opera troupes travelled around the provinces performing to Chinese communities on the island. Chinese musical instruments such as *claves*, percussion sticks; *corneta china*, Chinese oboe; and *tambores cu*, Chinese drums used in the lion dance—*cu* being the romanization of the Chinese word "drum"—found their way into Afro-Cuban music.

Roberto used to work as a bartender at Restaurant Pacífico. In 1994, he received a Chinese government scholarship to study martial arts and became a bona fide *wushu* practitioner and a good Mandarin speaker after two years. Our conversation alternates between Spanish and Mandarin.

After two years in China, Roberto married Tao Qi of Shanghai and brought her to Cuba. In 1997, they opened Templo del Cielo, Temple of Heaven, the only Chinese restaurant in town with an expatriate cook from China. (I suspect he is Roberto's brother-in-law; he is also surnamed Tao.) I had eaten there during my last trip, and the Shanghai noodle was surprisingly authentic.

"It was our idea to develop the cuisine, because real Chinese food is still unknown in Cuba," he says. "It's very difficult because there are very few Chinese spices and condiments here. Even though I'm Cuban, I sometimes feel Chinese with respect to training, seriousness and perseverance."

Having been chosen by his government, Roberto acts like a cultural ambassador. He refers to the preservation and promotion of Chinese culture in Cuba, and to the positive influence of Chinese philosophy. And he has become accustomed to wearing traditional Chinese clothing—"it's more comfortable and more of a Chinese feeling."

"Open up, open up. *Es el chino del barrio.*"

Our guide Luís is back, banging on the iron gates of the Chinese Cemetery, across the street from the National Cemetery. "I'm the Chinese from Chinatown," he shouts, "and I'm here with my family from the North."

The caretaker opens the gate without taking the dollar bills that Luís asked me to have in hand.

"He's even letting our camera in," he says. "I thought it would be more complicated."

I try to visit Chinese cemeteries everywhere I go. A cemetery can tell you a lot about the community. Besides, to an older generation of Chinese immigrants, dying in a foreign land is always on their mind—many want to go *home* when they die.

Wielding a machete, the caretaker escorts us through the cemetery grounds, speaking in a fast-paced and quixotic Cuban dialect. Valeria is having difficulty following his Spanish and makes a point of telling me that Peruvians speak the most standard Spanish in all of Latin America.

"You've to understand that many Chinese used to be very rich, and they have burial rites. After seven years, the bones are dug up, cleansed and put in tin boxes for storage in family crypts." He nonchalantly pries open a box with his machete to show us. There's a full set of human bones in there, all right. We are like archaeologists looking into a not-too-distant past. I don't know what the caretaker is going to do with the opened box.

The cemetery is quiet, leaves rustle, a stray dog lingers.

"We used to have nine employees. Then after the revolution, everybody fled," he says as we walk over to the Lung Kong pavilion, an elaborate structure in the shape of a pagoda with a crypt below. Lifting the floor cover, he motions me to go in. I find cemeteries creepy to begin with, much less stepping into an underground crypt.

"I'm going to follow you," says Kwoi as he pushes me on—he's too scared to go first.

Once inside, I find tin boxes marked with names, birthdates and native villages all stacked up eight high. There are many Kwans from my ancestral village. Life is strange: I've never been to the village my grandfather came from, yet halfway across the world, I continue to confront the ghosts of my ancestral past.

Back out in the spacious cemetery grounds, we walk among tombstones and pavilions, many of them engraved with the Chinese characters of family names. The plots and the tombstones are big and elaborate; the pavilions are like small houses. They remind me of those in Père Lachaise in Paris. The caretaker is right: the Chinese were once very rich.

Luís finds the tombstone of his grandfather, Enrique Chung, next to the bigger Chung pavilion, and becomes very emotional. Tears flow. His speech becomes incoherent. I'm not sure whether this is the first time he's discovered the tomb or if this is all just a show. I'm not even sure whether this is indeed his grandfather's name.

"My grandfather came by boat in 1928 from China to California and then to Cuba. He brought my father here as a young boy in 1942 to start a new life. My father worked as a cook at Luna de Oro, the same place where I work now. I feel very proud to be here with you. And you even helped me find the tomb of my grandfather. *Es increíble.*"

"The biggest dream in my life is to go to China," he continues as we make our way out. "I must still have some family in China, cousins, uncles . . . I don't know, we don't have any communication. It's far, far away, and a long, long time ago."

Then, he adds, as he closes the gates, "If the Chinese didn't come, we wouldn't have Chinese food in Cuba. We would have died with Creole food." He gives a wink. We all laugh.

It takes a little detective work to locate Casino Chung Wah. The four-storey building on Calle Amistad has only a small inscription in Spanish, *Edificio 'China'* (the word China in quotation marks), and four equally modest Chinese characters for "Chinese Benevolent Association."

A middle-aged woman who looks like she's in the Neighbourhood Watch motions me to take the elevator to the fourth floor—the lower floors were converted to apartments after the revolution. These apartments, and the association's rooms on the fourth floor, overlook a skylit courtyard.

The elevator doors open to an assembly hall with a stage where the flags of Cuba and the People's Republic of China are prominently displayed. I suspect they once displayed the flag of the Republic of China (Taiwan) and a portrait of Dr. Sun Yat-sen, modern China's founder who overthrew the Manchus (Qing dynasty) in 1911. It's a sign that China's United Front strategy—to win over the allegiance of overseas Chinese communities—has been effective here.

In Chinese communities everywhere, clan, family and village associations serve as protectors and family patriarchs—lending money to their members to start businesses, and providing food and shelter to those who have fallen on hard times. The Chinese Benevolent Association is the umbrella organization for all of them.

A young-looking Jorge Chau-Chiu, the general secretary, greets me and leads me into the president's office and the boardroom, the only air-conditioned spaces in the building. The rooms are filled with Qing dynasty furniture and antiques, gifts from the Chinese ambassador on the association's 100th anniversary in 1993. Paintings by Flora Fong, a contemporary Chinese Cuban artist, grace the walls. (Cuba also produced Wifredo Lam, an Impressionist painter who befriended—and was inspired by—the likes of Picasso and Matisse.)

In quick succession Jorge shows me the library, the activity rooms for tai chi and Mandarin classes, the medical clinic for acupuncture and herbal medicine, and the ubiquitous altar to Guan Di. I light incense for my namesake, his statue draped in blinking Christmas lights.

Jorge now takes me to a room filled with boxes of index cards. Until recently, the association functioned as de facto embassy and registrar of all *chinos*, pure and mixed-race. Each of the thousands of index cards contains a person's photo, name in Chinese and Spanish, home address, birthplace and ancestral village in China. It is Chinese tradition to trace a person's ancestral origin, even for those who are generations removed and born half a world away.

"Most of them are Chinese Cuban. There are only about 300 pure Chinese in all of Cuba today, maybe not even 300," he says as he pulls out a card for Carlos Chang of Santiago de Cuba. "Like this one, he's not pure Chinese. He has Chinese blood, but he wasn't from China."

The first boatload of indentured Chinese labourers landed on June 3, 1857. Most were on eight-year contracts to supplement African slaves—and treated no differently from them. Many did not even survive the journey from the transshipment port of Manila.

Yet 140,000 Chinese arrived and became part of the island's *mestizo* population, begetting the saying that a Cuban today is one-third Spanish, one-third African and one-third Chinese.

Early Chinese settlers demonstrated their loyalty by fighting in Cuba's Ten Years' War for independence from Spain, which ended in 1878. Two thousand volunteers sacrificed their lives, leading José Martí, Cuba's national hero, to proclaim, "There was not one Cuban Chinese deserter, not one Cuban Chinese traitor."

"It gives the Chinese respectability," Jorge says.

For the first three decades of the 1900s, there was a second wave of immigration from Guangdong, escaping poverty at home. Five thousand more came from California, to escape unbearable discrimination and racism in the US. The last wave, like Maritza's father and Alejandro, arrived in the 1950s, fleeing communism in China and uncertain futures in the colonies of Hong Kong and Macau.

I ask about photos of the old Chinatown. Jorge notes that all their historical photos were moved to government archives for safekeeping after the revolution. Was the association forced to hand them over to the government when ethnic distinctions were a social taboo? Or were they the ugly side of pre-revolutionary Cuba that Castro wanted to bury? A recent exile from Cuba would later tell me that it was a bit of both.

As Jorge locks up the record room and walks me out, I tell him that I am full of admiration for what the association has done—to protect and help the community while it was growing; and now, to painstakingly keep the record of a dying one.

"We are all very far from our roots," he reminds me. "And we have to take care of each other in a foreign land."

—-—

Lung Kong Restaurant's decor is straight out of a dance hall in 1950s Hong Kong. Dining tables with worn tablecloths, a Pepsi refrigerator next to the bar, ceiling fans rotating lazily and two giggling waitresses folding pizza boxes in the corner. Takeout pizzas are bestsellers in Chinese restaurants—customers line up for them, and, like all baked goods in Cuba, they are sold out as soon as they emerge from the oven.

It's mid-afternoon, and the restaurant is empty.

Fermín is waiting for me by the window. Someone has brought him a cola. He pulls a faded newspaper clipping from his pocket and unfolds it gently, revealing a photo of himself dancing in a white tuxedo. The caption reads: *El chino del carnaval.*

He inserts a cassette tape labelled *Canciones Cubanas*—a compilation of songs he recorded—into a portable player and starts singing along to his rendition of "Ilusión China."

It's my last day in Havana, and we are transported back in time. There's sadness in the room. Fermín is even more forlorn as he sings the last stanza:

> *Cuban woman of my dreams*
> *Come with me to Canton*
> *I want to enjoy it there with your love*
> *Love me a lot*
> *I love you with devotion*
> *You'll be the queen of love in Canton.*

As I say my goodbye, I am struck by the image of this man who once was a celebrated conga dancer. That time has passed. He is now living out his twilight years in a place where everything seems to be frozen in time. From another era. But like the buildings along the Malecón, there is beauty in the decay.

CHAPTER 11

The Great Escape

SÃO PAULO, BRAZIL

JUST BEFORE MIDNIGHT ON A MOONLESS NIGHT IN OCTOBER 1967, NINETEEN-year-old Lee Ho Shau and his friend plunged into the water and began their four-hour swim to freedom. It had taken them four days to get to the coast from their village. There was no turning back now.

Lee had been working in a people's commune since he was twelve, one of many agricultural collectives created during China's Great Leap Forward in 1958, which was undertaken to transform the country into a communist society and surpass the West. Instead, tens of millions died in what came to be known as the Great Chinese Famine.

The Cultural Revolution began eight years later, further throwing China into a decade of political and social turmoil. Like millions living in the south-eastern province of Guangdong, Lee wanted to escape. He looked toward the British colony of Hong Kong and the nearby Portuguese colony of Macau for possible refuge.

Hong Kong offered better economic opportunities, but it was situated at the other end of the Pearl River estuary. Macau, connected by land to his village in Zhongshan, was closer, but fleeing overland to Macau was both difficult and dangerous because guards constantly patrolled the border and would open fire indiscriminately.

Many became "freedom swimmers."

For four to six hours, they would cling to rubber tubes, football cores and other makeshift flotation devices, battling the cold, the tides and even sudden storms. Some were picked up by patrolling Chinese gunboats. The unlucky ones—attacked by sharks or overcome by cramps or fatigue—simply drowned.

For a year, Lee and his friend planned the escape to Macau. They scouted locations where they could slip into the water and consulted the almanac on the current flow and tides in the area. Although he was a good swimmer, Lee nonetheless trained to get into shape.

"An opportunity came up and we had to leave in a hurry," he recalls as we sit at his restaurant in a quiet neighborhood in São Paulo. Lee is in his mid-fifties but has not lost his swimmer's physique, firm and tanned.

Without proper travel permits, the two friends had to hike at night, as unfamiliar faces in nearby villages would arouse suspicion. When they reached the shore near Macau, they put their last sets of clean clothes into plastic bags.

"There were patrols with German shepherds passing by every twenty minutes. We waited for ten minutes after they passed and then, *po tung*," he uses his hand and a Chinese onomatopoeia to describe their jump into the water.

About half an hour into the swim, Lee's friend began to have cramps and decided to give up. Lee continued on alone. He was already in the water, he reasoned, and there was no turning back. A little later, he changed his mind and swam back to look for his friend.

"It took half an hour to find him," he says. "He asked why I didn't just leave him behind. I said, 'If we're caught, at least we'll be together. If we reach our destination, we'll get there together.' That's what friends are for."

Four hours later, they climbed ashore near Macau Electric's power plant, joining thousands of others who had made it that year. Not daring to flag down a bus, they found a sympathetic tricycle driver who pedalled them to safety at the home of Lee's aunt.

"I couldn't sleep that night. I was still in awe that I had made it," Lee says more than thirty years later.

"This would make for a great movie," I told him. Even if I've heard similar stories many times before, I am in awe of what he's done.

"Oh, it's nothing special," Lee says. "There's no choice if you want freedom."

Brazil is on edge tonight. Will Ronaldo be in top form? Will Brazil beat Germany to become the first country to win the World Cup for the fifth time? With the passionate and free-flowing style of football Brazil plays, a defeat in the hands of the machine-like German team would be a massive blow.

Kwoi, Mark Valino and I arrive in São Paulo two days before the 2002 championship match. The whole city is pumped, waiting for the big game on Sunday. *Nessun dorma*, nobody sleeps. ("Nessun dorma," from the opera *Turandot*, was the unofficial theme song of the 1990 World Cup tournament in Italy.)

São Paulo, with twenty million in its metropolitan area, is the largest city in South America—and the most populous city in the Portuguese-speaking world. It also has the largest Lebanese, Italian, Japanese and Portuguese diasporas in the world.

You can stroll along fabled avenues and through upscale neighbourhoods, visit the Botanical Garden in the heart of the city, admire the modernist architecture of the Museum of Art and linger around São Bento, the heart of the old city.

More often than not, you will also run into frustrating traffic gridlock and come across overcrowded slums and shantytowns, barefoot boys kicking a football on bare earth under a highway overpass and derelict industrial wastelands where factories, long abandoned by their owners, rust.

But today, there's an exciting party in town. People are making noise around the shopping district at Rua 25 de Março, cheering on the national side. Confetti and streamers, in Team Brazil's canary yellow and blue, are everywhere. Firecrackers pop in the air. Patrons spew from bars into the streets, blocking traffic. On the *avenidas*, cars honk incessantly, stopping traffic for no apparent reason other than to cheer the team on.

And the opening kickoff in Yokohama is still thirty-six hours away.

—·—

The steamed garoupa comes to the table glistening in a glaze of soy, ginger and scallion. The fish—which Lee Ho Shau and I bought in the morning at CEAGESP, the third-largest food wholesale market in the world—was cooked with the same subtlety and to the perfect degree of doneness as in the best seafood restaurants of Hong Kong.

We are having our first dinner in Restaurante Huang, which Lee has chosen to open in a tony, tree-lined neighborhood, Vila Mariana, with trendy eateries and a student-friendly atmosphere. The sign at the front says *Qualidade em Culinária Chinesa*, quality Chinese cuisine.

Jun Watanabe has joined us. He is tall and big for a Japanese. I first met him three months earlier, by chance, on my trip to the Amazon. He was working for a Japanese company in Manaus and has a good command of Portuguese. Having studied Spanish at university, the transition, for him, was *sem problemas*.

He is a mirror image of me: a Japanese who grew up in Malaysia and Singapore; while I, a Singaporean Chinese, spent my adolescent years in Japan. We both studied engineering in the US and ended up working elsewhere in the world. Although not totally fluent, we can speak each other's native tongue: he has a reasonable command of Mandarin, with a smattering of Cantonese, and I can converse easily in Japanese.

Watanabe moved to São Paulo a month before we arrived and is a great host, even arranging our after-hours entertainment—some of it too rowdy to be described here. I missed half of these nocturnal excursions, leaving them to Kwoi and Mark, who have more energy and alcohol capacity after a long day. But mostly, I enjoy eating with Watanabe. Having grown up in Southeast Asia, he knows his Chinese food.

There is a table of Taiwanese Brazilians upstairs. As the food is carried up, the same dishes are served to us downstairs: down-home watercress pork bone soup, a mixed platter of Cantonese barbecued meats, roast duck in lettuce wrap served with scallion and hoisin sauce (a healthier version of the Peking duck), and, *la pièce de résistance*, braised sea cucumber with Chinese mushrooms.

The latter dish is a perfect marriage of texture and taste. Chinese relish a wide variety of textures in their food; or as Fuchsia Dunlop, the first Westerner to train at the Sichuan Higher Institute of Cuisine, calls it, "mouthfeel" (from the Chinese word *kougan*)—as you'd get with jellyfish, duck tongue and chicken feet, for example.

The flavourless but high-protein slug-like sea cucumber lives at the bottom of the ocean floor. It is prized for its rubbery texture, as well as for its medicinal qualities—reportedly treating the likes of arthritis, high blood pressure, frequent urination and even impotence. The mushrooms supply the umami.

Wah! A truly moveable feast.

If Lee were an architect, this would be his masterpiece of eclecticism.

"Is this authentic enough for you?" The dinner is almost over when Lee comes out from the kitchen.

"I have died and gone to heaven." I just can't suppress my effusive praise.

"This dinner was made for our guests upstairs," he says. "The rest of my menu here is not authentic—it's just to fool the Brazilians!" He goes on to list the four top-selling Chinese dishes in Brazil: diced chicken with cashew nuts, beef with Chinese broccoli, sweet and sour pork, and shredded beef with onions.

"That's okay. They're what everyone here likes to eat," I say, trying to be sympathetic.

"Brazilians were taught to cook only with MSG and soy sauce, but not salt," he complains. "Chinese restaurants here have all been cooking this way."

I've eaten in Chinese restaurants the world over, and I know how challenging it is to maintain authenticity when customers' tastes don't conform to *real* Chinese food. Any cuisine will absorb foreign influence and incorporate new ingredients. Cashews are not native to China—Portuguese colonists in Brazil began exporting cashew nuts as early as the 1550s—but that doesn't make the diced chicken dish any less authentically Chinese.

"So cashew chicken is a truly Sino-Brazilian dish," he says with a laugh.

For me, the test for authenticity is one's ability to evoke the memory of a childhood meal. At this time, Lee's wife, Wong Yim Sheung, emerges with one of my fondest food memories: a tray of egg tarts that came straight out of the oven, piping hot.

"Wow, you're making your own egg tarts!" Kwoi jumps up in excitement. I've seen him devour egg tarts with gay abandon at dim sum lunches in Toronto.

"That's right. We're just learning. This is a small restaurant—we have to do everything ourselves," Wong says. I think she's trying a little too hard to be modest behind her sweet smile.

Watanabe takes a first bite and gives his Goldilocks pronouncement: "They're not too sweet, not too salty. They're just right."

"We're the only ones in São Paulo to make them like this." Lee beams. "Others are not as silky."

Daan tat is a popular item in Hong Kong bakeries and Hong Kong–style cafés known as cha chaan teng. The Cantonese egg tart has a delicate and creamy egg custard, sitting in a golden, flaky pastry—much lighter than its Portuguese counterpart, pastel de nata, which one finds on the streets here.

It is claimed that the egg tart was inspired by the English custard tart. I contend that pastel de nata (called *po tat* in Hong Kong), introduced to the Portuguese colony of Macau, was more of a major influence on the Cantonese version.

"*Sifu*, have you ever thought of passing your skills to the next generation?" Watanabe asks, using the Chinese word for martial arts master.

"I tried teaching both Chinese and Brazilians," he says with a sigh. "But they could never get it. There's nothing I can do about it."

"Is it that hard to learn?"

"I'm not sure. That's how I learned, watching my *sifu*. But it seems they aren't able to do so. The dishes taste different every day. No matter how many times I teach them, they still don't get it. I tried to teach them the proper way to roast, but they couldn't even control the rotation."

The next afternoon, I watch Lee spend four hours roasting a suckling pig, Cantonese-style, on a spit over a homemade porcelain-tiled charcoal pit at the back of the kitchen. The rotation, by hand, is slow, deliberate and constant. After it's done, a Taiwanese customer pulls up in her BMW, loads the succulent carcass with golden crispy skin into the trunk, and drives away happy.

—•—

"I'm usually the organizer who gets everything ready," says the fifty-year-old Wong Yim Sheung in an unassuming, but very determined, tone. "I was quite carefree. I didn't have to work at a farm, so I travelled around the district looking for ways to flee."

It's a hot and lazy afternoon at Huang. Wong and her husband, Lee, take a break from the kitchen and continue telling stories of their great escapes.

Wong and Lee were teenagers during the Cultural Revolution, when the Red Guards answered calls from Mao for a "continuing revolution"—persecuting anyone deemed to be "capitalist roaders" or "counter-revolutionaries." Both of them were considered "black elements" due to their backgrounds: his grandfather was a landlord, her father was a widely respected doctor. In other words, class enemies.

Wong had been planning to flee China since she was fifteen. "I had a burning desire to leave," she says.

She met Lee in his village while plotting her own escape. "I wasn't there for romance," she says with a laugh, looking over at her husband. "He was working in the farm and didn't have time to organize. When I arranged meetings, I asked him to come along."

"I wasn't allowed to take part in any political activities," Lee says. "It was at that time that I also started thinking about fleeing China."

They decided to flee together. But there was one problem: she couldn't swim. When he seized the opportunity in 1967, she couldn't follow him. "I began to learn to swim the following year," she says. "I was worried that someone might see me, so I started practising in small rivers."

Wong's first attempt in 1968, with three others, failed. They were caught in the mountains a few hours outside their village. She took full responsibility and confessed to masterminding the entire operation to the authorities. She was detained for ninety days, but continued to plot her escape even at the detention centre.

"People thought I was very brave. Maybe because I saw my family lose everything overnight. I had lost all my confidence in China." Four months later, she tried again with three other teenagers. It was very cold by then, but she didn't want to wait until the following year.

Like Lee and his friend the year before, the four of them walked sixty kilometres from their village to a bay across from Macau. They had no change of clothing and very little to eat. As they passed by a village, Wong says, "The dogs were barking and the villagers started chasing us. We just ran and ran until our feet bled."

After spending four nights in the hills, and getting lost a few times, they finally reached the coast. Even there, they had to evade the guard dogs and hide behind rocks whenever a flare went up. They slid into the water just before midnight, two boys and two girls, roped together.

Suddenly, one of the boys got cramps. The other boy helped by rubbing medicinal oil on him while the two girls dragged them along. Two hours later, Wong was worried, tired and wondering whether they would ever reach land.

The four used beacons from the shore to guide them, and the last one came from the chimney of Macau Electric. They dragged themselves out of the water exactly where Lee and his companion had landed a year earlier. Once safe, Wong immediately contacted her cousins in Hong Kong, who rushed to take the next ferry to Macau. They celebrated with a bottle of French champagne.

"I couldn't begin to tell you how overjoyed I was! I was so happy that I had completely forgotten how hungry I was. I hadn't eaten in days," she remembers. "But I always had confidence that I would be successful in *tau do*." She uses the Hong Kong expression for illegals crossing the Chinese border in the sixties and seventies, "stealing across."

Wong was not even eighteen.

By that time, Lee had been apprenticing at a well-known Cantonese restaurant. "Life in Macau wasn't bad at all. As I never finished school, I was determined to learn everything there was to know about cooking."

After a three-day reunion, Wong slipped into Hong Kong with the help of her cousins and got a job in a factory. The pay was "survivable," but, more importantly, she got her residency with the help of her employer. As we talk, she can't help but wonder, with a little sadness, how her mother permitted her to do such a dangerous thing. Her mother recently passed away.

"She had told me that it was my destiny," she recalls. "My dad also let me choose my way. They knew my goal was to get to Hong Kong."

"It's almost thirty years ago. It seems just like yesterday," her husband says, his voice tinged with nostalgia.

"He wasn't as bold as I was." She looks at him and switches mood. "I wasn't afraid of anything. People couldn't believe that I actually climbed over the mountains and swam across the sea."

"She's never worked a day in her life," he chides. "She couldn't even lift a five-kilo bag."

"I was the daughter of a doctor and never worked a day on the farm," she says with a laugh. "I couldn't even walk barefooted. I had to have my shoes!"

After two and a half years, Lee also sneaked across to Hong Kong, got a job through his relatives doing deliveries, and obtained his residency. But China's Cultural Revolution had spilled over to Hong Kong in the late sixties. Pro-Mao sympathizers in the colony demonstrated and eventually rioted.

Lee and Wong did not feel secure. Hong Kong, to them, seemed very small. Together, they made another life-changing decision—this time with less risk. Claiming they were engaged, they obtained tourist visas to Brazil, where Wong had an uncle.

"Wow, both of you are professional illegal immigrants," I say. We all laugh. Growing up in Hong Kong in the mid-sixties, I have heard all about freedom swimmers. Now, I've come face to face with two of them.

Lee and Wong landed in Rio de Janeiro in 1972. They married and opened a pastelaria in partnership with relatives. The entry points for Chinese immigrants to Brazil are pastelarias, fast-food snack bars selling pastels, deep-fried half-circle or rectangular thin-crusted hand pies filled with cheese or meat. Cantonese here call them *gok jai*, little puffs. The pie is said to have originated when Japanese immigrants adapted Chinese fried wontons to sell as snacks at street markets.

The food has come full circle.

I am so enamored of these little puffs that I stop two or three times a day at a pastelaria—there seems to be one in every corner—to sample them with their different fillings, washed down with caldo de cana, freshly squeezed sugarcane juice. Italian immigrants used to run the trade, but, in recent decades, Chinese have taken over.

"The Chinese make better-tasting pastels because they add MSG," Lee quips. I'm not sure if he is just playing on the stereotype of Chinese food.

The Lees moved to São Paulo after their son Luis was born and continued in the business of selling pastels. "Life was really difficult in the beginning," Wong says. "The children were young and our business wasn't going well. We didn't have enough capital, were just trying to survive."

Ten years later, a Taiwanese friend heard about Lee's roasting skills and encouraged him to open his own restaurant, Lua D'Ouro, or Golden Moon, in the Liberdade district. Over the following two decades, with a combination of hard work and entrepreneurship, the Lees launched five more restaurants. Restaurante Porto Vermelho (Red Port), where the family still lives upstairs, opened in 1996. Restaurante Huang, where we have our dinner, opened three years later.

Restaurante Huang Hei opened in São Bento the previous year. Popular with lunchtime office workers who get redeemable chits from their employers, the restaurant serves a *comida por kilo* ("food by the kilo") buffet where customers pay for their food by weight, a style popular in Latin America.

Just down the hill from São Bento is the Rua 25 de Março shopping district. The area is known for selling everything under the sun, in bulk and cheap: handbags, running shoes, electronics, toys, jewelry, as well as fake Guccis and Rolexes. Waves of Lebanese immigrants settled here in the nineteenth century. In the 1980s, more arrived from China, Korea, Greece and Portugal. The five-storey Shopping Oriental mall has more than 300 stores, run mostly by recent immigrants from mainland China.

When China opened its borders in the eighties, many started to immigrate to Brazil. The couple helped more than thirty of their relatives settle in the country. As Wong tells it, "Five or six relatives would come, and we would settle them into our restaurants. That's how it all started."

"Even now, with all our restaurants, if someone wants to join us, we'll cut them in," Lee says. "If someone needs a job, we give it to them." (The restaurant in Liberdade is now managed by his cousin.) As it was for many of the people we've visited, running a Chinese restaurant was a way to find a foothold in the new country, and provide the same for other new arrivals.

There were around 30,000 Chinese in Brazil when Lee and Wong arrived in the seventies. Many of them were paper sons, following elder immigrants from the same village in China. There is also a sizable Taiwanese community that arrived around the same time.

Brazil has not always been a destination of choice for Chinese immigrants. Central American countries such as El Salvador and Costa Rica have attracted more, because they are easier to get into. Others went to Paraguay then illegally crossed the border to Brazil. Today, there are more than 500,000 Chinese in the country, with almost 200,000 in São Paulo. Many came in the eighties illegally and became citizens through several amnesties.

Unlike many cities I have visited, São Paulo does not have a traditional Chinatown, but some Chinese immigrants began to open restaurants and shops in "Japantown" in Liberdade.

A large wave of Japanese immigration to Brazil began in the early 1900s, as the end of feudalism led to widespread poverty in rural Japan. Most came seeking jobs, especially on coffee plantations. Today, Brazil is home to the largest ethnic Japanese community outside of Japan, more than one million—almost two million if mixed-heritage descendants are included.

I take a walk with Lee in Liberdade one afternoon. A torii gate welcomes us at the entrance. There are Japanese restaurants and food stores, souvenir shops, Buddhist temples, art galleries and travel agents advertising cheap flights to Osaka.

Over the past two decades, Chinese and Koreans have moved in. The *feira de domingo* or Sunday market at Praça da Liberdade is an Asian street-food paradise: sushi rolls, yakitori (grilled chicken skewers), okonomiyaki (savoury Japanese pancakes), yakisoba (fried noodles) and gyoza (pan-fried dumplings). There are also Korean rice cakes and Chinese spring rolls.

A Chinese-owned grocery store sells homemade cured meat made by Wong in the tiny kitchen at Red Port—lap cheong (Chinese sausage), yun cheong (duck liver sausage) and lap yuk (cured pork belly).

"It's actually my husband's hobby," she says. "Our friends asked us to make these cured meats for them. That's how the business started."

I am already impressed with the couple's culinary skills. How much more do they need to prove? There is little to gain from selling homemade Chinese cured meat in competition with commercial manufacturers. And they surely can survive without roast suckling pig on the menu, ordered by a tiny fraction of customers.

But to Lee and Wong, it is less about making a living and more about passion—a passion for culinary art.

And there's another passion here: beef.

Watanabe takes me to a popular churrascaria, an all-you-can-eat beef extravaganza where roving waiters slice charcoal-grilled meats from large skewers directly onto our plates. All parts of the cow are in play: loin, rib, brisket, tongue and cheek. A huge salad bar sits in the middle of the room to remind us to eat a balanced meal. A miniature railway semaphore signal with red, yellow and green flags sits at each table. The only way to slow the onslaught is to raise the yellow flag. Or red, when you've had enough.

And if you get tired of the red meat, there's always the prospect of returning to Liberdade for a sashimi combo.

———

"I came back for many reasons. I was nostalgic for Brazil, for my family and for my people," Luis Lee says as we walk down Avenida Paulista, where the championship game would be aired the next day. "I want to find a good job so I can bring my wife here. Living in Brazil has many advantages these days. In some ways, I think I can have a better quality of life here."

Maybe it's World Cup fever, or maybe he just can't get Brazil out of his blood. Twenty-seven-year-old Luis had returned from Canada a few weeks earlier, sporting a crew cut. Having studied and worked there for a decade, he wants to move back here. But it's a complicated decision. He needs to convince his Venezuelan wife, whom he met in Toronto, to join him.

"Do your parents have a problem with you marrying a non-Chinese?" I inevitably ask.

"When I was growing up, my parents wanted me to marry a Chinese. It was always like that," he replies, nodding. "But I prefer Brazilian girls. When I fell in love with Carly, my parents understood that she was someone I want to share my life with. They've accepted her. Now, everything is fine."

What about racial discrimination?

Luis tells me that Brazil is very much a multicultural country, even more so than Canada. There are more people of Lebanese descent here than the entire population of Lebanon. And even though each ethnic group gets to keep its own culture, there is also a common and distinct Brazilian identity.

"Look, we're one country, all cheering for the same football team," Luis says. The night before, he took me to Forró Remelexo, a local dance club. Forró is a genre of music popular with the young. It originates from northeastern Brazil: a mix of country, Brazilian folk rock and disco beat. The dance style is as intimate as Argentine tango and as fast-paced as salsa. Luis is reticent. Dancing is not quite his thing.

His passion, however, is *futebol*.

"It's more than just a sport, it's almost a religion here," he continues. "Everyone has his favourite team, but during the World Cup we all come together for the national team." (Luis normally cheers for Pelé's Santos FC.)

Avenida Paulista is lined with Brazil's top corporations: Petrobras, Banco do Brasil, Telefônica Brasil. In the early morning, tens of thousands of fans will descend on Latin America's most famous avenue to watch the game.

But it's strangely calm and quiet this evening.

"What's your prediction?" I ask.

"Two to one. Brazil over Germany," he replies.

A nearby newsstand displays dozens of sports tabloids, most with a front-page photo of Ronaldo with his haircut for the tournament: a shaved head with a semicircular tuft in the front. I pick one up and ask Luis to translate the headline.

"We hope that Brazil will have the last laugh."

Dawn. The subway is packed with fans in yellow and green face paint. The bars have stayed open all night, and patrons are pouring into the streets. Jun Watanabe, with his six-foot frame, a Hawaiian shirt and a green-and-yellow jester hat, is bouncing up and down in the subway car like a big teddy bear. Luis, in his Seleção (or Selection, a moniker for the national team) blue, is more reserved but chants along.

The fans are standing shoulder to shoulder under a giant screen set up on the eight-lane boulevard. They go wild at every Brazilian attack, every missed shot at goal. Some are biting their nails, others praying to football gods with their eyes closed. Mark and I are perched on scaffolding below the giant television screen, scanning the crowd for reaction shots.

At halftime, I join Kwoi as he follows Watanabe and Luis in the crowd. Ronaldo scores the first goal; the crowd explodes. Watanabe cannot keep still and hugs anyone who passes by. Behind us, a band plays non-stop. Mayhem everywhere. Ronaldo scores again. The band plays louder. Watanabe and Luis hug each other and start dancing.

And then the final whistle. Brazil wins! *Penta campeões.* Five-time champions. On the other side of the world, shimmering confetti shrouds the Brazilian team on the podium. Here, a yellow and green paper rain falls. *Penta! Penta!* The crowd chants deliriously. Street parties are everywhere. Pastelarias, grocery stores and cafés are overflowing with revellers. Everyone is exuberant. Brazilian flags emerge though sunroofs. More firecrackers. And it's not even lunchtime yet.

In recent weeks, Brazil's national currency, the real, has dipped in value, and financial markets have suffered precipitous declines. But little matters now. All is well again. The nation can sleep soundly. The next day, Monday, is an instant national holiday. São Paulo, and the entire ethnically diverse and conflicted country, will celebrate together well into the night. And for the following week.

"I'm a Chinese Brazilian, but in many ways, I feel I'm more Brazilian than Chinese," Luis confides as we head back to his parents' restaurant for a celebratory lunch. When I ask how he feels about what his parents went through, he says, "My parents had a lot of courage fleeing China and coming to Brazil to start a new life here. They're well liked in the community. It's a really good thing that they tried to fulfill their dreams. My mother seems to be a quiet woman, but she's the one who makes decisions in our family. Many have said that they've never seen anyone with such a strong will."

"This is our home," Lee says as he joins us. "We came out of China as teenagers, spent five or six years in Hong Kong and Macau. But we've been in Brazil for over half of our lives."

"I'm used to living here now. Brazil feels like home," Wong says. "Brazilians are very passionate about life."

CHAPTER 12

Into the Heart of the Amazon

MANAUS, BRAZIL

THE MORNING AFTER BRAZIL WON ITS FIFTH WORLD CUP, I TRAVEL UPCOUN-try with my crew, Kwoi and Mark Valino, to the heart of the Amazon.

First stop: Rio de Janeiro. As an avid bossa nova fan, I must pay homage at Bar Garota de Ipanema, named after Antônio Carlos Jobim's 1962 hit song, "The Girl from Ipanema." Jobim composed the song's melody while sitting at that café-bar, watching a seventeen-year-old sashay to the beach. It is one of the most recorded songs in the world.

I imagine a tall and tan and young and lovely woman walking by me as I sip a margarita in the sun.

Then there's the obligatory cable car ride up to Pão de Açúcar, or Sugarloaf Mountain, to catch a glimpse of the setting sun casting a golden halo behind the statue of Christ the Redeemer. Looking the other direction, toward the airport named after Jobim, I take in one of my favourite city views in the world—rolling mountains, a sparkling blue sea and endless stretches of beach.

Next stop, Salvador, capital of Bahia state and centre of Afro-Brazilian culture. We hit upon one of the street carnivals that seem to be going on all summer long. Revellers gyrate with the pulsating, rhythmic music that has its roots in Candomblé—a fusion of Catholicism and Yoruba beliefs—as they wind their way along the cobblestone streets that slope down from the Upper City.

In a nondescript community centre in a jam-packed room with bare, baby-blue walls, we stumble upon a gathering where people are either in a spiritual trance or extremely intoxicated—they engage both body and soul in a hypnotic chant. Kwoi is pulled up onto a table, figuratively dancing with his camera while being cheered on by a group of women in Baiana dress. Mark, who's in his early twenties and always wearing a woolen skullcap during our travels (even in this heat), is so in awe of the moment that he's not sure how to react with his camera.

Night falls and capoeira comes to Praça da Sé.

Capoeira is an ancient African martial art, introduced by slaves and fused with Brazilian rhythms to disguise it as a dance. It's practised in pairs, which face off inside a circle of musicians. There is haunting, rhythmic chanting, mesmerizing percussion and the buzzing sound of the berimbau, a one-string bamboo instrument that originated in Africa.

And there's no better way to carry on with the festivities than by having our fill of caipirinha—a traditional Bahia cocktail made with cachaça (a spirit made from native sugarcane) mixed with lime juice and sugar. It's past two when we finally hit our beds and we have an early-morning flight to Brasília.

We get a twenty-four-hour respite there. The country's capital is an example of city planning gone sterile. Built from scratch in the mid-1950s, it is soulless and colourless, save for the modernist government buildings designed by Oscar Niemeyer, perhaps the country's most famous architect.

After five days of hopping on and off planes, we finally arrive at Encontro das Águas, or Meeting of Waters. This is where Amazon tributaries from Peru and Colombia join at Manaus: the dark-coloured Rio Negro meets up with the lighter sandy-coloured Rio Solimões, also known as the Upper Amazon.

Due to differences in temperature, speed and viscosity, the waters from these two massive tributaries run side by side for six kilometres in a two-toned confluence, like black coffee and caffe latte, that can be seen from space. This is the starting point of the Lower Amazon, which flows for another 1,700 kilometres to the Atlantic Ocean.

My contacts in São Paulo's Taiwanese community tell me Jack Sun's Restaurante Mandarim is the only *real* Chinese restaurant in the Amazon. Nobody else wanted to move there, they say; it's just too hot and humid. But *senhor* Sun was brave enough to go, and he's been there for thirty years.

The Mandarim is in a three-storey pinkish ochre Portuguese colonial building in Manaus's city centre, on the quiet Rua Joaquim Sarmento. It seats about sixty, with big, round tables for communal dining. There's another dining room upstairs for banquets and overflow, and the kitchen is on the third floor.

The first thing that catches my eye as I walk in are the two-tiered stainless-steel buffet counters in the front of the room. The Chinese decor in the dining room is sparse. A framed calligraphy piece with the Chinese characters for "Eating Is Health" hangs on a far wall.

Sun, on the cusp of turning sixty, is greying and balding slightly, and his shoulders stoop a little, but otherwise he's fit for his age. He leaves the restaurant's operation to his staff while he runs around attending to details, such as making sure that the buffet counter is clean and the steamers are still warm, and stirring soups and stews so they don't burn on the bottom.

The buffet is in a *comida por kilo*—food by the kilogram—style. At the end of the line, Sun's wife, Lina Wu, stands by the cash register to weigh each loaded plate and manages the customer flow with confidence and good humour.

"The economy is bad, and people watch how much they can afford to eat," Sun says, explaining the buffet arrangement. "This is a very fair way to calculate the charges."

Along with the usual pan-fried dumplings, fried rice and fried noodles, the buffet offers more authentic Chinese offerings, including oxtail stew, yee fu noodles with Chinese mushrooms, and fried eggplant with garlic and pork.

Sun's signature dish, however, is mapo tofu.

The Sichuan specialty, translated as "pockmarked granny bean curd," is challenging to do well and requires hard-to-find ingredients like Sichuan red chili, Sichuan peppercorn and fermented bean paste. The secret is in the peppercorn. It creates a tingly numbness in the mouth that Chinese identify as *ma*, as opposed to chili hot, which is *la*. The English words "spicy" and "heat" do not distinguish between the two.

"You pretty much have to fly in fresh Sichuan peppercorn from China," he says. "I couldn't get them here, so I use malagueta instead."

The malagueta pepper is widely used in Brazil, especially in the Bahia state. It's rated at 60,000 to 100,000 Scoville Heat Units, the scale that measures the spiciness of chili peppers, while Sichuan peppercorn ranges from 50,000 to 75,000.

Inevitably, the question of adaptation comes up. "Our customers are 98 per cent Brazilian, so we have to adjust our recipes to suit their taste," Sun says. "We offer up Brazilian dishes just to retain our customers. They don't care how authentically Chinese your food is."

Brazilian dishes at the buffet include feijoada (black bean and pork stew), farofa (a toasted cassava flour mixture), as well as moqueca (a cream-base seafood stew made with onion, garlic, tomatoes, cilantro and coconut milk).

And the sushi rolls are his nod to healthier eating. "Chinese food is very oily, but it doesn't taste good if you don't cook with lots of oil. Nowadays people prefer Japanese. It's light. It makes for good business."

When Chinese emigrate abroad, running a restaurant is a low-risk occupation—Chinese food is such a global phenomenon that there's always a demand. But it takes hard work, and long hours, to run a successful restaurant. The smattering of wrinkles and a certain weariness on Sun's face attest to that. He used to hire chefs from China, but they never stayed long, as the climate is too hot.

"And they all want to be their own bosses," he adds.

"Can the locals help?" I wonder.

"We're the only family-run Chinese restaurant in town, and they seem to like working here. As staff, they are okay, but I find them sometimes slow and irresponsible. It takes a lot of training and discipline."

This inertia, he believes, is due to living in a country that is too rich and too peaceful—there hasn't been a war here for hundreds of years. "They just want to have a nice life. That's good enough for them. Very different from us Chinese; we always want to get ahead, to win, to beat out the competition."

I load up on the mapo tofu at the buffet table. It hasn't lost anything in translation. The ground pork and medium-firm tofu are mixed nicely in a chili sauce made from fermented broad bean sauce (doubanjiang), sprinkled with chopped green onion, and oozing chili oil. My whole mouth is numbed and burning.

Oh, what a great feeling!

I finish the meal with Brazilian coffee, heavily sugared cold espresso served in a tiny paper cup from a thermos. It's commonly free in all restaurants. I love Brazilian coffee but wish they would serve it *sem açúcar*, unsweetened.

—•—

Manaus is a city with huge urban sprawl on the banks of the Amazon River, situated in the middle of the rainforest, equidistant from the Peruvian Andes and the Atlantic Ocean.

Floating docks that accommodate the river's fourteen-metre rise and fall are the heart and the soul of the city. People come from all over the world to see them. Ferries glide up and down the great river, stopping to load and unload passengers and goods. It's a one-week trip from Manaus upriver to Colombia and Peru. Passengers bring hammocks to hang on the upper deck of the boat—the Amazon's answer to a sleeper train. (There are no roads from the south. Everything has to be shipped or flown in.)

In 1967, Manaus was decreed a *zona franca*, free-trade zone. Migrants from all over Brazil and from neighbouring countries as far away as Chile flocked to the town in search of the new El Dorado. The city's population grew from 400,000 to 1.5 million.

Heavy tax incentives have attracted multinationals such as Samsung, Panasonic and Harley-Davidson, even though they have to ship their products for five days by barge to Belém, then for two days by truck to São Paolo, the distribution centre. Honda, for example, produces a million motorbikes a year at Manaus.

But the city still has the feel of a frontier town. There's a hint of lawlessness in the air. Liquor flows freely. People seem to be making a fast buck by whatever means necessary, legal or not. As I sit at a roadside poolhall-bar with a bottle of Skol, I find myself seeing gangsters and assassins everywhere. Everyone seems to be hustling. A couple of shirtless men at the next table are whispering to each other. A man in a camouflage outfit, also nursing a beer, shoots menacing glances at me.

A Portuguese Anne Murray comes over the loudspeakers. *You needed me. You needed me.*

Continuing down the road, I pass a crowded shopping district selling cheap electronics and toys imported from Miami and China. Everyone seems to be in a hurry. Imagine, then, my surprise when I turn down another street and discover an opulent Belle Époque monument, Teatro Amazonas.

Considered one of the most beautiful opera houses in the world, it was built, with marble from Italy, during the rubber boom years at the end of the nineteenth century. It's strangely quiet inside the gilded foyer, a world away from the streets. The building embodies a bygone era, and it stands as a highwater mark of extravagant indulgence in its mission to bring European high art and culture to the rainforest.

The opera house is also a reminder that this is a frontier town. Migrants—nineteenth-century Europeans included—flocked to the city from all over the world for a chance to strike it rich, bringing part of their old country with them.

Shopping at the local market is a ritual all Chinese restaurant owners share. I follow Sun early one morning to Mercado Municipal by the docks. The market is housed in a cast-iron building modelled after the iron and glass pavilions of Marché Les Halles built around the same time in Paris, in the 1880s.

Having shopped here for the past thirty years, Sun knows all the vendors by name. I'm amazed by the variety of regional fish, meat and produce available—from tropical fruits that I've never heard of to the myriad indigenous freshwater fish, including the "man-eating" piranha.

"Piranha flesh is very sweet, but the fish is very bony," he says. "Not suited to eating. Brazilians make soup out of them."

On our way back, he tells me he shops twice a week: "If you buy too much at once, like my wife, who buys for the whole month, the fridge gets overfilled and the food goes bad. The workers don't care. It's tough being a boss—it's very exhausting. I'm too tired to run it any longer, but I wouldn't pass it on to my sons."

He knows all too well how much work and dedication is involved in keeping his outpost restaurant alive in the middle of the Amazon. He made that choice more than thirty years ago.

Sun first learned about Brazil from an article in *Reader's Digest*: that the country was vast, but thinly populated, and welcomed immigrants from Asia, especially agricultural workers. Unlike the US, it was also relatively easy to get in.

During the Cold War era, the Nationalists placed Taiwan under authoritarian rule and martial law. The standoff between a "Free China" and a "Red China" on either side of the Taiwan Strait only added to the population's anxiety and insecurity. Many decided to emigrate.

Sun didn't like his job in Taiwan, and he wanted to see the world. He successfully applied for an immigrant visa by claiming he had worked on a farm, and set off for South America in 1967 aboard a freighter.

The two-month journey took him to Southeast Asia, the Indian Ocean and southern Africa. He has always been an adventurer, but every port of call—Hong Kong, Singapore, Maldives, Mauritius, Durban and Cape Town—opened his eyes to the Chinese diaspora. He also tasted Cantonese food for the first time in Penang, Malaysia, when his friend took him out for roast suckling pig.

He eventually disembarked at the São Paulo port of Santos and immediately fell in love with Brazil. The country, to him, was like a young man, full of new ideas and opportunity. It may have been underdeveloped, but it was developing faster than where he came from. Unlike the people of Taiwan, he found Brazilians to be passionate, positive and, most of all, polite. As Sun puts it, "They even say good morning to you on the bus."

Initially, Sun stayed with his cousin in São Paulo, getting to know the city and picking up Portuguese along the way. Within a year, he started to work in a succession of jobs: gas station attendant, long-distance truck driver hauling black-market goods to and from Paraguay, and company chauffeur.

But after two years, he grew tired of his nomadic life. ("I was constantly starving and barely surviving.") A friend advised him that if he were to cook Chinese food, he could go anywhere. He started out as a driver for a well-known Chinese restaurant and later became apprentice cook. Six years after his arrival in Brazil, a chef at the restaurant asked Sun to be a partner in opening a restaurant in Manaus. None of the other Chinese cooks wanted to go north, whereas he was single and carefree and had nothing to lose. He jumped at the opportunity.

Restaurante Mandarim was the first Chinese restaurant to open in the Amazon.

Sun's life changed dramatically a year later, when he took a month off to return to Taiwan for his father's seventieth birthday. He was introduced to Lina Wu at the birthday banquet.

"She was tall and very good looking, and I really liked her," he says as he flashes me a knowing smile. "It all started out as a joke. I asked her right there and then if she wanted to go abroad. She said yes, but didn't know how. I said I could help."

They were married three days later. When Lina asked what would happen if things didn't work out, Sun said they could divorce and she would still be a virgin, and he would just return to Brazil. They stayed in Taiwan for a month, each living in their respective homes.

"She was pretty brave to come here with me," he admits. "She was very young and I didn't have a career yet." His new wife had wanted to move to São Paulo, but he felt that the city was too dangerous. There were too many kidnappings and robberies, he argued. Manaus was quieter and simpler. And there were fewer Chinese.

A year after Sun and Lina returned from Taiwan, his partner at the Mandarim quit. ("He just couldn't take the Amazonian heat.") Thirty years and three boys later, the Suns have built a life for themselves in the Amazon.

—·—

"I miss the *peixarias* here," Eddy Sun says as he picks the remaining flesh off the bones. Peixaria means "fish market" in Portuguese, but in Manaus it also refers to a casual fish restaurant.

Eddy is the twentysomething middle son of the family. We are at Cabral's, a neighbourhood institution. The owner, *senhor* Cabral, is an avid fisherman who retired from Moto Honda da Amazônia a few years ago. His peixaria is basically an expanded street-food stall set up in an open area of a residential neighbourhood, next to a football field. There are three tables under a make-shift tent with dangling, naked lightbulbs. People drive across town to eat there, al fresco.

Cabral's calling card is fish. He serves two kinds, both fatty, sweet freshwater fish from the Amazon basin. Matrinxã, the bigger of the two, is wrapped in banana leaves and charcoal grilled. The pacu, a distant cousin to the omnivorous piranha, is deep-fried, but not before "a thousand cuts" are made to the body. The fish has countless tiny bones, and deep-frying makes them brittle and edible. We dip the fish into a fiery house pepper sauce and complete the meal with Brazilian-style rice—white rice fried with garlic and onion, then steamed.

"You don't get fish this delicious in the States. Everything there is so soulless and tasteless," Eddy tells me while taking another mouthful of rice. "Manaus is a fish town. When my friends and I go out, we eat at peixarias, not at churrascarias."

Having spent four years at university in Seattle, he identifies with Americans. But he is the quintessential Chinese son, returning home after getting a higher education abroad. He now works as a factory manager for a Taiwan computer chip manufacturer in the free-trade zone.

"When I was in Seattle, I acquired an American personality," he says by way of explaining his West Coast accent. "All my friends were Americans, so I hung out with them, acted like them and talked like them."

He laughingly adds he also ate like them, with forks, not chopsticks.

When he went to Taiwan for his job interview, and to visit his grand-mother, he morphed into a Chinese: "It was fun, and great to get back to my

Chinese roots. A good feeling. Deep inside I consider myself a Chinese, but Brazilian in spirit."

This fluid identity is familiar among the Chinese diaspora. We identify with certain parts of ourselves, based on experiences in different times and places. Everyone, it seems, is a chameleon. Some more than others. My speech and mannerisms change with the environment: Singaporean-accented English, Hong Kong–Cantonese loudness, Japanese quiet deference and straight-talking American mojo.

I ask Eddy about his Brazilian girlfriend.

"Well, girlfriends in different countries are different," he replies nonchalantly. "I've noticed, in America, you can't have more than one. And if you do, they'll leave you. Here in Brazil, it's the opposite. They know you probably have more than one, but it's not like they can do anything about it."

Unlike in southern Brazil, where there are a multitude of races, Manaus has very few Asians. What about racism and discrimination here? He pauses, takes a sip of beer, and acknowledges, "Yes, especially if you're the only Asian in the group. You can feel the tension. People would start yelling, 'Oh, there goes an Oriental.'"

And his reaction to these taunts?

"I've kind of adapted to that because there's not much I can do about it. So you kinda suck it up. I've a few Chinese Brazilian friends, born and raised here. But deep down, we're all Brazilians."

———

The soft-spoken and stoic Jack Sun I've come to know is not the Sun of yesteryear, and his wife was not the first woman he attracted to the Amazon. A young Polish woman named Alice fell in love with him when he was in São Paulo. She even came to Manaus twice during his first year to ask him to marry her.

"But her family opposed the marriage because I wasn't a Christian," he says. "She was a devout Christian and went to church twice a week."

Sun had no concept of religion at that time and didn't understand its importance in Brazilian life. Why didn't they marry if they were so much in love?

"She insisted I must first convert. I said, 'Let's get married first; and if I like it, I'll convert, not the other way around. Seriously, do you want to marry me or Jesus?'"

The second time Alice came up, she asked him to take her back to Taiwan. He refused. Taiwan was a conservative society, and interracial relationships were a rarity. He worried what people would think if he arrived with a blonde.

"I told her I'd be back soon. But she knew deep down that I would eventually marry a Chinese girl and forget about her."

When I ask to see Alice's photo, he tells me that he's burned them all. Any regrets?

"No. Maybe she never thought I would stay in Manaus for such a long time. And I never thought that I would be married in three days."

With no prompting from me, Sun invites me to his Taiwanese Presbyterian church and reveals that he converted to Christianity seven years ago. I'm surprised. He has never professed his faith before. Perhaps, deep down, he is still a loner and an outsider, looking for an answer to life.

The local Presbyterian church was established ten years earlier. His first association with it was purely social. The Chinese community in Manaus is so small that "if you want to socialize with other Chinese, you pretty much have to go to a church."

And since the Mandarim has always been open on Sundays, the Suns could only attend church *after* the restaurant closed, in the evenings, and on special occasions like Christmas and New Year's Eve. They eventually decided to close on Sundays so they could start attending services. Baptism came three years later.

"Christianity has really given me peace of mind," he says. "After that, we didn't go to church anymore because we believe deep down with our hearts, not just with actions."

On my last day in Manaus, I return to the Mandarim for lunch, to have the mapo tofu again. I ask Sun if he has ever thought about going back south after he retires.

"I'm getting used to everything here," he says. "The climate is nice here, no winter at all. Once you get older, you're going to hate winter."

There had been a few other Chinese restaurants in town, but his is the only one still in business. He bemoans the fact that all the others were getting old and tired, saying, "They all closed their businesses and left and no one in the next generation wanted to take over.

"I'm getting older, too, and don't have that much energy to take care of the restaurant," he continues. "Maybe in a few years, I will close the business or give it away. No matter how much I've been through, I tried my best to bring my children up, to give them an education. I just want them to have a normal life and do something else."

As Tahir Shah noted in his *House of the Tiger King: The Quest for a Lost City*, "the forest did not tolerate frailty of body or mind. Show your weakness, and it would consume you without hesitation."

Sun sounds discouraged, almost burnt out. At one time he must have had a fiery spirit of adventure to have come all the way to the heart of the rainforest to live and work. But he has found religion, serenity and fellowship on the banks of the Amazon and made this place his home.

CHAPTER 13

A Passage to India

MUMBAI AND DELHI, INDIA

I WAS ASLEEP AT A HOTEL NEAR AMSTERDAM'S SCHIPHOL AIRPORT WHEN THE second Iraq War began. I'd flown from Toronto the day before, made a same-day trip to Paris, and was scheduled to catch a morning flight to Mumbai for a rendezvous with Kwoi. But my Northwest flight was cancelled.

Airlines flying to Mumbai were being forced to fly around the war zone—good, I didn't want to get shot down by an anti-aircraft missile—adding three hours to an already long flight. This necessitated an extra crew shift, which Northwest couldn't fill.

No such problem for KLM's daily flight to Delhi, which takes a more northerly route, over Russia. I manage to get on that flight, with minutes to spare.

Two a.m. Delhi. Indira Gandhi International.

I'm in airport hell: signs and directions are unclear, porters want to grab my luggage and take it to god knows where, traffic is a nightmare and drivers from auto-rickshaws, taxis, private cars and minibuses accost me while I wait for an inter-airport transfer that never comes. I grab a taxi instead.

I had planned to overnight at the domestic airport, an hour away, where I'll be catching the first flight out. Instead, my driver talks me into sleeping over at a downtrodden hotel: "It's a small price to pay, *Baba*, for a few hours' sleep."

Something tells me that he's getting a commission on this.

"What took you so long?" Ajay Noronha asks half-jokingly the next day, when I finally walk into the coffee shop at the Holiday Inn Juhu Beach, where he and Kwoi are having breakfast.

"Ah, the war," I reply with my best Indian accent and head tilt. "The war, the horror."

Kwoi looks on with amusement. He, too, took a twenty-four-hour journey from Toronto to get here—all masked, transiting through a SARS-infected Hong Kong.

Ajay is Goan, and the cousin of a Toronto friend, Christine Pinto. He works at a television studio and makes documentaries on the side. I hired him as the second camera and soundperson on this shoot. We dive deep into production mode, with cameras and audio equipment strewn all over the hotel room. Outside, waves from the Arabian Sea are lapping onto the scenic beach. (Kwoi captured a sunset-on-the-beach scene as soon as he arrived.)

I would have liked time to relax after such a long journey. Instead, we squeeze into a yellow-and-black taxi with no air conditioning and plunge headlong into the noise, chaos and pollution of Mumbai traffic.

The monsoon season is still two months away, but the air is already humid and heavy. Fifteen million people live and work here. The city has the fast-paced business savvy of New York and churns out more movies than Hollywood.

Our taxi takes a tortuous route around the gridlock, spinning through detours and side roads. Auto-rickshaws fare better at weaving nimbly in and out of traffic. Sitting in the sauna—that's the only way to describe it—Ajay shares the story of a Canadian cameraman who was so freaked out by Mumbai that he turned around and took the next flight out. Ajay took his job.

———

It takes an hour and a half in this constant rush-hour traffic to reach Ling's Pavilion. The noise subsides as we enter Colaba, on one of the city's two peninsulas. It's the heart of British colonial Bombay—as Mumbai was then called—with a waterfront promenade that begins at the Gateway of India, an

Indian Arc de Triomphe built to commemorate the visit of King George V in 1911. Colaba is studded with high-end fashion boutiques, decades-old cafés, hip modern restaurants and outdoor stalls selling handcrafted souvenirs for tourists.

The restaurant is located on "Lansdowne Road behind the Regal Cinema," just around the corner from the heritage Taj Mahal Hotel. Lansdowne Road was renamed Mahakavi Bhushan Marg, just as Bombay changed to Mumbai, after the regional political party Shiv Sena came to power in 1995. The politicians were determined to reflect the city's Maratha heritage and to erase its British legacy.

On a trip a year earlier, Antoine Lewis, an Anglo-Indian food writer, introduced me to Ling's Pavilion. "There are more than five hundred places in the city that serve Chinese food," he said. "And this is the best and the most authentic."

That day, Lewis and I had, among other dishes, Cantonese-style salt-and-pepper jumbo prawns and Hakka-style steamed pork belly with preserved mustard greens.

The meal was simply sublime.

As I walk in this time, I can't fail to notice the restaurant interior is like a Ming tavern, straight out of a *wuxia* (martial art heroes) movie set. See the *Kill Bill: Volume 1* Tokyo nightclub scene. I expect a swordfight to break out at any moment.

The courtyard has a pebble-covered pond with a miniature waterfall. An arched Chinese bridge over the pond leads to a set of fake-stone stairs that lead to the mezzanine. The dining rooms feature Chinese decor and faux-antique Qing dynasty high-back chairs.

"People come from all over because they know we serve the best Chinese food in town," says Nini Ling, who greets me and takes me on a walk-around.

In his late fifties, Nini is a tall Chinese man with a dark complexion, sporting a light moustache and wire-rimmed glasses that give him a serious and dignified air. Although he and his brother Baba Ling are co-owners of the restaurant, Baba spends much of his time in Delhi managing the Imperial Garden and is opening another restaurant called New Nanking.

The kitchen is bright, spacious and clean. In its centre are prep stations where ingredients are lined up for each dish, ready for Chinese line cooks to stir-fry in high-firepower woks, all at Cantonese speed and efficiency. It's morning prep time. Five cooks are furiously waving around their cleavers, chopping, slicing, dicing, mincing, with spellbinding speed, on thick, round Chinese chopping blocks. It is as if I am watching a movie on fast-forward.

The art of cutting is fundamental to Chinese cooking, and the cleaver is an essential and all-purpose knife in Chinese kitchens. Chefs swear by it. It not only provides the proper weight for fast chopping but, perhaps most usefully, it is good for scooping up cut ingredients with its wide blade.

Martin Yan, chef and host of *Yan Can Cook,* uses it to the exclusion of all other knives, even when he's cooking a non-Chinese meal. He once minced a piece of ginger with one stroke of the cleaver in front of my eyes. It was like magic.

Johnny Chi, the charismatic head waiter, has been with Ling's since it opened twelve years ago, wooed by Baba after eighteen years of service at the Mandarin Restaurant across the street. Johnny's mellifluous Indian-accented English makes him a perfect restaurant ambassador.

Like when he tells me, "A lot of diamond merchants from Hong Kong come in here and they don't go to anywhere else. Sometimes they do try, but they always come back and say, 'Oh that food over there is not good. This is the only place where we get really authentic Chinese.'"

Bollywood stars and models come too. "You should see them. The girls are drop-dead gorgeous. And the boys, ooh-la-la," he says with a wink.

I'm confronted with difficult and delicious choices from a robust menu. But it's the section on sparklingly fresh seafood that intrigues me most: lobsters, crabs, prawns, oysters, mussels and squid "prepared in the style of your choice." There are dozens of options, ranging from "chili/garlic dry or gravy" to "steamed Cantonese style with minced meat, shiitake, preserved egg, and ginger."

At this time, Johnny comes out from the kitchen, with much fanfare, gripping a crab in one hand and a lobster in the other—just as in the better restaurants of Hong Kong where waiters pull *sang mang*, "live and ferocious," seafood from a tank and show it to customers before it's cooked.

"We only serve live seafood here. Look, they're moving." He wiggles the crustaceans. Their claws and legs move.

Ling's is famous for its live crab. According to Johnny, Korean and Japanese expats come several times a week "wanting really big crabs!" A customer once called from London to reserve one, weeks in advance, and Johnny didn't take him seriously until he actually showed up at the appointed hour.

I order crab in black bean sauce, jumbo lobster in ginger and scallion sauce, and deep-fried squid with chili. They're accompanied by Chinese greens ("from our own farm in Pune") as well as yee fu noodles made with Chinese mushrooms and fresh crabmeat.

I am about to order another dish when Johnny gives me an admonishing look, "I think you've ordered enough. Our portions are pretty good here. Your eyes are always bigger than your stomach. Let me get you these first. From more you can't make it less, but from less you can always make it more."

But Nini will have none of that. He insists that we try the chin jiew chicken. "My father is Chiuchownese," he adds.

For centuries, the Chiuchow (Chaozhou) region on the northeastern coast of Guangdong province has been a major point of emigration from coastal China to Taiwan and Southeast Asia. More than a million people of Chiuchow origin live in Hong Kong, comprising about a sixth of its population. Chiuchownese have their own distinctive cuisine and their own dialect—incomprehensible to other Cantonese speakers and to their Fujian neighbours to the north.

In this traditional Chiuchownese dish, diced chicken is stir-fried lightly with Sichuan chili, the *chin jiew* in the title. Loosestrife leaves, known as "pearl vegetable," served with the chicken, are deep-fried. They are dark green, crispy and paper thin. When loosestrife isn't available, as at Ling's, basil is used instead. The dish is as authentically Chiuchownese as it comes.

Members of the Chinese diaspora will always bring cooking from their native region. It's part of the link to their roots, and it's a food that will comfort them in a land so very far away.

The ever-jovial and loquacious Johnny doesn't look fifty. His fair complexion and handsome boyish looks belie his age, and the beautiful royal blue embroidered silk Chinese tunic that he's wearing makes him look even younger. For all I know, he could be a man of leisure, a playboy-about-town. His customers love him and shower him with expensive gifts from abroad. Others invite him to their homes so that they can cook for him. They treat him like family.

But Johnny has found his adopted family in the Lings.

"I'm happy here. Everyone is treated the same here, like a family. Both the brothers are good in their own ways, and both their wives are also very sweet, very friendly. Unlike other places I know, my God, they're so strict, like Hitler."

But he thinks Nini is too nice: "He's never angry, even when someone makes a mistake. Sometimes I get upset and tell him, 'You are too soft, you should be a little harsher.'"

Baba, to him, is the opposite: the extrovert and the more aggressive businessman. "But deep down, Baba is soft and kind. I remember when my mother died, Baba told me, 'Johnny, you don't need to worry. You work for me and I'll take care of you.' Those sweet words were just so touching. I'll never forget."

Later, Johnny volunteers that he's half Polish. His mother was a refugee from Warsaw when she was a teenager. Following the Soviet invasion of Poland at the onset of the Second World War, up to a million Polish nationals were deported to gulags in Siberia and other parts of the USSR. After 1942 more than 10,000 Polish refugees from Soviet camps migrated to India through circuitous routes across the Middle East. (The maharaja of Nawanagar state took in 500 orphans.)

I am reminded of the Jews who found refuge in Shanghai after fleeing Nazi Germany. They boarded ships in the south of France and sailed through the Suez Canal to Mumbai, hoping British India would take them in. When they were refused, the ships sailed on, and the Jews eventually found their way to Japanese-occupied Shanghai, where they settled in the city's Restricted Sector for Stateless Refugees, better known as the Shanghai Ghetto.

Johnny's father left Hong Kong for Mumbai in 1947, just before Indian independence. He met his future wife at a refugee camp in the Maharashtra state and brought her along.

"It was love at first sight," Johnny says. "My mother was gorgeous, and very religious. She was Roman Catholic and prayed the whole day. When I lost her, I thought I lost the whole world. But life has to go on."

Growing up biracial in India was not easy to begin with, but it must have been really difficult when neither parent was Indian. I ask whether he is ambivalent about his identity.

"No," he says without hesitation. "Wherever you are born, that's your country, that's your home, this is your land."

And he has always thought of himself as Indian.

"Except when I look at myself in the mirror. I say, 'Oh no, I'm not.'"

The next day, Johnny takes me to a restaurant where he has butter chicken for lunch almost every day. I notice that Chinese fried rice and noodle dishes take up half of the menu.

Raphael, the owner and Johnny's friend, explains: "This trend started in the late eighties when everybody wanted Chinese food. We had Chinese cooks who taught us how to prepare this food, and that's how it all started. Chinese food is lower in cholesterol, lower in oil, less chili, and all that stuff."

On our walk back, Johnny plays a prank on a street vendor. It's a friendly gesture—they know each other—but I wonder aloud, "Do you ever get into trouble?"

"It's not that I don't get into trouble," he teases. "Everyone gets into trouble, but I always get out of trouble faster than I get into it."

I tell him about the trouble Kwoi and I had gotten into that morning at Churchgate station. We were filming on the platform when a ticket collector spotted us and hauled us into the stationmaster's office. We offered to erase the offending video, and I instinctively handed over a bundle of rupees. I didn't expect a receipt, and none was given.

"Ah, you got into trouble, yeah?" He gives me an oh-I've-heard-this-before look. "You are not to photograph any government buildings or infrastructure here."

I'd encountered the same sort of trouble in Kolkata a year earlier, when I took pictures of the Writers' Building that housed the state secretariat of West Bengal. Security demanded I hand over the film, but I did a quick switch and gave them an unexposed roll instead.

But nothing beats the time I was travelling in Tibet, in the mid-eighties, when my video camera caught a pro-Tibet demonstration in Lhasa. That incriminating footage was discovered by Chinese border guards just as I was walking across to Nepal, and I was detained for three days. They finally let me go after making me erase the offending footage.

Now I understand why Ajay decided not to accompany us to Churchgate, saying he would meet us later, at the café by the cricket oval across the street. As an Indian national, he would have been in worse trouble. We are tourists, until we are not.

—•—

Nini Ling's father, Yick Sen Ling, arrived from Hong Kong in 1937 to help run his uncle's furniture and curio shop, the Chinese Museum. But his passion was cooking. He bought the Nanking across the street from his uncle's shop when it went up for sale at the end of the Second World War. That same year, he married Mary Correa, a Roman Catholic from Mangalore in southern India.

Opened in 1934, Nanking was the oldest and, at one time, the only Chinese restaurant in the city, a dining destination for diplomats and luminaries, including Prime Minister Nehru.

"It was a simple eating-house, and that is where we have our humble beginnings," Nini recalls as we sit in his tiny office on the ground floor, looking out at the courtyard. "I don't think people would come to a place like that anymore. Now, any restaurant has to be very opulent and look very expensive to be successful."

The elder Ling was well known for his generosity and kindness, which he passed on.

"We never distinguish people by their social status. We accept everybody as they are," Nini says. "It has to be a give-and-take with the staff. They have to be comfortable and happy working at your place."

In 1962, military skirmishes broke out between India and China over the Himalayan border, and the loyalty of the Chinese community in India was questioned. The Sino-Indian War lasted only a month, but it left an indelible and far-reaching impact on India's Chinese community.

"We went from being brothers to enemies overnight," Nini adds with a sigh.

Those with a Chinese surname, Chinese ancestry or even a Chinese spouse were targeted. They had to register at the local police station, and their movements were restricted. Indian companies were forbidden to employ people of Chinese descent, and Indians were discouraged from patronizing Chinese restaurants.

Nanking's business suffered, and the family feared deportation to an internment camp: "We always had a suitcase packed with all the woollies and stuff because Rajasthan was quite cold. Even though we've always considered ourselves Indian, and my dad came before India was even an independent country, we were always called *cheena*. I guess because we have Oriental features. In the eyes of the government, my mom was also considered a *cheena* because she married a Chinese."

Even when tensions cooled, stigma and suspicion remained. India's already small Chinese population was further decimated when many returned to China or emigrated abroad. Mumbai's Chinese quarters at the Naval Dockyard—where Chinese with shipbuilding skills were employed before the war—was reduced to a handful of families and a single Chinese temple.

Nini left in 1969 to study in California, where he married Nancy Nguyen, a Vietnamese immigrant. It was the height of the Vietnam War, not a good time to become American immigrants when they, too, were subject to the military draft. The couple decided to immigrate to Canada after their studies, and there Nini went on to a successful career in computer engineering.

Eighteen years later, his father asked him to return to India to take over the Nanking.

"I guess Chinese like their families to be together, and I'm the number-one son, so it was up to me to take over the business," Nini explains. "I was in a dilemma as to whether I should obey my parents or just do what I wanted to do. There was a lot of soul searching. But my wife agreed to it, so we decided to give it a try."

"I really didn't know he was Chinese," Nancy says as she joins us at the table. Warm and friendly, she mixes easily with the customers and ensures the restaurant runs smoothly. "I always thought he was Indian. Life turned out quite nice for both of us. We have a happy marriage. I never expected I'd go on to live in India, but I have been here sixteen years."

Baba's wife, Mandy Shi, who also helps manage the restaurant, brings her signature chocolate layer cake, just baked, to us. She was born to Chinese parents in Assam, a state in northeastern India that borders the Himalayan country of Bhutan. The family moved to Kolkata when her father opened a restaurant there.

Was she looking for someone Chinese to be her partner?

"No, not really, but I always felt that it would be nice if he were Chinese. We would be more suited to each other, and it would be easier to get along."

How did the Sino-Indian conflict affect her?

"We were nervous. At that time lots of Chinese were being taken away. They shut all the Chinese schools down and took the teachers away as well."

And there was no choice about her citizenship.

"If you had a Chinese father, you had to get a Chinese passport. Only in 1975, after marrying Baba, was I able to switch to an Indian passport."

The Nanking was forced to close temporarily in 1990 when the building was under renovation. By this time, Nini and Baba had opened Ling's Pavilion around the corner, and they decided it was time to close the Nanking permanently.

—•—

It's 6:30 a.m. All is quiet at the Sassoon Docks. Fishing boats have already come in overnight to unload their catch. A few pigeons flutter above. The docks, established in 1875, are a monument to Mumbai's mercantile past and its thriving fishing economy.

The Sassoons are a long line of wealthy Sephardic Jews from Baghdad ("the Rothschilds of the East") who settled in Bombay in the eighteenth century. From there, they spread across Asia, Africa and London, accumulating immense wealth through banking and trade, especially in opium. In Hong Kong, Baghdadi Jews from India—primarily the Sassoon, Kadoorie and Belilios families—worked in tandem with the British Empire and dominated business and government in the colony.

Nini is meeting us at the Sassoon Docks Fish Market, the largest in Mumbai. "Fish is something you have to get every day. Especially in Chinese cooking. It's a perishable commodity that goes bad very fast."

The noise inside is palpable, almost unbearable. The stench of fish permeates the morning air. Guts and blood drip everywhere. Homeless cats roam freely, trolling for breakfast. The voices of vendors and buyers are a jumble as they badger and yell at each other for the best bargains. One seller shows off a fish as long as he is tall.

Kwoi is in his element. He grew up near a wet market in Hong Kong ("If it ain't movin', I ain't eating it") and prefers fresh live seafood any day over "packaged dead fish from pristine North American supermarkets." I cringe as I watch him, in his rubber sandals and shorts, slosh through pools of dirty water to chase down a fishmonger with his camera. He's not afraid to go where other cinematographers dare not.

Nini is buying seafood for his brother's restaurant in Delhi, too. The seafood he selects will be packaged and shipped out on the 2 p.m. flight. (An earlier 7 a.m. flight took care of the lobsters, which came in the evening before from the Arabian Sea.)

Nini, Baba and middle brother Didi, with his Punjabi wife, all live in a high-ceilinged three-storey house a block from the restaurant. This is impressive real estate they inherited from their father, who moved the family into the home in 1942.

"We used to be able to see the Gateway of India from here, but now it's blocked by the extension of the Taj Mahal," Nini says as we gaze from his third-floor apartment window. "Today, unfortunately, there are only a few people left in the house. We have lots of room and nobody here."

The home is tastefully furnished with articles that are probably left over from his father's China Museum days: delicately carved Qing dynasty–style furniture in the living room, exquisite porcelain and lacquerware in tall display cabinets, and ink-brush painting and calligraphy scrolls hanging on the walls.

"When are you going to retire?" I pop the inevitable question.

"Yesterday," he says with a laugh. "There are a lot of things in life I'd like to do at this point. It's probably better to do it while I still can." Nini fell in love with Goa some years ago and dreams of retiring there to run a bed and breakfast.

"What's Baba like?"

"Different in every respect. He's quite an extrovert, you know, and I'm more of an introvert. I don't like the limelight too much."

"You think he's going to succeed in Delhi?"

"I'm sure he will. We've generated a tremendous amount of goodwill from my dad's time, which we are now capitalizing on and expanding."

"What about the future of the restaurant after you and Baba retire?"

"That's the million-dollar question. I don't know. I guess we'll have to cross that bridge when we come to it. That's a tough call. Once you're in the business it's really hard to get out."

———•———

Roly-poly, in his signature safari suit, Baba is the youngest of the three Ling sons, and the most adventurous—venturing into unknown and potentially risky territory to bring authentic Chinese food to upper-middle-class Indians in Delhi.

Imperial Garden offers fresh green vegetables ("Indian dishes are all overcooked vegetables"), fresh seafood ("flown in twice a day from Mumbai"), and homemade sauces ("we make our own soya and chili sauces"), and it has built a following of loyal customers.

Baba is the quintessential foodie. He loves to eat and to taste. When he was young, he used to follow his father to the market to see how fresh the food was. They would return to the kitchen, and his father would teach him to cook.

"In Indian Chinese cooking basically everything is red or everything is black. Today our food is neither red nor black, it's more on the authentic side," he says. We are sitting across from each other at a large, round table in the basement room that the restaurant uses for private banquets and overflows.

"We have a lot of steamed food, which retains the natural flavour. And to get that sort of flavour, you have to get the freshest ingredients.

"Coming into Delhi, I knew seafood was going to be the backbone of our organization, but I never knew at the time that I could sell so much seafood here," he continues. "All my Singaporean customers tell me that our chili crab is better than the real thing."

Singapore-style chili crab is made with ketchup and soy sauce, stir-fried over high heat with garlic, shallots and chili, then steamed at a high temperature and finished with green onion and lime. Sounds simple, but it's difficult to do well.

The trick is in having enough firepower (high BTU) and a well-seasoned wok to produce what the Cantonese called *wok hay*, literally "air of a wok." Grace Young, who offers a more apropos translation in the title of her book *The Breath of a Wok*, calls it "that prized, elusive, seared taste that comes only from stir-frying in a wok."

Baba believes in goodwill and karma. I remark that this is very Buddhist, but he says it has nothing to do with religion. It's just common sense. He says, "I never look at a worker as a worker. We eat together, joke together. That's why we have people working for us for so many donkey's years. Whatever I do, I do it from the bottom of my heart, yeah."

Not satisfied with his success at this restaurant, Baba is resurrecting the Nanking brand in the affluent neighbourhood of Vasant Kunj, known simply as VK. It will be three times the size of his current restaurant, adorned with traditional Chinese decor and interior lighting designed by an architect friend from Malaysia.

Everybody says Nini looks very much like his father, while Baba inherited his mother's looks and temperament.

"My mother is really the backbone of the family," Baba says. "Daddy was a weak person; anyone could bully him. But not Mommy. And the good things from both of them are coming to me today. I feel I stand out here being Chinese. India is what gave us and made us what we are today. But our roots are Chinese, and our eating habits are still Chinese."

He signals the wait staff. "Okay, let's eat."

With that, the chili crab appears at the table. It's a huge king crab, chopped into a dozen pieces, with its pre-cracked shells draped over with a sweet, salty and spicy tomato chili sauce thickened with egg. We dig in—licking the shells and scraping the orange roe into our mouths, then sucking the legs and digging in with our fingers to extract the succulently sweet meat from the claws.

The mouthfeel is incredible, the taste superb. This is what eating a crab is all about.

CHAPTER 14

Tea in the Himalayas

KOLKATA AND DARJEELING, INDIA

I'VE ALWAYS WANTED TO TAKE TEA IN DARJEELING AND GAZE AT Kangchenjunga, the world's third-highest peak.

My afternoon tea, with a chicken sandwich, on the rooftop of Hotel Valentino offers a commanding view of the valley below. I've grown up within British colonies and have taken on the habit of having afternoon tea, especially with a chicken sandwich—hand-shredded dark meat on buttered toast, as only a Brit would make it. (Don't ask me why, but chicken tastes better hand-shredded. All kinds of regional Chinese cuisines feature hand-shredded chicken dishes.)

But Kangchenjunga is nowhere to be seen. The Himalayas are shrouded in a heavy mist.

"The weather is always changing," says Samuel Yeh, the stocky sixty-year-old hotel owner with a grey flannel jacket: "One moment you get sunshine and the next moment it's very misty. But that's part of the beauty of Darjeeling."

Samuel fell in love with Darjeeling on his first visit twenty-five years ago and convinced the family to build a hotel here.

Kwoi, Ajay Noronha and I flew from Kolkata to a small airport in Bagdogra, then took a three-hour taxi ride up the mountain to Darjeeling.

The weather cooled as our four-wheel-drive traversed deep valleys, crossed torrential rapids and wound through narrow roads. We travelled through a misty, almost mystical, landscape dotted with tea plantations and monasteries.

Closer to town, the road runs parallel to the Darjeeling Himalayan Railway, a UNESCO World Heritage Site. The narrow-gauge tracks run for eighty-eight kilometres from New Jalpaiguri to Darjeeling, where they resemble a trolley route in the heart of the city, with passengers hanging out from carriage doorways.

Urban development is more intense as we get closer to town. Shops and low-rise houses line both sides of the narrow road, which makes a U-turn just before the city centre. Trucks, minibuses and taxis hog the road, honking their way up and downhill. Pedestrians often push past each other on the even narrower sidewalks. What was once a sleepy hill station nestled among majestic mountains is overdeveloped, congested and polluted.

My romance for the hill station is fast being shattered.

Where is my Shangri-La?

"During the British times you were only allowed to build cottages here," Samuel later tells me, with nostalgia. "You weren't allowed to ply the roads with heavy trucks. But now it's all changed, totally changed."

The four-storey Valentino stands on a narrow street, a steep climb from where our taxi drops us off. Three Nepalese women carry our heavy bags strapped to their heads.

It's the off-season. We seem to be the only overnight guests, but a table of young Indian customers is dining in the restaurant. They're in a festive mood and seem more interested in drinking than eating. The dining room is lit by fluorescent lights that emit a strange blue-green hue. We are like ghosts dining in semi-darkness.

The menu is typically Indo-Chinese. Vegetable pakoras (Indian fried snacks) and momos (Tibetan steamed dumplings) are offered as appetizers. Hakka chow mein is a yellow mix of cabbage, bean sprouts and noodles in a curry powder. There are a variety of meat dishes covered with a thick, brown sauce. But no seafood.

"Wow, mysterious meat cooked in an even more mysterious sauce," Kwoi says, alarmed, as he looks over to see what the other table has ordered. There's an obsession with gravy in Indo-Chinese cuisine. Nowhere else in the world are you likely to be asked whether you like your dishes "dry or with gravy."

"Hey, don't be a food snob," Ajay chides him. "This is Chinese food we Indians want."

I ask to see the kitchen. Seven Indian men and two boys are hovering around, with no Chinese in sight. Two people are actually cooking. Kwoi asks one of them to give him a "wok fire," basically a huge flambé, so he can capture a dramatic shot of "man at wok."

We place our order, asking for less gravy, wash down our meal with prodigious quantities of Kingfisher beer, then call it a night.

Darjeeling is situated near the 3,000-kilometre border between India and China. In October 1962, China invaded disputed border territory, sparking a war. Although it lasted only a month, the loyalty of Indians of Chinese descent, who had been in the country for more than two centuries, was called into question. They were treated as enemy aliens.

Soon after the end of the war, the Indian government passed an act allowing for the "apprehension and detention in custody of any person suspected of being of hostile origin." This applied to anyone with a Chinese surname or even a Chinese spouse. About 10,000 Chinese Indians were held at desert internment camps in Rajasthan, a seven-day train ride, in bare boxcars, from Kolkata. Like the Ling family, Samuel remembers his bags were always packed, not knowing when a knock on the door would come.

"They came at night, without notice, and put you in a truck. We were treated like prisoners of war," Samuel says without rancour.

The detainees were accused of being spies, but not a single charge held up. In 1964, many were forcibly and arbitrarily deported, breaking up their families. It wasn't until four years later that the last of these prisoners was released.

After the war, Chinese Indians could not hold any job except in the restaurant, tanning and shoemaking industries. Their movements were restricted. They were required to report to designated police stations once a month, and until the mid-1990s they had to apply for special permits to travel more than a few kilometres from their homes.

"If you were born and bred in Kolkata, you stayed in Kolkata," Samuel says. "You were not allowed to go anywhere outside the city. It was a very difficult period."

Many left, and their numbers in all of India dwindled from 30,000 to about 3,000. Those who stayed struggled to survive despite great hardships. But survive they did, carving out new lives for themselves.

I tell Samuel that Japanese Canadians and Japanese Americans, too, were deemed enemy aliens after the Pearl Harbor attack, put in internment camps in the interior of the countries and stripped of their civil rights.

—·—

I return to Kolkata to visit three of Samuel's brothers—Samson, Stephen and Henry—at the New Embassy Restaurant, located on Chowringhee Road, which runs along the eastern edge of the Maidan. Often referred to as the "Lungs of Kolkata," the Maidan is an expansive green space in the middle of an otherwise polluted city. Inside the park sits the white-marbled Victoria Memorial, the city's most celebrated landmark. The domed building, now a museum, was built to commemorate Queen Victoria's reign—and it's probably the country's starkest reminder of the British Raj.

Residents of Kolkata are well known for their volatile political activism and have frequently elected leftist governments. No surprise that, on the way to the restaurant, we are confronted by an anti-war demonstration, staged by the Communist Party, to protest against the second Iraq War—in front of the US consulate located on, irony of ironies, Ho Chi Minh Road. Red flags flutter everywhere, shimmering in the golden glow of a late-afternoon sun, while the voices of protest from trucks equipped with loudspeakers drown out the cacophonous traffic.

The single-storey New Embassy Restaurant stands out among its taller neighbours with its pagoda-style overhang and baby-blue arched door with red Chinese decor. The windowless, white-tiled dining room is small, seating fewer than thirty, dimly lit by fluorescent lights and cooled with two air-conditioning units. When customers enter through the swinging front doors, a bit of natural light sneaks into the room. Several tables of office workers are quietly having lunch.

After the dust, the heat and the noise, the restaurant feels like an oasis.

"Our menu is a little different from the one in Darjeeling," Samson Yeh says as he greets me. Sturdy, balding, with a greying moustache and an air of authority, he is the sixty-four-year-old patriarch of the family of seven brothers and four sisters. Four of the brothers run the New Embassy and its sister restaurant, Valentino, in Darjeeling.

The menu is ambitious, featuring more than 100 dishes: a dozen options in each category of soup, rice, noodles, prawns, fish, chicken and crab, and more than twenty vegetarian dishes including, in a nod to India, chili paneer. There are only three pork dishes. And this being a majority Hindu country, there's no beef on the menu.

Indo-Chinese cuisine was born when Chinese immigrants had to stretch their cooking to accommodate a new environment and new ingredients. Cantonese and Hakka cuisine became currified, and chili, coriander and cumin made their way into the wok. Deep-frying became prevalent.

I order a few items from the menu to sample the cuisine: chili chicken, paneer in garlic sauce, Manchurian fish. Like what I had up in Darjeeling, everything is coated in a thick, brown gravy.

"Yes, it's our native Hakka cooking adapted to the tastes of our Indian brothers and sisters," Samson tells me at the end of the meal. "Our restaurant can't depend on Chinese customers; hardly any of them come. My customers are 200 per cent Indian."

Then he adds, "They like Chinese food, but mostly they like chili chicken."

I'm glad he mentions chili chicken. I've eaten it so often in Toronto that I am determined to track down the original recipe on this trip.

"This dish was created by our Hakka people a generation ago," he explains. "They thought it suitable for the local people. Indians like a little bit of chili hotness. They like their chicken fried. And if you put some fermented soybean paste on top of it, it all becomes very tasty, you see."

There are 1,001 ways to make chili chicken. This is the New Embassy way: chicken pieces are lightly coated in flour and fried until they are golden brown and crispy. Then, they are stir-fried with onion, ginger, garlic, red and green chilies, cumin and coriander powder. The sauce goes in last: dark soy, rice vinegar, honey and a healthy dollop of fermented soybean paste, along with the addition of chopped cilantro before serving.

Can a dish not created in China be considered authentically Chinese?

Like chili chicken, General Tso's chicken wasn't created in China— people in Hunan, the home province of General Tso Tsung-t'ang, a Qing dynasty statesman and military leader, have never heard of it. In researching for her book *The Fortune Cookie Chronicles*, Jennifer 8. Lee uncovered two competing claims for the origin of this dish. Both from New York City, in the 1970s.

"You can tell it's American from the deep-frying, the sweetness, and the broccoli," Jennifer told me. "Broccoli is not a Chinese vegetable, and General Tso certainly never saw a stalk of broccoli in his life."

So, what, in fact, constitutes a *good* Chinese dish? According to Samson, "Chinese food must have colour, aroma and taste. You'll have a good dish with the three combined. Missing any of these elements, then it's not up to standards."

Running a restaurant with such an ambitious menu is daunting, and it's doubly challenging in a small and poorly equipped kitchen with only one wok. I ask how difficult it is to train his Indian staff.

"We don't allow them to work at the wok right away. They wash dishes first, then they learn prep work—which ingredients go with what dish and how much. Only after that do we let them stand by the wok to watch and learn."

Samson comes across as a stern village schoolteacher. Kwoi catches him on camera slapping an Indian employee on the head when a dish doesn't taste just right. As Samson explains it, "My policy is that if you satisfy yourself, then you can satisfy customers. If you're not satisfied, the customers won't be satisfied."

Two of the Yeh brothers, Stephen and Henry, work in the kitchen. At the end of a very busy day, I gather the three brothers together in the dining room and ask whether they ever fight.

"We do fight sometimes, but we don't keep it inside or take it seriously," Samson is the first to admit.

"There will always be clanging when you wash dishes," Stephen chimes in. "But as long as dishes are cleaned, it's okay."

"Because we're Hakka, we're a big family," says Henry. "We have to be very united—otherwise we'll be defeated."

After a pause, the patriarch sums up, "Many of the Yehs here are related. We have the largest extended family in all of India."

———

Samson's Hakka grandfather came from Meixian county in Guangdong and opened a shoemaking shop in Kolkata. Like many who had emigrated overseas, Grandfather Yeh went back to China to father his children. Samson's father arrived in India as a nine-year-old and eventually succeeded his father and expanded the shoemaking business substantially.

Samson has worked in the family business since the age of fifteen. His father died four years after that, and he became the patriarch of the family: "I know this was my responsibility. I am the oldest child in my family, I have to take care of everyone. I'm very dutiful and I always try to face all the difficulties, never try to avoid them."

With the decline of the shoemaking industry in the early seventies, the brothers decided to go into the restaurant business and opened the New Embassy.

Hakka people take pride in their large, conservative families. The entire Hakka family often will live in a single household. Marriages are usually encouraged or arranged with other Hakka, to keep it all in the clan, so to speak.

The Embassy Villa, a five-storey family house the Yeh family built, is on a side street not far from the Maidan. Shady tropical plants line the lane leading to the front door. Inside, each of the floors is delicately adorned with traditional Chinese designs and motifs. Each of the four brothers in the restaurant business occupies one floor, with his family. An open staircase connects the floors and unites the family home. (Three other brothers live elsewhere. The sisters, alas, don't count, as they have married out of the family.)

Hakka *tulou*, commonly known as "roundhouses," are rural dwellings unique to the Hakka in the mountainous areas in southeastern Fujian province. Built as early as the twelfth century, they are enclosed earthen buildings, usually circular in structure, and can be up to five storeys high and house up to 800 people, like a medieval fortified city. (In the 1980s, the CIA thought that they were missile silos.)

Collectively, these roundhouses have been declared a UNESCO World Heritage Site, deemed "exceptional examples of a building tradition and function exemplifying a particular type of communal living and defensive organization in a harmonious relationship with their environment."

That pretty much sums up the essence of Hakka families everywhere.

"The Chinese in India used to live in miserable conditions," Samson says. "You've been to many places around the world, and you can see how the Chinese endure hardships without complaints. We are patient, we persevere. We are the Sons of the Yellow Emperor, Descendants of the Dragon. We all start from scratch and work hard to achieve our goals. Like the saying 'Slowly, slowly, catchy monkey.'

"We adapt to new environments, not the other way around," he adds.

The Chinese began to arrive in Kolkata, then called Calcutta, in 1778, around the same time the British designated the city as the capital of British India. It is from this "Shining Jewel in the Empire" that Britain extended its rule, via the East India Company, east to Singapore and what was then known as Malaya. In the aftermath of the Opium Wars, its reach extended to Hong

Kong, which the Brits forced China to cede for ninety-nine years. (Hong Kong was handed back to China in 1997.)

Situated in the state of West Bengal in northeastern India, Kolkata is the most accessible city by land from China. Almost anyone with Chinese heritage in India can trace their roots back to what is now the fountainhead of their community. The Chinese population in the city peaked at 20,000 before it fell, after the 1962 Sino-Indian War, to only 2,000 today.

As I drive along Sun Yat Sen Street, named for the founder of modern China, I see the remains of a once-vibrant Chinese district. The area looks empty and dilapidated, with abandoned temples and boarded-up stores.

There is, however, a buzz of activity at the breakfast bazaar. You can have your fill of puff pastries, spring rolls and pork buns standing in the middle of the street or stroll around the small wet market watching shoppers and vendors haggle, as neighbours look on while sipping their chai.

Hakka Chinese in India specialize in two occupational niches: shoemaking and tanning. The Hindu caste system forbids work with leather—considered unclean—for all but the Untouchables. Chinese have no problem scooping up work that Hindus will not touch. Leather work is one of the major industries of West Bengal, providing employment to tens of thousands of Untouchables.

I visit Jessica Yeh and her father, Shih Yen Yeh, at his Ah Tiam Tannery in Tangra. Jessica is a university student in Toronto, but she is home for the summer break. When I was looking around for a contact in India's Hakka community, a professor friend of mine introduced me to Jessica, who is part of the clan that runs the New Embassy.

Tangra is formerly a marshy low-lying land east of the city. Around 1910, a handful of Chinese shoemakers moved there to start their own leather production plants and to work as shoemakers. The enclave grew further in the 1950s when the Chinese community, facing displacement from central Kolkata, relocated there. It once housed more than 600 Hakka Chinese tanneries.

The first thing I notice is the stench in the air and the dirty water flowing all over the ground and through storm gutters on the side of the road:

pollution emanating from the tanneries. Otherwise, the area is a fully functioning Chinatown, with Chinese and English schools, retail and wholesale stores, Buddhist temples, restaurants and associations, as well as a Guan Di temple, omnipresent in Chinatowns around the world.

Jessica's father is Samson's first cousin. He treats me to a meal at Kimfa Restaurant. We have Hakka chow mein, chili chicken (said to be created right here in Tangra) and another Tangra original, chicken lollipops. The "lollipop" is essentially a chicken drumette, with the meat cut loose from the bone end and pushed up, creating a lollipop appearance. It's eaten with a Szechuan sauce.

"I am sorry that the smell is so bad around here," the elder Yeh says. "We have no choice. Hakka people are either cobblers or tanners in this country."

The Indo-Chinese community now calls Tangra home, but there is a question as to how long this will last. Once again, the Indian government has created a feeling of instability for their community. Several years earlier, it announced a timetable, requiring them to move out of Tangra to the eastern fringe of Kolkata. Officials claimed the tanneries are environmental hazards. Yet again, they are facing an uncertain future, with another dislocation and a further test of their adaptability and resilience.

It's Kwoi's birthday. On the way back from Tangra, Ajay and I buy a cake from a bakery on Park Street and celebrate the occasion with a thali dinner at Kewpie's, a Bengali restaurant. This is the second time we have marked Kwoi's birthday while eating our way around the world.

—•—

Curiously, each of the distinct Chinese groups in India found a niche: Cantonese commonly were carpenters; Hakka, cobblers and tanners; people from Hubei, who came during the Sino-Japanese war, dentists; and people from Shandong, silk traders.

An occupation popular with all these groups is restaurateur, and so many Chinese women own beauty salons that they almost have a monopoly in Kolkata. This morning Samson takes me to the Sunflower Beauty Salon, which his wife Patsy runs with her two sisters-in-law—wives of Stephen and Samuel—as well as her daughter-in-law, Sabina.

A sociable young woman, Sabina is Nepalese and from Darjeeling. She met Samson's son David there, in college. The couple live on the same floor of the villa as Samson and Patsy. I am curious about her experience marrying into this large Hakka family and the cultural adaptation that is expected of her.

"To be frank, I have had no adjustment problem marrying into this family," she says while leaning at the cash desk. "Except when it comes to working. We open at seven and close at seven. I used to cry a lot whenever my mother-in-law was not around and nagged my husband because I wasn't used to working this hard."

Did her parents have a problem with her marrying a Chinese Indian?

"Not really. I thought my parents would have a problem, but they were very understanding. They had only one wish: they wanted me to get married according to our Buddhist custom, and that's what we did in Darjeeling. And later we had a church wedding here in Kolkata. My father is Buddhist, my mother is Hindu, and my husband is a Christian."

———

Born in India, Samuel Yeh feels no ambivalence about where his future lies. He loves the country, and he loves Darjeeling: "This is our homeland. We're staying here, our homes are here, our land is here."

There is often a perception that India, a functional democracy, lags far behind China in social development and poverty eradication. "The problem is that Indians are too proud," he explains. "They are too proud to admit that they are behind."

Democracy, he tells me, is a nice thing, but sometimes you need an authoritarian regime to make things work. He admires Indira Gandhi, who ruled India with an iron fist. "That was the medicine that India needed to take herself out of poverty and underdevelopment, and to join the developed world."

For years, Chinese Indians lived under British rule and were denied citizenship. They carried on their lives with passports from the Republic of China, issued by Taiwan, which they either carried on arrival or got passed down from their fathers.

After India's independence in 1947, Chinese Indians were considered ethnically and nationalistically distinct. Those born before independence had to apply for Indian passports, which were not easily granted.

"Even if you were born and brought up in India, you're still categorized as Chinese. You are forever a foreigner," Samuel bemoans. "They just put you under the Chinese category. They don't care. You're of Chinese descent, you should be in that group."

He recounts visits to other parts of India where, with a single glance, hotel receptionists registered him as a foreigner. He protested that he is Indian and has citizenship papers to prove it. At first, they didn't believe him, but when he spoke in Hindi, they started smiling, "Yes, you're Indian."

"So, do you consider yourself Chinese or Indian?" I ask.

"I'm Chinese, of course," he says. "But if you want to continue to stay in India, you have to obtain citizenship. You have to call yourself Indian."

—•—

"I guess you can say that we have an Indian accent," Robert Yap says with a laugh when I ask him what makes Indo-Hakka people different from all the other Hakka in Toronto.

I go along with the quip: "It's hard to get it mixed up with the Jamaican accent."

It is estimated that there are more than 25,000 Hakka immigrants in Toronto, with those from Jamaica and India comprising 75 per cent of the community. Others come from countries such as Mauritius, South Africa, Trinidad, Peru and Suriname. There are also Hakka in Tahiti, but I doubt many of them have made it to Toronto.

Yap and I have lunch at Federick's, which has a predominantly South Asian clientele. The eatery is one of many Indo-Hakka restaurants that sprang up in Toronto in the 1990s, particularly in areas with a large concentration of South Asian immigrants. (For reasons no one can explain to me, Federick's and Waldorf are among the most common names for Chinese restaurants in India.)

In Toronto, Indo-Chinese is synonymous with Indo-Hakka—a cuisine that amalgamated the subtlety of Chinese cooking with the heat of India.

We have Hakka fried rice, chili chicken and Manchurian beef. Manchurian sauce, reportedly created by Nelson Wang at his China Garden in Mumbai, is made by simmering garlic, ginger, sugar, soy and cayenne or red chili paste. It is a spicy cousin of the sticky sweet-and-sour sauce that coats billions of American Chinese chicken balls.

"This is a lunchtime hangout for Indian and Pakistani taxi drivers," he says between mouthfuls of fried rice. "They come here because they crave the kind of Chinese food they knew back home."

Yap's father immigrated to India from Meixian county in Guangdong province at a young age, in 1937. The elder Yap was in the dry cleaning and restaurant businesses, and the principal of two Chinese schools. He was also president of the Overseas Chinese Association of India and acted as the de facto representative of the Taiwan government in Kolkata, processing visas, among other consular duties. (In 1950, India became the second non-Communist country to recognize Mao's China, and Taiwan's diplomatic status was downgraded from embassy to representative office.)

Yap says that "1962 was a very scary time. It lasted for more than fifteen years. Everybody wanted to leave."

He came to Canada in 1973, as an eighteen-year-old, studied engineering, and eventually rose within the ranks to become a power utility executive. His father immigrated to Toronto a few years after him but continued to go back to Kolkata to run the family business. The entire family—seven brothers and two sisters—eventually came to Canada.

"We have a very large family here," he says. "I know Samson Yeh's family well . . . Most of their children are over here." (Yeh and Yap are different phonetic renderings of same surname in Chinese, meaning "leaf." Yeh is the Mandarin pronunciation, while Yap is in the Hakka dialect.)

Among what may be the most diasporic people on Earth—the Chinese—the Hakka are perhaps the most diasporic regional or linguistic subgroup. From several counties in Guangdong and Fujian provinces in southern China, Hakka migrated first to Southeast Asia in the eighteenth century; then, in the nineteenth century, to areas around the Indian Ocean and the South Pacific, as well as to the Caribbean and the Americas.

There are estimates of anywhere from 80 to 100 million Hakka around the world.

Chinese have been emigrating for centuries, seeking a second homeland in which to raise their families free of war, political strife and famine. The generations that follow may find themselves migrating again from their adopted country. Now "two degrees" from China, they become, for the lack of a better term, second-generation transnational migrants.

This is especially prevalent among second- and third-generation Chinese in post-colonial Commonwealth countries, like those who came to Canada in search of prosperity and stability, hoping to avoid social unrest, political turmoil and ethnic persecution.

But it hasn't always been an easy road. In 1979, a television network perpetuated anti-Chinese racism when it broadcast a newsmagazine segment called "Campus Giveaway," alleging Chinese Canadian university students were taking the rightful places of Canadians. In fact, these "foreign students" were Canadians themselves, either citizens or immigrants. The story was met with protests, with which I was involved, resulting in a national movement to demand equality for Chinese Canadians.

Yap are I are both of the same generation, each of us immigrating to Canada in the 1970s. So this fight for equality came at the right time, for us. We all come from different places, but we all end up in our "rightful place" in the world.

CHAPTER 15

Last Tango in Argentina

BUENOS AIRES, ARGENTINA

"WOULD YOU LIKE TO RETIRE TO CHINA?" I ASK THE SEVENTY-ONE-YEAR-OLD man sitting next to me as our taxi meanders down the streets of Buenos Aires. A light rain falls.

"I can't go home. It's too complicated. There are too many problems every time I go back," says Foo-Ching Chiang from the shadowy interior of the cab. Through rain-splattered windows, yellow streetlight beams dance across his weathered face.

Chiang has been in Argentina for more than half of his life. I found him through six degrees of separation. My sister has a friend whose aunt, Eileen, lives in Rio de Janeiro. It was during a lunch with Auntie Eileen, within view of Pão de Açúcar, that she brought up that her stepson lives in Buenos Aires.

This connection in Argentina prompted me to send Kwoi, my cinematographer, to scout ahead. Kwoi was in a cyber-relationship with a woman from Buenos Aires, and I was all too happy to send him there for a Christmas "getting-to-know-you." That was when he connected with the stepson, Stephen Wu, who took him to meet his good friend of many years, Foo-Ching Chiang.

I ask Chiang if Argentina is his home. Today is the feast day of Santa Ana, and we have just come from a San Telmo church concert that opened with the national anthem.

"Yes and no. For me the concept of home is fading," he says. "I empathize with your internationalism. It's the only way out. The Earth is so small and our time here so quick. I see myself as a member of this Earth, so, for me, the concept of national boundaries is troubling."

"A lot of people want to be buried in China," I say, not expecting an answer.

"I told my children to scatter my ashes to the sea." The rain is pelting harder against the taxi window, and I've found my kindred spirit.

The soft winter light, faint smell of Gauloises in the air, and misty vistas of a lush green countryside on the ride in remind me of taxi rides from Paris's Charles de Gaulle airport. With its cosmopolitan air, fashion sense and boulevard cafés, Buenos Aires lives up to its reputation as the Paris of South America. Even its Jewish garment district, with *milongas* (tango dance halls) in abandoned lofts, reminds me of Paris's Thirteenth Arrondissement.

Through another three degrees of diasporic separation, Kwoi found us a gorgeous, high-ceilinged Parisian-style apartment in the city. The apartment belongs to a French diplomat, Valerie Tehio. She and her Chinese writer-husband are on vacation with their toddler son, leaving us this luxurious accommodation, which even comes with a maid who dutifully lays out breakfast every morning.

Ajay Noronha and his wife, Sarada Ramaseshan, are already waiting for us at the apartment when we arrive. The couple came all the way from Mumbai for this shoot, arriving the day before via Air Canada's nightly Toronto-to-São Paulo non-stop. It's the only way I could get our Indian nationals to South America without transiting through the post-9/11 US.

Luz Algranti arrives last, just as we are sitting down for breakfast. She's our local fixer and interpreter, whom Kwoi found through his now former cyber-girlfriend. Sometimes the film crew falls into place like pieces of a jigsaw puzzle.

Casa China is a three-storey building on Calle Viamonte, just blocks from Teatro Colón in the heart of Buenos Aires. Two heavy red doors, each adorned with the Chinese character for "fortune," open to a skylit inner courtyard decorated with Chinese artifacts and motifs. A half-moon arch, like those in classical Chinese gardens, leads to the restaurant hall.

Chiang conceived the concept of Casa China a few years after he arrived in Argentina in 1964. He imagined it as a home away from home for the handful of Taiwanese families who lived there at the time. It would become a gathering place for future generations to enjoy the food and to socialize with each other.

"The future of the world rests with those who can hand over to future generations the essence of life and hope," he wrote in his essay "The Casa China Story." He also envisioned that, once the People's Republic of China established diplomatic relations with Argentina, more Chinese would make their way here and he would expand Casa China, bringing vibrant Chinese cultural centres to different cities.

In this remaining Casa China in Buenos Aires, tai chi, cooking and Chinese medicine classes are held on the second floor. There's even a Sunday-evening tango class for Chinese immigrants. Chiang lives on the third floor.

María Alejandra Gerolami has been working at Casa China for four years. This afternoon, dressed in a blue Chinese tunic, she's demonstrating the iconic Chinese culinary export chow fan (fried rice).

A long prep table with a propane stove is set up in the hall upstairs. She works quickly and offers up cooking tips—always use cold, preferably two- or three-day-old rice; break up the rice chunks with your spatula; cook the harder vegetables first, then beat in the eggs. As she melds ingredients such as water chestnuts, bamboo shoots and Chinese mushrooms into the dish,

María describes the culinary alchemy of arriving at the right mix of colours, taste and aroma.

Fried rice is perhaps the most versatile and the most encompassing of all Chinese dishes. As long as your rice is done right, you can mix in any kind of ingredients during the stir-frying. My favourite is lap cheong (Chinese sausage). And there are just as many styles: Yeung Chow (Yangzhou), Hokkien (Fujian), Chiuchow (Chaozhou), Hakka, Peruvian and—only in India—Singaporean.

"Everyone is very happy when they leave here," María explains to the class. "The food is prepared based on where people are coming from. There're people who like more vegetables, there're people who don't eat pork, or spicy food. It all depends on who's here. Okay, I will write it down step-by-step for you. *Sin preocupaciones*." No worries.

Chiang now takes me to the basement kitchen to meet his chief cook Yafang Jiang. He introduces her as his niece from China, and there's no reason to doubt him. After all, they have the same surnames—Jiang and Chiang being the Mainland and Taiwanese romanization, respectively, of the Chinese character for "river."

However, this kind of family relationship can sometimes be stretched. Chinese restaurant owners around the world have been known to bring over distant relatives—even unrelated people with the same surnames from their own villages—to work at their establishments. It's a way out of China, and into immediate livelihoods, for these new immigrants.

He now proves that he is still the master of making spring roll skin.

"The secret is when you mix the flour with the water, it should neither be too dry, nor too wet. You have to wait a few hours, then you can do it." He spreads a dollop of dough onto a flat, round pan. "The temperature of the pan has to be just right. If it's not hot enough, the dough will stick."

"The dough is a little wet today," his chief cook comments, to no one in particular.

So, the flour mix can be different from day to day. And the art of making paper-thin spring roll skin lies in adjusting to the variations in every batch depending on the ambient moisture. Chiang continues to make more skin on the flat stove as he talks, until his niece asks him to stop—he is in her way.

"I kind of do this as a daily physical exercise," he says with a laugh. "I feel that as long as we have these skills, we'll have no problem surviving here."

On December 13, 1937, after the outbreak of the Sino-Japanese War, Japanese soldiers marched through Nanjing's city gate and, in a matter of weeks, killed more than 200,000 civilians in what is known as the Nanking Massacre. Shortly after that, Chiang was sent there to live with relatives. He was seven.

Chiang was born in 1931, in Jiangsu province in eastern China, and was orphaned during the early stages of the Chinese Civil War between the Nationalist government and insurgent Communist forces. By that time, Nanjing was in Japanese-occupied territory and the seat of the collaborationist government. But no one talked about the horrific event, not even his relatives years later.

Following the end of the Second World War, Chiang lived for a short time in Shanghai before moving to Taiwan in 1947, when he was sixteen. It was two years later that Chiang Kai-shek's Nationalists fled to Taiwan.

The Nationalists controlled the social, cultural and political agenda in Taiwan, which had been populated by Chinese who had mass migrated across the Taiwan Strait after Dutch colonizers were expelled in 1662. (The Dutch called the island Formosa, a name that was commonly used until the 1970s.)

Life in Taiwan was not happy for Chiang.

He never finished school and only held odd jobs. When asked to join the governing Nationalist Party, the Kuomintang, he refused, not wanting to be drawn into the "whirlpool of politics." The Kuomintang's preoccupation was with recovering the Chinese mainland from the "Communist bandits." Chiang's sympathies, however, lay with local Taiwanese who resented the new arrivals.

"It was very childish. You were either a friend or an enemy—there was no in-between," he says, evoking the sentiments of a young generation in Taiwan at that time. The Communists had already established a new republic on the mainland, and these young people didn't see the point of fighting over a lost cause.

Chiang was soon conscripted and served on the tiny island of Jinmen, the first line of defense in southwestern Taiwan, within shelling distance of China's guns across the strait. He brought along an English dictionary and a copy of *The Old Man and the Sea*.

Like his hero Hemingway, Chiang has always been his own man—self-taught, a loner, a romantic and a non-conformist. It was during his time in the barracks that he wrote a thirty-eight-page love letter to his fiancée detailing the cruelties and injustices of war. For his pacifist rebellion, he landed in solitary confinement for four months.

Chiang married his fiancée after his discharge but could not hold down a regular job. After the birth of their two children in the late 1950s, he saw no future in Taiwan and wanted to leave the island, but travelling abroad was restricted. An Argentine diplomat couple he had met in Taipei arranged for the family to migrate to Argentina.

—◦—

La Boca once was a working-class *barrio* settled by Italian immigrants from Genoa. Now it's an artists' colony and tourist destination with rows of brightly painted houses by the dock. The rough neighbourhood is home to Maradona's equally rough Boca Juniors *fútbol* team—two police officers come by to tell us to watch our camera gear.

I bring Chiang to the dockside in the old port—close to where his family would have disembarked forty years earlier after their month-long journey from Taiwan—and ask about his first impression of the New World.

"*Las chicas como estrellas en el cielo*," Chiang enthuses. Girls like stars in the sky.

I am interviewing him in Spanish through our interpreter, Luz. I grew up in an English-speaking world and am always fascinated by Chinese diasporic communities who speak in languages other than English. Chiang's Spanish is serviceable, using mostly the present tense, often dropping plurals and auxiliary verbs, and mixing up the genders. All this I would learn from my translator weeks after I came back from South America. It's okay, I would tell her—the Chinese language has no conjugated verbs or gendered nouns.

"We didn't know that Buenos Aires was so modern and so beautiful," he continues. "And in truth, I had a lot of faith because the city was so big and it surely had space for us."

When he arrived, there were only about 200 Chinese in Buenos Aires, mostly Cantonese. He noticed they were not well off, "so they had to work very hard." I ask about the Chinese grocery and electronic goods stores in Belgrano, where the city's Chinatown is located.

"That came later, settled by immigrants from Taiwan and China in the 1980s," he tells me.

After a few months of odd jobs, Chiang moved his family to the provincial capital of Córdoba, where the city is smaller and the people closer and friendlier. When he approached the American consulate for work, he was told there were no jobs for him because he did not speak Spanish.

But, could he cook?

Just like that, he was hired to prepare family meals at the consulate. He thus joined a long line of Chinese immigrant cooks without a culinary background.

Like so many Chinese immigrants to Latin America before him, Chiang became a small-scale purveyor of empanaditas, turnovers, made from his home kitchen. It was the consul general who encouraged him to turn these little empanadas into spring rolls. Soon, with the help of his wife, he set up a miniature factory making up to 600 spring rolls a day.

He eventually moved his family back to Buenos Aires, convinced that there was a bigger market there. With word of mouth and publicity, he began to mass-produce frozen spring rolls for supermarket chains—"one was owned by the Rockefellers"—becoming the Spring Roll King of Argentina.

—-—

The journey to South America had opened Chiang's eyes to the world of the Chinese diaspora. The freighter his family took from Taiwan stopped in Hong Kong, Singapore, Malaysia, Mauritius, Mozambique and South Africa before rounding the Cape of Good Hope to South America. He was surprised to find Chinese settlers everywhere: Port Louis, Maputo, Durban, Cape Town, even São Paulo and Montevideo.

Taiwanese of Chiang's generation, who came in the 1950s and 1960s, were not the first Chinese immigrants to settle in Argentina. The first wave, mostly Cantonese-speaking from southeast coastal regions of Guangdong province, came between 1919 and 1949. But Chiang now tells me that a tribe of Chinese of unknown provenance had come from France after the First World War to settle in the northeast region of Chaco, near Paraguay.

They became *gauchos*, Argentine cowboys.

It was the Chinese in Chaco who made a profound impression on Chiang. When he made a trip there, he saw children two generations removed who could not speak Chinese. He thought about his own children: "If they don't speak Chinese, the Chinese culture will be lost."

I bring up the more than 140,000 workers in the Chinese Labour Corps, recruited by the British and French during the First World War to provide support work and manual labour behind front lines. Most of them were repatriated back to China after the war, but could some of them have made their way to Argentina? He is aware of them but insists that those who came to Chaco were not from the same province in China as those behind the front lines in Europe, nor had they ever served in France.

In the late 1960s, Chiang made several extensive trips around the world "to look at how other Chinese migrants live." His curiosity into the Chinese diaspora has informed his worldview. He learned, for example, about how racism pushed Chinese railroad workers to migrate from the United States to Central and South America—but not to Brazil or Argentina, he hastens to add, because of two continental barriers: the Andes and the Amazon.

After his travels, he crafted a cultural manifesto, and he sent me a copy before I arrived in Argentina. The document, written in Chinese and translated into Spanish and English, offers his vision of Chinese culture playing a big part in "life harmony and world peace." It delves into, among other things, the yin and yang of life forces and the preservation of 5,000 years of Chinese culture, and draws inspiration from *Future Shock*, *The Aquarian Conspiracy* and the philosophies of Russell and Krishnamurti.

He also cites Beethoven's Ninth Symphony as a major influence in his life, quoting Friedrich Schiller's poem "Ode to Joy," which Beethoven used in the final choral movement of the symphony:

> *Thy magic power re-unites*
> *all that custom has divided*
> *all men become brothers*
> *under the sway of thy gentle wings.*

I quote back a Chinese saying: "Within four seas, all men are brothers."

—•—

"It's just a short hop across the Andes," says Chia-Yin Chiang, who flew in from Santiago de Chile in the morning for one of her frequent visits with Chiang. She comes to see her father to have "one of these long conversations that both of us enjoy having from time to time."

In her mid-forties, and having lived away from home for the past fifteen years, Chia-Yin appreciates the opportunity to spend time with her father. I find all this very touching and tell her so. Chinese men of a certain generation are not usually open and expressive enough to have long chats with their daughters like that.

"Our family has become disjointed. We don't have time to meet each other. One lives in the north, the other in the south. How do we maintain our family unity?" she says.

We are on the balcony overlooking the skylit courtyard just outside Chiang's living quarters. While setting up, Kwoi peeks inside. The room is filled with old and dusty furniture, unkempt and stockpiled with old Chinese newspapers. It reminds him of depressing places where "elderly uncles" lived their remaining years in 1950s Hong Kong.

"My father had rough times in life, first in his childhood during the Sino-Japanese War, and later in Taiwan during the Cold War, then coming to Argentina without knowing anyone," Chia-Yin continues. "But I think that has strengthened him instead of weakened him. It has provided him with unbounded optimism about life.

"Argentina is not an easy country to live in. In 2002 we had the worst situation," she adds. Chia-Yin, a UN economic development specialist, is referring to the country's economic crisis in which the peso lost more than half of its value.

"Every time I called and told him that I worry for him, he would say 'Why worry? This is normal. We've always lived like this, in uncertainty, in chaos, so you shouldn't be too worried.'"

Chia-Yin stood out as *china*. When they were growing up in Córdoba, she and her younger brother were the only Asians among the 2,000 students in their school. Classmates came up to her to stroke her hair and look at her eyes. "I felt like a Martian," she recalls. "In fact, I escaped from school one time feeling uncomfortable and unwanted."

She did not date during her adolescence—she was always helping out in the restaurant, working at the dessert table when she was nine and helping out in the dining room at age thirteen. When she was nineteen, she was left in charge of the restaurant for three months while her father went on a world tour with her brother. "Those were the hardest months of my life."

She anticipates where I'm going next with my interview: "Yes, of course, my father expected me to marry a Chinese. When I was twenty-one, he went to China and brought the son of a childhood friend of his to Argentina, thinking that we would probably hit it off."

She didn't dislike the young man—they spoke the same language and he was very pleasant. However, he had grown up in China, while she's from the West. "We didn't have the same outlook in life. We were just incompatible."

Partly to get away from her father's matchmaking, Chia-Yin left to study in New York. She was in her twenties and found the city exhilarating. "It was the 1980s; New York was on top of the world. I was stimulated by the diversity of people, hearing these different beautiful languages spoken."

When the Falklands War broke out in 1982, the situation back home made it impossible for her family to support her. A friend urged her to apply for work at the United Nations, since she could speak three official UN languages. She accepted the only position available, a secretarial job, working by day and completing her graduate studies in the evening at New York University. The UN eventually promoted her to a permanent job as an economic development specialist, posted in Geneva.

Even though Chia-Yin was in her thirties and living in Europe, Chiang tried again to interest his daughter in a prospective husband from Taiwan. Again, she thought the young man was interesting but, again, incompatible.

After seven years in Switzerland, she became homesick and wanted to be near her father. She applied for a job at the UN's Latin American headquarters in Santiago de Chile. By that time, she had met an American physicist.

"As our friendship turned into a romance," she says, "he decided that Geneva was no longer interesting without me there and he would come with me to Chile. That's when we decided to get married."

Since her mother and brother now live in New York, it was also a way for her to be near her father.

Foo-Ching Chiang was introduced to Yong-Fen Liu when she was in junior high school. Four years older than her, he treated her like a little sister. They were married several years later, in 1957.

"It was her mother's idea," he tells me, speaking in Mandarin. "Her mom liked me a lot. She was a great woman. She even came to live with me in Argentina in her eighties and told me, 'I would like my life to end with you beside me.'"

But immigrant life in Argentina was not a happy one for Liu.

"I found my mother crying one day," Chia-Yin remembers. "My mother comes from a very comfortable and well-to-do family. She was sad because there was no money to go back to Taiwan."

The couple soon grew apart in Argentina, and Liu eventually moved to the US to join their son in 1981. "I wanted to set her free, so I made no effort to retain her," Chiang explains. "She spent an hour every day doing her makeup, living like an aristocrat. I just wanted to live a simple life.

"People are excited to be married before their twenties; but after a while, when you start having responsibility, you cannot be as impulsive as before. In our times, responsibility was very important to us. And I still feel a sense of responsibility for my wife and my mother-in-law."

Chia-Yin confides to me that if she were to choose between her father being alone and uncared for, or having someone care for him in his old age, she would choose the latter, "for his own good." She also told her mother that if she ever finds a suitable companion in New York, to "go ahead."

"I don't feel like they should limit their choices because of some traditional Chinese views of family life. We're all adults. I think what matters the most is their happiness. And if they're happy, whether living alone or with someone else, that's up to them. That's their choice."

Stephen Wu, through whom we made contact, and Chiang have been friends for as long as Chiang has been in Argentina—forty years. Seven of us, including Wu's father-in-law, pile into an old Mercedes and make our way to Wu's country house just outside the city.

Porteños is a generic Spanish word meaning "port people," but Buenos Aires residents have adopted the term for themselves. Porteño country houses are essentially family homes with large yards just outside the city limits, far away from the port area.

Wu was a magician and ran a circus—which is where he met his Italian wife, a trapeze artist. One of their sons now runs the circus. Wu became a successful businessman—he talks business non-stop in the car with his father-in-law.

Wu comes from a wealthy and well-connected family. His father was a high-ranking military officer during the Sino-Japanese War when the Nationalists and Communists were busy fighting the Japanese, and each other. Names of Nationalist leader Chiang Kai-shek and collaborationist leader

Wang Jingwei crop up in our conversation, but he gives no indication which side his father was on.

"The whole society was like a fishnet—everything was connected, but it was hard to tell who's good and who's bad," he quotes his father.

In 1949, on the eve of the Communist victory, Wu's family moved to Brazil with a large group of émigrés. (Which is how Auntie Eileen, Wu's step-mother, ended up there as well.)

As we drive into Wu's country house, I can see that his plot is larger than most, fenced in by walls and trees, with a stream running through it. In the front yard, to one side, is an abandoned circus trailer. Helpers are now laying out a parrilla feast—various beef parts cooked on the backyard brick grill. We are about to consume half a side of cow in one sitting.

"That's enough meat to feed an entire village back in China," Kwoi says with a straight face. He is exaggerating, of course, but not by much.

We are eating on the patio. Parts of the animal arrive in succession—ribs, sirloin, flank, shank and brisket (Chinese love brisket for its exciting tex-ture)—charred and grilled to perfection. Wu insists that we try everything. They are all tender and luscious, oozing burned fat.

I've had enough after a few rounds. Where's my red semaphore?

The atmosphere is idyllic, the conversation collegial. The winter sun shines warmly and spreads a golden hue across the garden. Beer, wine and liquor flow freely. After lunch, with glasses of cognac in hand, we walk around picking fruit from the trees. I am drunk with the scene. Thousands of miles away from China, at the other end of the world, and for a fleeting afternoon, we meet as if long-lost friends.

Wu is in the mood to talk, which prompts Chiang to open up as well. They speak of love and mistresses, about Chiang's separation from his wife, the universe and the world, and liberation from family entanglements.

"All his friends hope he and his wife can get back together as soon as possible," Wu says in a loud enough voice to make sure that Chiang hears it.

"You've got to respect a person's choice. A person has her right to do things she wants," Chiang rejoins. "It is not appropriate to use family to bind two people together."

"I have lots of girlfriends, but I still want to be with my wife all the time." I'm not sure whether Wu's saying it in jest.

"I told my wife that she has three choices," says Chiang. "If she wants to live with our daughter, she can go live with our daughter; if she wants to stay with me, we can live together; or she can live with our son in New York."

Chiang elaborates for us his concept of love, of the romantic and pla-tonic varieties, and about the need for a companion to take care of him at his age. When I ask whether he's still in love with his wife, he answers only in generalities, with comments like "What's love, anyway?"

—•—

San Telmo, with Spanish colonial buildings and cobblestone streets, is the oldest barrio of Buenos Aires. Sunday is when Porteños and tourists alike descend on the neighbourhood to eat, shop and have a good time. As we walk through the area filled with antique shops, flea markets and tango dancers in the street, Chiang becomes animated and explains how he came to open his own curio shop in the barrio.

"I've been to many Chinatowns, but the souvenir shops are all small and crowded, unlike mine," he says as we walk into his store. This is where I meet a long-time friend of his, the seventy-year-old shopkeeper Shou-Chang Wang. Wang shows me the products on the shelves. Chiang is right: They are laid out like gallery pieces.

I suggest we all go to the café-bar next door where a handful of men are nursing their coffees and their Camparis; pictures of Carlos Gardel, the patron saint of tango, hang on the walls; and a football game is on television.

"I jumped ship in the seventies. Nothing really to worry about; I wasn't robbing them," Wang speaks to us in Cantonese. "Argentina is resource rich, and that attracted me right away." He uses the Chinese expression "jump ship" to describe how illegal immigrants, often working in merchant marines, would go ashore and vanish into a foreign country.

"Right now, my wife, my children and my grandchildren are all ghosts," he says. "*Así es la vida.*" That's life. Here Wang uses a part-derogatory, part-endearing Cantonese term *gwei*, ghost, for white Europeans—Chinese see themselves as "humans" in the Celestial Empire; all others are "ghosts."

Wang left his wife and children back in Taiwan when he jumped ship in Argentina. After his wife died, his relationship with his children back in Taiwan ended. "I lost contact with them."

He reminds me of older Chinese who left China as young men. Living apart from their original families—often in hardship—and in countries with restrictive immigration policies, these men would marry and have second families in the New World. I encounter these stories everywhere I go in the Americas.

——•——

I've always liked the tango: its seductive and sensuous music, and the eroticism and sexual longing in the dance. And I've always wanted to find a Chinese restaurant owner who could tango the night away. Sadly, Chiang cannot. And I'm reduced to filming him trying to dance with the rest of the tango class in Casa China, or filming him watching a pair of tango school students dancing in a bar-restaurant.

Bar Sur is a tango parlour in San Telmo. Its checker-tiled floor hosts nightly tango shows for tourists, who arrive by the busload. On our last night in the city, after another round of carnivorous excess at a nearby parrilla and yet more Mendoza Malbecs, we walk with Chiang to Bar Sur.

He stands at the entrance but doesn't go in. The lighting near the entrance is a warm orange glow. Cobblestones glisten after the rain. It is cool, and he instinctively pulls up his collar, a cigarette dangling from his mouth. Kwoi back-steps with his camera, like a human dolly, to pull wide on Chiang. Through the camera, I see a loner standing in front of a tango bar, in the country that gives us the melancholic dance.

Afterwards, I call a taxi to take him home and watch as the car disappears into the mist, hurrying into the night.

CHAPTER 16

Have You Eaten Yet?

LIMA, PERU

THE DECOR, THE NOISE AND THE SMELL HERE REMIND ME OF A TYPICAL HONG Kong restaurant. It's Sunday. The restaurant is packed with large families—young and old—eating Chinese food.

But we are in Lima, in Chifa San Joy Lao, one of the oldest eateries in the country's Chinatown, Calle Capón. Everyone here is Peruvian. And everyone drinks Inca Kola with their chifa.

Kwoi and I, accompanied by Ajay Noronha and his wife, Sarada Ramaseshan, flew in the day before from Buenos Aires for the final stop on our four-year, five-continent odyssey.

I am having lunch with Fabiola Castañeda Chang, who promised to introduce me to the owner of the restaurant. She is the third cousin of Valeria Mau Chu, the Chinese Peruvian friend who interpreted for me in Cuba a year earlier.

"Chifa is a Peruvian word for 'Chinese restaurant' *and* 'Chinese food,'" Fabiola tells me. "Like we say '*vamos a comer chifa*,' let's eat Chinese."

We are having a delectable dim sum combo of ja kao (shrimp dumpling), siu mai (pork dumpling), wantán (wonton), enrolladito primavera (spring roll) and—something new to me—chicharrón, which is akin to Cantonese BBQ roast pork.

Right on cue, Luís Yong Tatje, the owner, walks up to our table to introduce himself. I recognize him right away. I saw him on a Channel 2 cooking show just this morning on my hotel TV. He was wearing a blue embroidered Chinese tunic, as he is now, making Peruvian fried rice.

"We do not serve jasmine tea with Chinese food in Peru," he says. "When you have chifa, you have to have Inca Kola. This weird cola drink that outsells Coca-Cola."

The fifty-two-year-old Yong is flamboyant and gregarious—and balding—and has what the Chinese call *fu gui xiang*—that rounded and benevolent "wealthy and noble look" that many cherish. (Interestingly, baldness is also part of this look.) It's a sign that the person comes from a good background, enjoys good fortune and *eats well*.

So where did the word *chifa* come from?

"My Cantonese grandparents would say *chui fan*, 'Let's cook rice.' My Hakka grandfather, in his dialect, would say *chi fan*, 'Let's eat rice,'" he explains. In Chinese, *fan* means "cooked rice"—which is different from *mi*, the grain—and is often used to mean "meal."

"Since three of your grandparents were Chinese," I muse, quickly working out the math in my head. "That makes you three-quarters Chinese."

"I might be a *mestizo*, but I'm 100 per cent Chinese in my culture and thoughts," he says.

"I'm only one-quarter Chinese," Fabiola adds. "But I get called *chinita* all the time." *Chinita* is an endearing term for "Chinese woman."

Without my asking, Yong goes into a dissertation on all that is good about China's 5,000-year cultural and philosophical traditions. But most of all, he extols the holistic health benefits of Chinese food. He's got the medical qualifications—he has been a practising gastroenterologist and surgeon for more than twenty years and only recently quit his profession so that he could devote his full time to his restaurant.

"Eating and food are important in Chinese culture," he says emphatically. "The way we eat, the food we take in, all help harmonize the yin and yang in our body."

San Joy Lao, the restaurant's name, literally means "Mountain Sea

Pavilion." The term "mountain sea" (*san hoy* in Cantonese) brings to mind *The Classic of Mountains and Seas*, a compilation of mythic geography and beasts that likely dates back to the fourth century BC. It evokes expansive landscape, mystique and beauty.

This being Sunday, the whole family is helping out. While Yong tends to the kitchen, his wife, Blanca, greets customers and directs them to one of the two split-level floors. Daughters Vanessa and Veronica help out wherever they are needed.

The third-floor kitchen is spacious, organized, well lit and well equipped. It certainly ranks in the top three kitchens I've seen. (The other two are in Trinidad and Mumbai.) Yong is supervising his kitchen staff, scrutinizing each dish before it is served. A true showman, he occasionally stir-fries at the wok, throwing up big flames for our cameras.

"I learned Chinese cooking from my father, and my mother made excellent Peruvian food," he says as he glances sideways at one of his line cooks. "So, we have both Chinese and Peruvian cultures in our family. That makes me proud and happy."

Yong took over the dilapidated San Joy Lao in 1999. "Because of my character and personality, I'm not good at running a clinic. But running a restaurant is different. Although it doesn't pay well, it gives me tremendous personal satisfaction. It allows me to combine food with medicine."

As Fabiola said, chifa refers not only to the restaurants but to the food itself—dishes that blend Chinese and Peruvian cuisine: fusing spices, ingredients and cooking methods. Unlike other countries that consider Chinese food "ethnic," chifa is so deeply ingrained in the Peruvian diet that it has become, itself, Peruvian. In fact, you could say the country nationalized Chinese food and made it its own.

There are between 20,000 and 30,000 Chinese restaurants in Peru—more than half of them in Lima—which is a large number for a country of 27 million. In fact, there are more chifas in Peru than all other kinds of restaurants *combined*.

Chifas started in Lima around the turn of the twentieth century and spread to the remotest corners of the country. In the 1970s, the cuisine was "exported" to neighbours such as Ecuador, Chile and Bolivia, influencing traditional Andean and coastal dishes. Over time, it emerged as a new kind of authentic Peruvian cuisine.

"There's a saying that if there's a menu, there's chifa," Yong enthuses. "Putting a chifa restaurant in Peru is a guaranteed business."

In fact, the distinction between Peruvian and Chinese food is often blurred. Many Peruvian restaurants devote a large portion of their menu to chifa dishes, while others just call themselves a chifa, serving *comida chino peruana*.

Lomo saltado is typically Peruvian and considered a national dish. But the dish is Chinese in origin: cubes of beef filet, marinated in soy sauce and stir-fried with a combination of ginger, red onions, green onions, tomatoes, red pepper, garlic, cilantro, fermented black bean sauce and ají amarillo.

Here are the Peruvian twists: ají amarillo is the yellow chili pepper, with a slightly sweet flavour and plenty of heat, so common in Peruvian cooking; French-fried Inca gold potatoes are either stir-fried into the wok or served, with white rice, on the side; and pisco, a liquor made by distilling fermented grape juice into a high-proof spirit, is often substituted for Shaoxing cooking wine.

"We have conquered Peruvians through their stomachs." Yong might have said this as a joke, but there is plenty of truth to it.

Chinese food has become mainstream, and words such as *sillao* (soy sauce), *chaufa* (fried rice) and *kion* (ginger) are part of Peruvian lingo. Peruvian dishes that bear the description *saltado* are usually of Chinese origin. In Spanish, *saltar* means to jump or to skip, a good description of food that is stir-fried in a wok.

"I didn't even know it was Chinese food," says a diner at San Joy Lao eating a plate of tallarín saltado, Chinese Peruvian fried noodle. "It's hard to tell which restaurants are Chinese, which dishes came from China. It's all Peru."

Calle Capón literally means "castration lane"—it got its name when pigs from the nearby Mercado Central were brought there to be castrated, to fatten them up for better tasting chicharrón, "pork belly."

The Chinese settled around the Central Market in the late 1800s, after they were released from indentured labour. They established businesses, associations and guilds, transforming the area into Lima's Barrio Chino. The number of Chinese workers arriving in Peru grew rapidly, comparable in size to those who settled in Cuba and California during the second half of the nineteenth century. Lima's Chinatown, together with those in San Francisco and Havana, was among the three largest in the Americas.

"My grandparents lived on the outskirts of the Barrio Chino," Yong says. "The Chinese were motivated to do that because they could find all the fresh food and vegetables from the market, and they could find a place where it was easier to survive, for work or commerce."

Having experience as cooks in the haciendas to the north, many who settled around Calle Capón opened their own *fondas*. These cheap but popular restaurants serving Chinese food came into direct competition with the *picanterías*—Peruvian eating houses that serve their food *picante*, hot and spicy.

More formal chifas evolved from the fondas. The first chifas opened in Barrio Chino in the 1910s and soon proliferated throughout Lima. In the 1950s, they spread to every single town and village across the country.

One of the six original *grandes restaurantes* that flourished in the 1920s in Lima's Chinatown, San Joy Lao was indeed *grand* in its heyday, with customers dancing well into the night to a live orchestra. But as the Barrio Chino fell into decline in the 1970s, these opulent restaurants lost their lustre and were overtaken by newer and more efficient eateries.

In 1968, the military junta imposed currency controls that made imports prohibitively expensive. Soy sauce, oyster sauce, five-spice powder and different kinds of fermented bean pastes became scarce. Chinese food went into decline.

That changed when President Alberto Fujimori instituted a free-market economy in 1995. Chinese businesses prospered again, and the community collaborated with the city government to restore Barrio Chino. In 1999, a rejuvenated Calle Capón was launched on the 150th anniversary of the arrival of the first indentured Chinese labourers in Peru.

Calle Capón, the lane where pigs were castrated, became a tourist destination with stereotypical trappings: lantern-shaped street lamps, pagoda-style kiosks and a red *pailou* (traditional Chinese arched gateway) topped by a green roof at the entrance. The pedestrian-only street is paved with tiles engraved with names of donors and twelve concrete discs, each displaying an animal of the Chinese zodiac.

Revitalized businesses fill both sides of the lane: chifas, banks, souvenir stores, electronic goods stores and one-hour photo shops. Jirón Ucayali (the street that includes Calle Capón) extends past Mercado Central and features a string of Chinese-run chicharronerías selling chicharrón.

Chicharrón is popular across Latin America, with national variations. It can be anything from a crunchy, deep-fried pork rind snack to a fried pork belly dish. In Peru, it's boiled with seasonings and spices until all the water evaporates and the meat is then fried in its own fat. The Peruvians even made a sandwich out of it, pan con chicharrón, a popular breakfast item for people on the run.

"Everyone makes chicharrón, but it never turns out like when the Chinese do it," Yong boasts. "Because at the end of the cooking, when it's fried golden, we add a little bit of soy sauce to give it that extra flavour."

Yong's father, Felix Yong Loo, born to immigrant parents from China and trained as an accountant, started a popular chicharrón sandwich shop, Sanguchería El Chinito, in 1960.

There is even a local street song about Chinese chicharrón vendors:

> Chinese chicharrón vendor
> Who eats chicharrón sandwich
> Add less fat and more meat
> The chicharrones will taste better.

Although the Chinese made their mark in the chicharrón business, the *grandes restaurantes* define Chinatown. And they are thriving. Chifa Ton Kin

Sen, at one end of Calle Capón, is consistently full. Salón China Restaurante, two doors down from San Joy Lao, is just as popular. Then there's Chifa Thon Po, named after the Song dynasty poet, painter, statesman and gastronome Su Dongpo, who purportedly created Dongpo pork, Hangzhou-style braised pork belly, which I'm sure is on the menu.

"We rescued a tradition," Yong says, perhaps speaking for all the chifa owners. "Owning a restaurant is nothing new for us. Chinese always knew how to handle food. The important thing is that through Chinese food, we were able to spread our Chinese culture."

But not every chifa is as busy as San Joy Lao, and not every owner is as prosperous or as happy as Yong. On a dreary day, Alfonso Koc Fong, a second cousin to Fabiola, takes me to Chifa San Luís in a nondescript suburb of Lima, a world away from Calle Capón.

Fifty-year-old María Yiu, a family friend of Alfonso and the owner of the chifa, walks in dressed in tight jeans and high-heeled alligator boots. When she was twenty-two years old in Hong Kong, a Chinese Peruvian cook came calling, looking for a bride.

"It was my mom's idea. She said it was better to get married to a guy who is mature and steady," Yiu says. "I was a *fei nui*, a greaser. I had a boyfriend at that time, but my mom didn't like him. I had no other choice."

What did she think of her future husband?

"I didn't like him at first. Maybe because he was just a cook, and he wasn't really good looking. I always dreamed about marrying those white-collared guys. I don't know, maybe it was meant to be."

Anxious to adapt to her new country, the new wife even changed her Christian name from Mary to María. But all these years have taken a toll on her. Three children and several chifas later, she is separated from her husband.

Does she want her children to take over the chifa?

"I don't want them to do that. Other than my kids, I have no one here. If I could, I would sell everything and go back to Hong Kong to take care of my parents. All my friends and relatives are back there."

She starts sobbing. I signal for a close-up on the tears running down her cheeks.

"Everything I do is for my children. If I take them back to Hong Kong, they don't really speak Chinese. It would be too difficult for them. I hope they can go to the US or Canada. Wherever they want. I don't really like Peru. I haven't been treated well here. This has never been my own country. Peruvians look down on us Chinese."

It's not the first time I've heard about this being the fate of someone who married overseas, like a mail-order bride. When the marriage breaks down, and you are stuck in a foreign country that was never your home, going home to your own family becomes the ultimate goal.

—•—

On October 15, 1849, a boatload of seventy-five indentured Chinese labourers arrived in Peru from Macau after a four-month trip aboard Manila–Acapulco galleons. Every Chinese Peruvian I meet knows this precise date. In no other country—save, perhaps, Cuba—is the arrival of indentured Chinese labourers cited with such exactitude.

It is the first thing Isabelle Lausent-Herrera mentions when I sit down with her to learn about Chinese immigration to Peru. She is an anthropologist at the Instituto Francés de Estudios Andinos, and her research focuses on the Chinese Peruvian community.

"When Peru effectively abolished slavery in the mid-nineteenth century," she says, "the country needed coolies to work."

Coolie is a Hindi word meaning "migrant labourer," popularized in the sixteenth century by European traders across Asia. By the nineteenth century, it was used for Asian workers under contract to plantations that had been formerly worked by African slaves.

The Chinese phonetically rendered coolie as *ku li*, "bitter strength," from the expression *chi ku*, "eat bitter" or "to endure hardship." It is a characteristic the Chinese have turned into a virtue, relating it to a similar idiom, "Bitter first, sweet later." An unintended consequence is that it may have conditioned the Chinese to accept racism and discrimination as part and parcel of immigrant life.

The first wave of imported workers was sent to coastal sugar plantations and agricultural farms in the north. Interestingly, through their cooking in the haciendas, the Chinese first introduced rice cultivation and established rice as a staple of the Peruvian diet.

"The Chinese couldn't miss their rice in their daily meal," says Lausent-Herrera. "And that daily ration of rice was written into their contracts."

The second wave of Chinese immigrants toiled in guano mines on several islands off Peru's northern coast that are collectively known as Guaneras Islands. Guano, the accumulated dung of seabirds and bats, is rich in salt residues and used in fertilizer. It was so valuable that Peru fought the 1879 War of the Pacific over the control of the commodity.

Railroad workers came in the third wave. Henry Meiggs, an American railroad builder and robber baron, became a *chinero*—a contractor of Chinese coolies—when he heard about the hard-working nature of the railroad workers in California. He moved to Peru in 1868 and, in partnership with the country's president, used coolies to build two railroads, one across the Andes.

All told, more than 100,000 Chinese arrived in Peru over twenty-five years. Almost half of them perished due to abuse, exhaustion or suicide from loneliness. It was only in 1874, amid international outcry, that the inhumane trafficking of coolies stopped.

When these indentured labourers were freed, those who did not return to China moved to Lima to open businesses and eateries around the Mercado Central. Yet racism and xenophobia persisted. The Chinese were blamed for everything wrong with society, such as high food prices and the lack of jobs. They were also disparaged for their "unhygienic" eating habits. ("Eating rats" was a popular refrain.)

During the War of the Pacific, Chinese labourers sided with the invading Chilean army, counting on Chile's promise to emancipate them from bondage in Peru.

"After 1883, every Peruvian blamed the Chinese for this betrayal," Lausent-Herrera says. Branded as *traidores* (traitors), the Chinese were targeted and murdered. It was not until the 1890s that anti-Chinese pogroms stopped.

This is in stark contrast to the Chinese in Cuba, where 2,000 of them joined the rebels in the war for independence, and a monument in Havana honours them with José Martí's words: "There was not one Cuban Chinese deserter, not one Cuban Chinese traitor."

Nevertheless, the Chinese in Peru persevered and thrived, first opening grocery stores, then moving into the chicharrón business and eventually opening restaurants. According to Lausent-Herrera, there's a saying, *el chino en la esquina*, the Chinese at the corner—referring to a small grocery store at the corner of each city block. These stores grew to become wholesalers called *tambos*, from the Incan word for food reserve.

"The Chinese stores would extend credit to other Peruvian customers and thus built up trust between the two people," she says. "The Chinese have always been hard workers. They educate their kids and slowly work their way up in society."

Peruano chino comprise only 3 per cent of the country's population. But by some estimates, up to 20 per cent of Peruvians have Chinese ancestry. They are called *tusán*, which is a romanization of the Chinese word for "native born." The country's only Olympic gold medallist, Edwin Vásquez Cam, is a *tusán* who won the fifty-metre pistol event in the 1948 London Games.

Perhaps no one epitomizes Chinese Peruvian success more than Erasmo Wong, the King of Supermarkets, who started with a small store in 1942, just like "the Chinese at the corner." Now there are billboards everywhere for E. Wong supermarkets. He is widely seen as a patriotic Peruvian, treating his employees and customers well.

——–—

"I don't have any conflict with holding both Peruvian and Chinese cultures in my heart," Luís Yong tells me as we tour the oldest Chinese temple in Barrio Chino, on the rooftop of a three-storey building. "I believe in the synergy of the two cultures."

Growing up, he wanted to dispel the myth that Chinese only stay in Calle Capón. A good education often offers a way out: "Among the three brothers, we have two doctors and a psychologist."

His knowledge of both medicine and Chinese holistic health practices informs his passion for food. This is what he says about ginger: "When you mix onions with ginger, they work together in the respiratory system to get rid of the mucus in our bronchial tubes."

And on soy sauce, "It's a main source of vegetable and oil proteins. Soy products, like tofu or soya sauce, provide antioxidants that protect you against cancer. Breast cancer in Chinese women is rare. Prostate cancer in Chinese men is also rare, and that's due to what they eat."

But it's not all about health. Chinese food, he says, must appeal to the senses: it has to look good, smell good and taste good. And a Chinese dish must have the five flavours—salty, sweet, sour, spicy and bitter—he says, as he counts with the fingers of his right hand.

"Like five-spice powder," I say. The "five-spice" in Chinese cooking is usually made up of fennel, cloves, cinnamon, star anise and Sichuan peppercorns. They complement the five concepts in Chinese philosophy: wood, fire, earth, metal and water.

"The Chinese also have a sixth flavour, umami," he adds, holding up the index finger from his other hand. Umami was identified by a Japanese researcher in 1908 as glutamates found in foods such as shellfish, fish sauce, mushrooms, cheeses and soy sauce. Glutamate is the G in MSG.

On our way out, Yong can't stop himself from repeating, "Chinese cuisine is very much associated with that mystic energy of qi. If our qi flows without hindrance, then our yin and yang are in harmony. And that's what we do when we cook. It's not just a culinary art. It's a combination of philosophy, feelings, knowledge and health."

If that is not cultural ambassadorship, I don't know what is.

—·—

The Yongs live in a three-storey house in a quiet, gated neighbourhood next to the Japanese embassy. At this point, my curiosity gets the better of me. Didn't a revolutionary group take hostage hundreds of high-level diplomats, government and military officials and business executives here in 1996?

"No, not here. It was at the ambassador's residence in San Isidro," Yong replies. "Although the whole incident is referred to as the Japanese embassy hostage crisis."

Given the country's brushes with the Shining Path and other revolutionary movements—which President Alberto Fujimori was credited with suppressing—it is not surprising to find gated communities everywhere in Lima. That's also why I asked Kwoi to take off his Israel Defense Forces fatigues before he deplaned. Don't want to get killed in the crossfire.

I was expecting chifa, but we are treated to more pan con chicharrón brought in from El Chinito. Blanca is at her gracious best, making sure we have enough to eat. We have jasmine tea. Chopsticks are laid out on the table.

"Try this—this is how we make char siu here." Yong puts a plate of what looks like Cantonese barbecue roast pork in front of me. It doesn't taste like the real thing, but it certainly has that five-spice flavour.

Blanca and Yong met at a party, and it was love at first sight. But her integration into the community has not been easy. "I moved in with his family. There were things I couldn't adapt to. But, little by little, I became part of the community. What can I say? It's like a rock, they're like this," she says, holding both hands together in a tight grip.

Little by little, she learned to savour Chinese food. "Now I love it. At first, I didn't know how to eat with chopsticks. Now I eat with, how do you say it, *fai chi*. That's what has been great, marrying an Oriental."

I ask the two twentysomething daughters whether their father would like them to marry a Chinese Peruvian.

"Yes, he would like it, but . . .," Veronica, the younger one, replies first. "I don't know if it'll happen. I don't think so."

"In my case, I don't know what will happen," Vanessa chimes in. "Whether he's Chinese or Peruvian, my father would respect the decisions we make. I would like to marry someone who's a go-getter. It's not important what his race or colour is, as long as he's a good person. And even if he's not Chinese we'll convert him *poco a poco*."

Little by little.

We all laugh.

"Being married to a Chinese makes me the happiest woman in the world," their mother says, turning serious. "I always tell my daughters that I would like for them to meet a man like their father, someone who's a good son, good brother, good friend and a good spouse. And imagine my Chinese grandchildren looking like their grandfather with their little Chinese eyes."

We laugh some more.

"Our lives are simple and modest, but our great wealth is family unity," Yong says as he comes back from the kitchen. "This family virtue came from my parents. I learned from them respect for our parents, our older brothers, the value of family, fraternity and solidarity. Rather than explaining this to my daughters, I teach them by living it.

"*Una familia unida es fundamental*," he adds. A united family is fundamental.

"My wife doesn't like the host flirting with me," Yong whispers as we walk into the studio at Channel 2 Cable Express. We are going on La Chola Energía's *Cosas de la Vida* ("Life Things") program. In Peru, *chola* is an endearing term for a woman of Indigenous origin. The host is in a traditional Incan dress, doling out hugs and kisses. I try not to ruin her heavy makeup as we give each other light pecks on both cheeks.

La Chola opens the show: "That nice music, that affection, that love. Who's here? Who has arrived? Doctor Yong. Let's give him a big applause. Doctor Yong is presenting to all of you with all the love in the world. He fills our stomachs and fills our souls. The soul which we all need in order to keep going. Good morning, Doctor."

In a twenty-minute cooking demo, Yong makes stir-fried beef with broccoli and tofu, all the while bantering with La Chola and extolling the virtues of each ingredient he tosses into the flat-bottomed wok: beef, broccoli, red bell pepper, green onions, tofu, fermented black bean paste and soy sauce.

"And along with everything else, we add this incomparable Peruvian product," he says, adding ají amarillo and instantly rendering the dish *chino peruano*. "Remember that Chinese men here cook well for their women, because there's a Peruvian expression, 'Full stomach, happy heart.'"

La Chola is wrapping up: "A program for the Peruvian people, for the people we love, and our show is to teach you to eat nutritiously, healthily, exquisitely and economically, but always with the concept of the Andean condor and the Chinese dragon."

At this point, she pulls me onto the set. Kwoi is filming me. Ajay is filming Kwoi filming me. I'm getting my Warholian fifteen minutes of fame on Peruvian television.

"Peruvian people and families, although this is a cooking demonstration, I'd like to point out the other value of this program," Yong gives his patented speech. "The value I learned from my Chinese ancestors, the same value my Peruvian brothers taught me: friendship. The kind of hospitality found in few other places in the world."

In his red embroidered tunic, he put his hands together and bows, giving thanks in Cantonese, Mandarin and Spanish: *Doh tse, Perú. Xie xie, Perú. Muchas gracias, Perú.*

Epilogue

KEN HOM'S CHINESE COOKERY DEBUTED IN 1984 ON BBC. IT WAS A HUGE SUC-
cess, and the companion book became one of the bestselling cookbooks ever
published by BBC Books.

Hom went on to write thirty-six more cookbooks and continued
appearing in a number of prime-time BBC TV series that have sold throughout
the world. He single-handedly made Chinese food approachable and accessible in the United Kingdom. So much so that 65 per cent of all British kitchens
now have a wok.

But he has never run a restaurant. Instead, from his homes in France
and Thailand, he travels tirelessly, promoting Chinese cuisine, and remains
passionate about restaurants worldwide and the ever-evolving state of the
Chinese diaspora.

I've only met Hom once—in 2006, in Paris, when I came down from
Amsterdam to have lunch with him at a Sino-Laotian restaurant in Belleville,
the city's second *quartier chinois*. Save for a chance encounter several years
later at a Chicago restaurant, we lost contact. While finishing this book in 2021,
I thought I would reconnect with him. We chat over Zoom—he is in Bangkok,
and I in Toronto—as another wave of the pandemic ravages the world.

"I felt immediately at home," he says when I ask about his going to Hong
Kong for the first time.

"Coming home at the ripe old age of thirty," I tease.

"I couldn't believe it. Everybody looked like me, spoke in Cantonese, the
dialect that I understood. Everything, the smells, the food, talked to me. It
was amazing."

"It speaks to your origins, growing up as a Cantonese kid. It's as if you always have one foot firmly planted on Chinese soil."

"That's what saved me. I grew up in Chicago's Chinatown and always felt like a foreigner. In my formative years, I only ate Chinese food. My mother was right: we Chinese cook better."

In the 1980s, Hong Kong was a place of slick modernity, very different from what his parents left behind. Hom would have discovered that he spoke colloquial Cantonese laced with a country-bumpkin Taishanese accent—he would have used archaic idioms and syntax, and come across neologisms and slang he'd never heard.

For any member of the Chinese diaspora, going back to your roots takes on special significance. I had the same experience at age thirteen, when I went back to Hong Kong for the first time. I'd left Hong Kong in the arms of my grandmother when I was only ten months old. That same coming-home feeling was palpable when I visited Beijing's Tiananmen Square on my first trip to China. I was twenty-six, and I felt a sense of home in a country that I never knew.

I have had three nationalities: British (albeit as an overseas subject), Singaporean and Canadian. But no matter that I have held different passports, and passed through different cultures, deep down I know that I'm ethnically Chinese. Or ethnic Han Chinese, to be precise.

"It's funny because Chinese in China always asked me, why do I feel Chinese?" Hom recalls. "I tell them because I was never fully accepted in America, and being Chinese is the one thing I could cling to."

"People in China look at us funny," I remark. "In their eyes, we're foreigners. They don't see our ethnicity. That's why we don't have that Han ethnocentrism, that centre-of-the-world, descendants-of-the-dragon attitude."

So, what does it mean to be Chinese? Is it our nationality or our ethnicity? That we are born inside the country of China, or that we eat Chinese food?

Because we don't have a centre, we are left to negotiate around the periphery. This marginality is something that all diasporic Chinese navigate, no matter where we go.

Hom started working in his uncle's kitchen when he was eleven. He was cooking "professionally" during his high school days. But by the time he went off to university in Berkeley, California, in the early 1970s, he didn't want to do cooking anymore.

"I only gave cooking classes in my kitchen as a way to support myself," he says over Zoom. "I never dreamt it would become a career. But cooking is therapeutic, and I was able to make a living sharing my culture."

"I was living in Berkeley at that time," I tell him.

"You could've come to my class," he says with a laugh.

"And you became a celebrity in the early eighties with an immensely popular cooking show in the UK. How did they find you?"

"I had a cooking school in Hong Kong, and BBC came calling."

"What? You were teaching Hongkongers how to cook Chinese?" I can't believe what I just heard.

"No, no. It was an early form of gastro-tourism." He laughs some more. "I had set up a kitchen in Mong Kok and brought Americans over for cooking classes."

He also took his students on excursions: to wet markets to shop for live chickens; to the New Territories to buy directly from the fishermen and have the seafood cooked by restaurants along the pier; and to eat at a restaurant in Sha Tin well known for its deep-fried whole pigeon, with the head on. (Hong Kong is said to have the highest per capita consumption of pigeons in the world.)

"They couldn't believe it. They'd never experienced it before," he enthuses. "I think Hong Kong has some of the best food in the world."

"I reference the food in Hong Kong quite a bit," I say. "Not only in the context of what *real* Chinese food can be, but also to talk about my childhood food memories."

"That's why your project is so fascinating. Food tells us who we are and where we come from."

The term "Chinese food" covers an area four times larger than Western Europe and the eating habits of more than a billion people, featuring cuisines from fifty-six ethnic groups—including Manchus, Mongolians and Koreans—as well as the Han majority. You could say that there is really no such thing as "Chinese food"; and, equally, that there are just as many hyphenated Chinese foods around the world.

"What I find is how pragmatic and adaptable we Chinese are," Hom says. "Wherever we are, we make things work."

"Like that unique blend of Chinese and Peruvian cuisine called *chifa*," I add. "It's a matter of survival."

"Chinese immigrants in the UK would take over fish-and-chip shops and add curry," he says. "Why? Because that's what people want, so give them what they want. It pays the bills."

"Right. I only eat Chinese and Indian when I go to London." I play up the curry bit. "It's cheap and tasty, and you know what you're getting."

—•—

Hom is a youthful seventy-two-year-old. He has a shaved head, a perfect tan and the physique of a fighting Shaolin monk—firm and supple, with a bit of a belly. In his autobiography, *My Stir-fried Life*, he writes about being mistaken for the Dalai Lama by a young girl at the Bangkok airport.

He became a household name in the United Kingdom. To this day, he still professes his undying love for the country and its people, who took him into their homes and especially their kitchens.

But does he have the same feelings for the US?

Hom's native country is reeling from anti-Black and anti-Asian racism these days, and he says he feels lucky to have moved to France where, he believes, they don't have the same history of racism as in America. He was also lucky that his entire adulthood in the US was spent in Berkeley, a place so different from the rest of the country—"very tolerant and very open"—which shielded him from the discrimination that he faced when he was growing up.

So it came as a shock to him when, on his first book tour in the US, people would say to him, "How come your English is so good?"

"We all get that, all the time," I say to assuage him.

"Nobody in France says that," he replies. "In fact, across Europe, they look upon me as someone from an ancient civilization, even though I'm not."

Perhaps it's the respect of history that Europeans have that a young country like the US doesn't. The Chinese, especially, tend to take a longer view of things. One time, when asked by André Malraux what he thought of the French Revolution, Chinese premier Zhou Enlai famously said, "It's too early to tell."

"I can't begin to tell you how many times I've been told in the States: 'You can't possibly be American,'" he continues. "Really? I told them I was born in Tucson, Arizona. Racism is something I grew up with, but there's no other place I can go. I'm an American."

Racism is something that all Asians face in North America. The Chinese have the Chinese Exclusion Act, yellow peril and kung flu to thank for that. We almost beg for another Bruce Lee to save us.

What about knowing his roots?

"My mum would say, never forget where you came from. That's why this anti-Asian hate comes as a shock for a lot of young Asian Americans. They thought they were Americans all along, and then all of a sudden, bam, what's happening?"

He fell in love with France, like everybody does, and permanently moved there in 1997. "I love France. There's no other place I would live other than in Asia. It's always been my goal to leave the US."

Hom became a consultant to Cathay Pacific in the early nineties, devising the Hong Kong airliner's menu and working with the catering team. After that, he flew around the world doing different cooking stints, "in the air, on land and at sea."

Then Bangkok's Oriental hotel—where W. Somerset Maugham and Joseph Conrad once stayed—brought him on as a guest chef. When that gig was over, he made the city his second home—"it's quite affordable, unlike Hong Kong or Singapore." Besides, the food is just as he likes it: spicy.

To me, a home is about finding a community where you feel you belong—physically, emotionally and spiritually.

I have six homes: Jiujiang, the ancestral village in southeastern China I've never visited; Hong Kong, the cultural hybrid where I was born; Singapore, where I came of age and where I retain my earliest food memories of satays, rojaks and Hainan chicken rice, among myriad multicultural offerings; Tokyo, where I spent my adolescent years watching Japanese baseball and Spaghetti Westerns; Berkeley, where I learned about jazz and Asian American identity politics; and my current home, Toronto, where I found my voice in Asian Canadian activism.

This multiplicity and layering of language, geography and culture befuddled my university friends in Cleveland, Ohio. The two other Asians in my fraternity house came from much simpler backgrounds: a Japanese American from Hawaii and a Chinese American from nearby Youngstown, Ohio.

"So where are you really from?" they would ask. "I'm from everywhere," I would tell them. "I'm an internationalist."

For Kwoi, the experience of travelling around the world with me left an indelible impression. He was born in Hong Kong, but to him the place is like a campground and a transit point where a person has no sense of identity. He doesn't identify with Canada, either, and "felt like a freak all the time" growing up.

During the 1990s, he worked at different times in Canada and Hong Kong. Hong Kong is like a bad girlfriend, he once said. When he's with her, he wants to leave. And when he's away, he misses her.

As Kwoi says now, "After I worked on the series, I felt a lot more at peace with myself because I discovered a belonging, a global belonging. I want to be a global citizen."

Which brings me to another global citizen, Jun Watanabe. When he was four, his Japanese parents moved to Malaysia, where his father took up a job in the public health system as a surgeon. After Watanabe's sojourn in Brazil, where we first met, he married a Chinese Malaysian and moved to Kuala Lumpur to work for a Japanese company.

Ten years later, I caught up with him over a Nyonya lunch in Malacca, Malaysia, where his family now lives. "Nyonya" is the cuisine of the Peranakans—Chinese who settled more than six centuries earlier along the Malacca Strait, intermarrying with local Indonesians and Malays. The dishes that emerge from their kitchens are a blend of Chinese and local spices, ingredients and cooking techniques.

It is *truly* fusion. We had many of my childhood favourites: Penang laksa—a seafood-laden noodle soup that is aromatic, tangy and spicy; and bubur cha-cha—a coconut milk dessert flavoured with pandan leaf, containing pearled sago, sweet potato and taro.

I had reached food nirvana.

Watanabe is, in a sense, a modern-day Peranakan. Or, as he told me, "I'm becoming Malaysian." What he was trying say is that—just like Chiang, the Chinese restaurant owner in Argentina—he sees himself as a member of this Earth.

But perhaps more than being a global citizen, I feel connected across the Chinese diaspora. As in, we are one world.

Like the Wang family in Turkey. I feel a bond with them. I can empathize with what the next generation had to go through growing up in a foreign country—their experience, their education, their sense of initial displacement, and yet, how quickly they found their sense of belonging, not to one country, but to the world.

This is a family that straddles many nations, cultures and identities. They may be anchored in Turkey, but they are also emotionally attached to Taiwan, to China. It's not easy for a family to retain its Chinese heritage—especially for the next generation, for there are no national or cultural boundaries when it comes to love and marriage.

Perhaps this is the way we need to survive in the postmodern world, each one of us trying to juggle little pieces of our identity puzzle.

—·—

"Life's normal here," Hom says about Thailand, where he's weathering the pandemic. "Today's paper reported that there have been just ninety-six deaths since the beginning. And this in a country of 70 million."

The pandemic exposed a schism between Asian and Western attitudes toward society and community—that sense of collectivism that is the antithesis to Western individualism.

"Americans will say that their freedom and liberty are being threatened, and it's their right *not* to wear a mask," I lament.

"It's all about me, me, me," he says. "Guess what? Asians get with the program. They put on masks from the beginning. There's no bitching about 'why are we doing this.' When you put on a mask, you are protecting other people."

Perhaps it's true that Asians are more disciplined. Or maybe just more deferential or, dare I say, more obedient to authorities—to their parents, to their teachers, to their elders. But that doesn't explain New Zealand and Australia, two non-Asian countries that successfully fought the pandemic to a draw.

Hom continues: "A doctor tells you something, you listen. And if you're not going to listen, why bother? This drives me absolutely bonkers. Even all my friends in France tell me that's because we do as we are told. Well, no, we do what we're told because we know what's good for the community."

"I can't wait till the pandemic is over so that we can get back to travelling and eating," I tell Hom.

"When you come visit me in Bangkok, I'll take you out for glorious street food. There's nothing like it in this world. Then you should come by my place in southwestern France, and I'll make you my specialty, Peking duck."

Peking duck in the French countryside? I really look forward to that.

Acknowledgements

THIS BOOK WOULD NOT HAVE BEEN POSSIBLE WITHOUT THE HELP OF MANY people. So many to thank.

First to Talin Vartanian for editing and helpful suggestions during the early stages of my writing; my sister Nicole Kwan for early reviews and fact-checking on "things Chinese"; and Michelle Kuan for reading through the manuscript with a critical eye. And to my readers Angie Wong, Dora Nipp, Richard Fung, Paul Jewell, Anthony Pierre, Frédéric Geisweiller, Monika Mérinat, Frank Wania, Jun Watanabe and Luz Victoria Chang de Siu, each of whom reviewed various chapters.

I am especially grateful to Chris Casuccio at Westwood Creative Artists for believing in me and guiding me through the writing process; and to Letecia Rose for introducing us.

To the Douglas & McIntyre team, Anna Comfort O'Keeffe for taking a chance with a first-time author; Pam Robertson for trimming and pulling different story strands together into a coherent whole; Caroline Skelton for her meticulous editing and fact-checking; and Iva Cheung for her fine eye.

I drew inspiration from conversations with chefs Ken Hom, Susur Lee, Alvin Leung and Martin Yan; writers Grace Young, Linda Anusasananan and Jennifer 8. Lee; as well as scholars Allen Chun, Glenn Deer, Lily Cho, Walton Look Lai, Henry Yu and Jenny Banh. A version of "Last Tango in Argentina" was published in *American Chinese Restaurants: Society, Culture and Consumption* edited by Jenny Banh and Haiming Liu.

Thanks, Anthony Bourdain, wherever you are.

This book is a memoir of my four-year adventure to find stories from the Chinese diaspora. The title came from the 2004 "Have You Eaten Yet?"

exhibition at the Museum of Chinese in America, New York, where I first showed episodes from my *Chinese Restaurants* documentary series.

I was lucky to travel around the world many times over during the making of the series with my director of photography Kwoi, and his crew David Szu, Mark Valino and Ajay Noronha. They shot with grace under pressure, enduring exhaustive travel, tight kitchen spaces, not-quite-real Chinese food, bare minimum lodgings, a landslide, two bomb scares, over-inquisitive border guards, aggressive security agents, the SARS pandemic, the Second Intifada and maybe a lurking sniper or two in the West Bank. Lucky none of us was hurt, or landed in jail.

These stories would not have been possible without the research of Carrianne Leung, Heather De Peza, Rosey Ma and Fabiola Castañeda Chang; as well as on-location interpretation by Valeria Mau Chu, Luz Algranti and Alfonso Koc Fong.

I am indebted to my storytellers back home in Toronto: Linda Tse, associate producer, who gave me story ideas; Susan Martin, who co-wrote the voice-over script with me; and Zinka Bejtic and Ricardo Acosta, editors, who helped shaped these stories on film.

They were greatly assisted by an unsung team of transcribers and translators: Laura Cowell, Frances Kushner, Sherry Xie, Maureen Nolan, Una So, Shulamit Elmaleh, Rehan Shahabun, Marilyne Wong, Rehan Nisanyan, Xinlan Wang and Zoey Chen. They laboriously produced transcripts from hours and hours of interviews in English, Cantonese, Mandarin, Hakka, Spanish, French, Portuguese, Hebrew, Arabic, Turkish, Norwegian, Swedish and Mauritian Creole.

To all my restaurant owners, their families and friends, and fellow travellers who appeared in this book, you are the *original* storytellers.

To Marietta, Nicholas and Saskia, who had often wondered where their husband/father disappeared to for long periods at a time, I hope this project justifies your love and patience.

This book is for Anthony B. Chan (1944–2018), who embarked with me on a media journey that knew no bounds and co-founded, with Paul Levine and me, *The Asianadian*, the magazine that helped kickstart a progressive Asian Canadian movement in the late 1970s.

In memory of Jim Wong-Chu (1949–2017), who first invited me to the LiterASIAN festival he founded, and who convinced me that visual storytelling is just as much part of writing as anything else. He was a mentor to us all in the Asian Canadian writing community.

Permissions

Excerpts from the lyrics of *Feelin' de Vibe* by Anthony Chow Lin On, published by Laundry Music, transcribed by Anthony Pierre.

Excerpts from *The Hakka Epic* by Joseph Tsang Mang Kin, published by The President's Fund for Creative Writing in English, Mauritius.

All photos courtesy of Tissa Films.

Index

ON THE MENU

About the Author

Photo by Cedric Sam

CHEUK KWAN was born in Hong Kong and grew up in Singapore, Hong Kong, and Japan. He has also lived in the US, Saudi Arabia, and Canada, and speaks English, Japanese, French, and several Chinese dialects. Kwan is the co-founder of *The Asianadian*—a magazine dedicated to promoting Asian Canadian arts, culture, and politics. His *Chinese Restaurants* documentary series braid his personal experiences with his love of travel and appreciation for Chinese culture worldwide. He now resides in Toronto, Canada.